FROM MAIN STREET
TO STOCKHOLM

From Main Street to Stockholm

LETTERS OF SINCLAIR LEWIS · 1919-1930

EDITED AND WITH AN INTRODUCTION BY

Harrison Smith

HARCOURT, BRACE AND COMPANY

NEW YORK

COPYRIGHT, 1952, BY
MELVILLE H. CANE AND PINCUS BERNER
EXECUTORS OF THE ESTATE OF SINCLAIR LEWIS

*All rights reserved, including
the right to reproduce this book
or portions thereof in any form.*

first edition

PRINTED IN THE UNITED STATES OF AMERICA

Contents

Introduction ... ix

MAIN STREET
I. The Beginning of a Career ... 3
II. Publication and Success ... 37

BABBITT
III. Creation Abroad ... 71
IV. A Reputation Established ... 104

ARROWSMITH
V. The Scientist as a Hero ... 121
VI. Travel on Two Continents ... 159

ELMER GANTRY
VII. Portrait of a Preacher ... 193
VIII. Trouble in Kansas City and Boston ... 233

DODSWORTH
IX. Marriage and Divorce ... 249
X. The Nobel Prize ... 269

Index ... 303

Introduction

When in December 1930 Sinclair Lewis rose to his feet in a palace in Stockholm to deliver the most unconventional Nobel Award address to which that distinguished gathering has ever listened, he made two contradictory statements. He said that he had always been fortunate; and later that the American novelist must work alone, in confusion, unassisted save by his own integrity. If Lewis, as the first American to receive the Nobel Award for Literature, was not at that moment the most celebrated novelist in the United States, he was soon to become so when the American press, through the most vocal of its columnists, editorial writers, and literary pundits, blazed with indignation at his attack on such sacred institutions as William Dean Howells, Mark Twain, our universities, the Academy of Arts and Letters, and the New Humanists. Neither of his two statements was quite true as far as his own life was concerned. No man can be called consistently fortunate who has had to work for ten years alone and in confusion, and Lewis had endured the indifference of critics and the public to his novels before *Main Street* brought him fame almost overnight. For eleven years before the Nobel Award he had been assisted by the devotion and ingenuity of a young publishing house. Aside from a forgotten book for boys written under a pseudonym, he had published before he came to Harcourt, Brace four novels which had got him nowhere near his goal, and he had worked for a score of magazines, newspapers, and press associations until in 1914 he became an editor of George H. Doran's flourishing publishing house. What he wanted of life was freedom from routine tasks so that he could devote all of his energy to writing the novels that were forming in his mind.

He learned in the hard school of experiment how to write short stories for two or three magazines and for George Horace Lorimer, the famous editor of the *Saturday Evening Post* who had given a chance to many youthful writers and who had created a national institution out of a small magazine. They were not very good short stories, as Lewis well knew, but they served their purpose. He was aware finally that he had won the long battle for freedom. The drama of his startling rise to fame was soon to begin. The publisher he needed was waiting off-stage, though neither Alfred Harcourt nor Sinclair Lewis was at the moment conscious of it.

The involvement of these two men in each other's fortunes came about when Harcourt was in the trade department of Henry Holt and Company, and Lewis was respectably performing editorial and publicity functions across the street in the office of George H. Doran and Company. Harcourt had been brought up in New Paltz, a village in upper New York state; Lewis in Sauk Centre, an equally small community in Minnesota. They began to take lunch together in the ornamental grill-room of the old Waldorf on Fifth Avenue, and the narrowness and oddities of village life often proved to be a more interesting topic than books and authors. Lewis had a passion for the little people submerged in the cities and the crossroads of America; he had written about them in his unsuccessful novels, and he had an idea stirring in his head that would not let him alone.

Even in those early days he was one of the most stimulating rapid-fire conversationalists in America. He was also a youthful reformer with the illusion that the lot of men and women would be bettered if their faults could be pointed out to them. In the course of these meetings Harcourt realized that he had found a writer who had a capacity for enthusiasm and indignation, an astonishing memory for detail, and a new approach to contemporary American life.

The die was cast the day Lewis walked into Harcourt's office at Holt's, shut the door and said, "Alf, I'm going to write that small-town novel you've been pestering me about. The title is *Main Street* and don't you mention it to a single person." Then the wheels began to turn. In 1916 Lewis gave up his editorial work with Doran to devote himself to writing. Two years later he drove across country to the West Coast with his wife, Grace Hegger Lewis, in their Ford, and then back to Sauk Centre and his father's house to write a serial for Lorimer based on the trip. This was *Free Air*, the first of his books published by Harcourt, Brace, an innocently romantic and adventurous story of a small-town garage hand who fell in love with a girl from Brooklyn while she was motoring through the Middle West.

In the spring of 1919 Alfred Harcourt resigned from Henry Holt and Company. He wrote Lewis at Sauk Centre that he did not know what he was going to do, whether to accept a post with another house or start his own firm. Lewis wired Harcourt to meet him in New York the following Sunday morning. "What I came on to say is," he told Harcourt at once, "don't be such a damn fool as ever again to go to work for someone else. Start your own business. I'm going to write important books. You can publish them. Now let's go out to your house and start making plans."

He was taking a risk that few ambitious young writers would have contemplated, for it meant that he was leaving an established publishing house for a business venture that even in the best of times is hazardous. He had given his word; he was loyal, yet he was shrewd enough to sense that a firm headed by Alfred Harcourt and Donald Brace might succeed and would give to the books he was to write the enthusiasm and devotion he hoped for.

There was another aspect to his decision to gamble with his future. Sinclair Lewis had a morbid fear of loneliness, perhaps the most obvious trait in his complex nature. He wanted to have friends. He liked and was charmed by women, but as in the case of so many men, the company of the most devoted and intelligent woman could not take the place of the conversation of male companions. But his friends were always drifting away from him. They could not keep up with him; or they could not endure for long the close scrutiny of an endlessly inquiring mind, or the long satirical monologues in which he imitated with astonishing virtuosity the accents of characters he had not yet brought to birth. Oddly enough he never parodied women; but the voices of long-winded men in smoking cars, of Babbitts and Elmer Gantrys and the men who knew Coolidge were always echoing in his friends' ears.

Sinclair Lewis was determined to alter America's conception of itself. Early in his career he foresaw that he might win the Pulitzer Prize and the Nobel Award. He was linked with a publishing house from which he could safely wander to whatever part of the globe he pleased, and he felt that others who might join the enterprise would also be friendly associates in his ambitious design. The letters in this book, drawn from the files of Harcourt, Brace and Company, tell part of the story, from the founding of the firm to Lewis's last letter written in 1931 from Germany, where he had retreated after the Stockholm ceremonies were over. They do not tell all of it. Part of the story was developed in conversation rather than letters, for Lewis was spending a certain amount of his time in and around New York. This was particularly true of the period preceding the Nobel Award and at other times indicated in the notes that go with the text. During the later years when he was gaining all he might have hoped for it is evident from his letters that his interest lessened in the way in which his victories had been won. He had become used to large figures and no longer was eager for the latest news and reports from the office.

Lewis had for several years served the company unofficially as a scout and as its envoy in England and France. After *Babbitt* was published in London, there was an immense curiosity about the man who had revitalized American literature, so that he was welcomed everywhere. Harcourt, Brace had acquired an extremely important list of British writers—John Maynard Keynes, Lytton Strachey, E. M. Forster, Virginia Woolf, and others of the Bloomsbury group—and to him they were all part of the firm. He describes in his letters the parties and dinners he attended, the houses he lived in, and his travels in England, France, Italy, and Germany.

Through this correspondence the reader can discover the admirable qualities of Sinclair Lewis which were often not apparent to chance acquaintances or even to those who met him frequently. He was unfailingly courteous and thoughtful of those who were associated with him. His opinions of the writers he met through his connection with the firm were shrewd. Occasionally his evaluation of the work of a young writer with whom he had made friends was too generous, though he always surrendered gracefully and rarely argued with the editorial opinions of the office. Though he was desperately anxious for success, he wanted others to take advantage of the expanding opportunities for American writers. He was not jealous of those who shared the limelight with him, or angry at adverse or unfair criticism. When one of his books failed to live up to his hopes, like *The Man Who Knew Coolidge*, or *Mantrap*, he revealed his anxiety but never did he hint that he was disappointed in his publisher. These letters reveal a brilliant and dynamic man, deeply concerned with social problems, generous, restless, often unhappy, meticulous in his financial affairs, and almost exhaustively so in the accuracy of the details with which he surrounded his characters, so that the notes which he made before he began to write a novel were often as long as the completed manuscript. There are certainly no letters in the history of American publishing quite like this correspondence between Harcourt, and other members of the firm, and Sinclair Lewis.

HARRISON SMITH

MAIN STREET

ONE

The Beginning of a Career

[1919]
315 South Broad Street,
Mankato, Minn.
June 12

Dear Alf:

Working hard on *Main Street*. Like this town immense. I wrote to Herbert E. Gaston (director of Nonpartisan League publications) about the NPL book, and he writes that he'll get in touch with you. He's soon going to Chi and may go on to NY. You might write him, especially if you've settled yet where your office will be. If he doesn't do the book, he'll know the best man to do it.

Lots of luck! Much regards to Mrs. Harcourt and Ellen Eayrs.[1]

Zever,
slewis

117 Lorraine Avenue,
Mount Vernon, N.Y.
June 16

My dear Lewis:

After some confusing offers of rather extraordinary jobs, everything is cleared up, and we are going after our own business. I think the firm name will be Harcourt, Howe and Brace.[2] Howe is at the moment the head of the English Department at the University of Indiana; the author of a set of school readers of which Scribner's have sold 5,000,000; editor of their Modern Students' Library; and a corking fellow of about forty

[1] Harcourt's assistant.
[2] Incorporated as Harcourt, Brace and Howe, July 29, 1919.

who can give us a hook-in on school book business. He brings some capital, but so many fine books are showing up that I think we shall need all we can get. Do you really want to put some money in? We'll give you preferred stock with at least 6% dividends guaranteed. I don't think we will need it until late in the fall, but of course we want to know what we can count on. Now be absolutely frank about this.

Do you know *Free Air* is making a hit? My neighbors and their wives are saying it is one of the most interesting and refreshing things they have seen in the S. E. P. (Saturday Evening Post) for some time, and people in the trade are talking about it. Brace hears the same report. You have heard from Bobbs-Merrill and probably from a good many other directions. At any rate, set yourself down and, with all the skill you can muster, write to Henry Holt and Company (our correspondence is in their files) explaining, if you wish, how you came there because of personal relations with me, and ask them to let you have the *Free Air* contract back. I think you will get it all right. You might address E. N. Bristol [1] direct.

Things look rosy to an unbelievable degree. We're off in a cloud of dust!

Ever yours,
Alf

Mankato, June 16

Dear Alf:

Here's a carbon of a letter from me to Holt Co. *Main Street* goes apace (none of your biz *what* pace). Doing nothing else, and really am under way. Got an office address yet?

Zever,
SLewis

[*Enclosure*]

Mankato, June 15

Dear Mr. Holt: [2]

I wonder if I can, without impairing our good personal relations, ask for the return of the contract on my book *Free Air?*

There are two disconnected reasons. First—as I wrote to Harcourt long before there was the slightest hint of his severing connections with Henry Holt and Company—you'll find the letter in the files—when I

---

[1] Vice president and treasurer of Henry Holt and Company.

[2] Roland Holt, son of founder and president of Henry Holt and Company, and vice president of the company.

started to work to add to the ms to bring it from the present serial length of 56,000 words to a length suitable for book publication, I found that it would be such a long job that I cdn't with the work already in hand, do it till sometime next year. And in its present short form it hasn't quite the dignity I want in my next book. Now as other tasks may keep coming in and preventing my properly enlarging and developing the book, I don't like to have a contract for it out, even with the understanding that it's not to be published till I do properly complete the work.

Second, despite my long and hearty respect for the Company and my personal liking for you and others, yet after all Harcourt has always been the man in the firm whom I have best known and with whom I have done business, as book reviewer and fellow publisher and author, and while I don't know what his plans are, I want to be loyal to him and stick by him.

I understand that one of the fundamental principles of the Company has been to hold authors by their own desire rather than by the semi-compulsion of contracts, so I put this directly to you, and hope that you will see it in the decidedly friendly light in which I see it.

I am here in this Minnesota town for the summer—and I like it; like the friendliness, the neighborliness, and the glorious sweeps of country round about.

Sincerely yours,
Sinclair Lewis

Mankato, June 19

Dear Alf:

I like the name The Harcourt Company better than Harcourt, Howe and Brace, just because it's shorter, but the other is good too. Just how much time can I have before I decide about taking some stock? I certainly would like some, but of course just now my problem is that I'm writing *Main Street* and living on what I have ahead, and as I can't tell how long it will take me I don't dare to invest and risk having to go back to short stories before I want to. I certainly ought to have some ahead next fall, but don't know now, so don't like to promise. I also don't know yet about the musical comedy version of *Hobohemia*[1]—when Smith[2] will finish it and get it on. If I got a wad out of that, I'd like to put it into your business—a real investment.

[1] Lewis's first play, a satire on life in Greenwich Village, produced in New York February 8, 1919.
[2] Harry Bache Smith. Librettist who collaborated at different times with Victor Herbert, Irving Berlin, and others.

Free Air seems to be making a great hit here too, but I still suspect that it'd be wise to put it off till after *Main St*. Before getting your letter I'd written to Roland Holt; if I don't hear satisfactorily from him, I'll write to Bristol, as you suggest. GOOD LUCK!

As ever,
sl

Mount Vernon, N.Y.
June 23

Dear Slewis:

I raise my two-year-old Panama to the letter you wrote Henry Holt and Company. You wrote before you received mine suggesting such a letter, and I am glad because the letter couldn't have been improved upon. It might have been less good because of some hang-over from my letter. We'll treasure it as a model.

I arranged with Gaston Saturday morning for a book on the Nonpartisan League.[1] He is getting right at it. Things are coming along unbelievably well for us in every direction.

Ever yours,
Alf

In care of Tobey and Co.
5 West 50th St., New York
June 27

Dear Slewis:

Don't tear your shirt about capital. We have enough to turn over on. We should not need any from you until late fall or the first of the year. It could be left that if you do want to put money into our business and with the money conveniently in hand, we should be delighted to have you in to the extent and in the fashion that will make you feel most comfortable.

I keep hearing about *Free Air*, and my hunch is that if we let that wait a year or so, it is going to be pretty stale and that the impetus which the enjoyment of the serial has created will be lost. Don tells me they have sent your contract back from Holt's. What I really wish you would do is to get *Free Air* into the best shape you can by the first of August and let us make a book of it. You ought to make up your mind about this right off and perhaps let us have a telegram, as we have to make a fall list by

---

[1] *The Nonpartisan League* by Herbert E. Gaston, HB&Co., 1920.

the first of next week. If you do take my point of view, very shortly after you have sent the telegram, mail us a description. Also send us the first chapter or two to make a dummy. Then we can get advance orders this summer. Gehrs [1] is going to stay at Holt's until the first of October, but we have made arrangements whereby he can sell our fall line on his summer trip for them—and I am afraid our line will get all the emphasis to which it is entitled!

I am sending you a copy of the results of our last week's activities. We are getting a book or two a day and all first-class ones. That is, we are going off with a bang. We have no quarters yet, but we have a temporary place at 5 West 50th St. which I hope we can make permanent. The lawyers are working on the incorporation, and in a week or ten days we shall be all set and going.

As ever,
Alf

Mankato, June 30

Dear Alf:

In answer to your letter I wired you I'll finish *Free Air* for book in two or three weeks. I'm sending you today the first 166 pages, all ready to print, so that you can not only make a dummy but really start setting.

Go ahead and make up a contract when you are ready—no hurry. I do NOT want an advance. But equally, you don't get anything on movie rights—I have a wire from Brandt [2] saying Famous Players offer $3000 for movie rights.

I've tried to make a résumé of the story, without success. I enclose my abortive attempt. I hate writing abt [3] my own stuff—did too much of it at Doran's.

Getting lots of good letters about the story, praising it heavily. It should be especially pushed in Minn, NDakota, Montana, Washington. Here's an idea for an ad:

> Whenever you see the sign
> FREE AIR
> before a garage think of
> the one book that makes motoring romantic
> FREE AIR

---

[1] August H. Gehrs, sales manager of the new firm.
[2] Carl Brandt, New York literary agent.
[3] Lewis often used this form of "telegraphese," dropping vowels from words, and it has been retained throughout.

Or something like that. We ought, somehow, to be able to take advantage of the publicity implied in all the tens of thousands Free Air signs before garages and filling-stations.

Oughtn't the book to have four or five charming illustrations: I think Arthur William Brown or Dean Cornwell would do em better than Gruger did in the Post; still, Gruger's were pretty good, and we cd probably get em from the Post cheaply.

As ever,
sl

Mankato, July 3

Dear Alf:

Hard at work on end of *Free Air*, and it's going fine. If Louise Bryant, wife of Jack Reed and my good friend, comes to see you, be extra nice to her and buy her a —— Oh gosh, you can't, even 2.75%.

sl

Mankato, July 14

Dear Alf:

Miss Eayrs asks me to send her the original *Free Air* Holt contract, for use in making new one. Two changes are that you are NOT to pay me an advance, and that you don't get anything on movie rights. You can come in on dramatic rights. There won't be none!

I've received check for *Free Air* movie, and I can now, if you want to monkey with so small a sum, invest $2000 in the firm. That's all I'd better venture now. Later in the year I may be able to increase that considerably. No way of telling. But I'd sure be glad to invest the two thousand now, if you'd like.

Ought to have the new part of the book done, but between heat and long continued plugging I got so tired that I laid off for a week and took my dad on the long motor trip I told you about—he enjoyed it enormously; saw the places he knew as a kid but hasn't seen for from 30 to 50 years. Now I'm back on the job and will hustle the end of the book thru.

I wonder if you can work any publicity in combination with the movie production of *Free Air?* Ought to be something good in it. It's been bought by Famous Players—Carl Brandt can probably tell you who is doing their publicity. They'll probably be pushing the picture at just about the time of publication of the book.

Zever,
Sinclair Lewis

Tell Miss Eayrs to quit working so hard. I know her!
Why don't *you* try to buy rights to earlier books from Hoyns?[1] No further word from him since the last letter I sent you.

5 West 50th St., N.Y.
July 19

Dear Lewis:

Now that we know the length of *Free Air*, Brace has sent it to the printer; meantime we have used the serial version to have a jacket made that is a wonder.

I am so glad you had that trip with your father. The year before my dad died, we drove to Niagara Falls and back, and it's a rare and dear memory.

We would really like very much to have your $2000 in the business. Our articles of incorporation go to Albany Monday, and we shall be ready to issue stock as soon as it can be printed. You had better keep the money in your bank until I write you that the stock is ready to exchange for it. I believe and hope it will be a good investment for you.

We have found offices after tramping all over this town at 1 West 47th St., the first floor and basement in a nice old private house, and you will never have a warmer welcome anywhere, except in your own home, than when you come to see us there. I think we shall have an extra room upstairs with a bed in it for such wandering wayfarers as you, so don't go to a hotel the next time you come to town until you have found out if we haven't a comfortable place for you.

You know I sort of expect a killing for *Free Air*. We are going out for one, anyway.

Zever,
Alf

Mankato, July 22

Dear Alf:

I'll be sending the rest of *Free Air* to you in less than a week. I think the new stuff is more than up to the rest of it, and it's in no sense padding. In fact, when I originally planned it, I'd intended to have in all this Seattle matter, then stopped short because I didn't want to make my first Post serial too long. Grace[2] says it's the best part of the story.

---

[1] Henry Hoyns of Harper and Brothers, publishers of Lewis's earlier novels, *Our Mr. Wrenn, The Trail of the Hawk, The Job, The Innocents.*

[2] Grace Livingston Hegger and Lewis were married at the Ethical Culture Church, New York, on April 15, 1914.

In view of this, of the fact that I've added almost 30,000 words—nearly doubled the story—it's important for your salesman in talking to book dealers to emphasize that only about half the story appeared in the serial. And how about putting that on the jacket? Or is it better not to admit on the jacket that it has appeared as a serial? If such an admission is made, there should certainly be a good note about the new half—Milt up against city social complications—the small-town garage man going to the opera in his first evening clothes. Think that over for jacket note, and use or not as seems best to you. It *might* do something to counteract the bad effect of Post serialization, and mite be so worded that those who liked it in the Post will get the book. It might also go into a literary note.

Glad you've found offices, and many thanks for your warm welcome to them.

Sincerely,
SLewis

Here's a true literary note. I've heard of several people who are now driving from Middlewest to the Pacific Coast because of reading *Free Air*.

Mankato, July 25

Dear Alf:

Next Thursday, July 31, just after mailing you the end of *Free Air*, Grace and I are going to start motoring East. If you should need to get hold of me before I go, you could telegraph me. I don't know of anything you'll need to wire me about, however, and I'll reach the East sometime after the middle of August.

We're going to spend the winter in the East—just where, we don't know yet. We'll look for a house on the way. It probably won't be more than a hundred or a hundred and fifty miles from NY. We're going to look at West Chester, Pa., where Hergesheimer lives.

Check:

So that I'll be sure to have it in to you, I'm enclosing the check for two thousand for stock. Yea, I'll trust you, even tho I know your weakness for large lunches. You can have some stock made out in my name, and HOLD the stock.

Proofs:

I don't know when you plan to issue *Free Air*, so I don't know whether I'll be East early enough to read proofs—you can't *count* on me to do it till after September 1st. Do NOT hold up the book. If someone reads proofs for me, have them change the population of Gopher Prairie (the first town where Claire stops for the night) to make it agree with

[1919]

Main Street. When I read proof for the Sat Even Post, I transferred those corrections to the book ms, and that will help some—tho of course Brer Author can always find some new changes.

I would wait here for the proofs, but I'm all in—been grinding too long and hard, need a vacation bad, and it's a good stunt to use it in this Eastern trip, as we'll be going East anyway. We plan (unless it gets too hot) to go down thru Tennessee and Virginia, so it'll be quite a trip. By the way, if they want to go, I'll take Father and Mother at least as far as Chicago.

PHOTOGRAPHS:

I'll have some new photos taken when I get East, and there ought to be some bully snapshots along the road, peculiarly appropriate to *Free Air* publicity.

ADS:

Think over the use of the "When you see a Free Air sign in front of a gas station, thing of the one book that," etc. and the plan of having ads in the motoring and sporting journals, and maybe an inch or two or three in the S.E.P.

ADVANCE COPIES:

(*Lewis sent in at this time a remarkably complete list of the most important American critics, newspapers and magazines carrying book reviews.*)

I can't think of anything else to insult you with—this is my last shot at you (giving you a chance to reply, at least) before I hit the road. But don't wire me, "You poor fish, don't you suppose I know a little about the publishing business?" I'll assume that answer, and save money for . . . my firm!

Back to work copying the bloomink book.

As ever,
S Lewis

1 West 47th Street, N.Y.
July 28

Dear Mr. Lewis:

Mr. Harcourt and I moved to this address [1] last Monday. We spent one week in a tiny cubby-hole in the basement, encircled with piles of trash and paint pails. From where we sat, we could see legs descending the stairs to call upon us; after a time sufficiently long to guess at the owners of the legs, a head would appear. We entertained a lot of distinguished

[1] These were the first quarters of Harcourt, Brace and Howe, and this letter was written the day before the firm was formally incorporated.

visitors; even Mr. Ellery Sedgwick's [1] legs called upon us, and he was impressed—how he didn't say. This morning we moved to a lovely room on the third floor where we shall be until the first of October. After that we shall all be in our rightful quarters on the first floor. The explanation of all this is that Mr. Harcourt has taken the first floor and basement of an old red brick house; he could get the basement at once, and the first floor on October first, so for the sake of being at the permanent address, we are going to be in this house. He will write you fully about all this as soon as he has time. I write this so that you shall be in on the first struggles of a poor but honest young man!

Sincerely yours,
Ellen Eayrs

July 28

Dear Lewis:

I think you will get this reply to your good letter of the 25th before you leave. I am glad you are taking the trip. It will do both of you a world of good. I've sold the Oldsmobile and bought a Ford. The latter is cheaper to run. The new car came yesterday, and it was fun finding all the grease cups.

I hereby acknowledge the check for $2000. We cannot issue stock to you until you sign our stock book in person. We'll have it all ready for you when you come in.

I hope you won't be disappointed when I tell you that the book will not be illustrated. With present costs of manufacture, the book would have to be $1.75 instead of $1.60. Gruger's drawings were not good, and the other people were not within reach for a hurry-up job, and I'd rather have the $500 for extra advertising, window display posters, etc.

When you get East, find out whether my house is vacant or not before you camp out here. Sue and Hastings [2] are going up to Dorothy Canfield's [3] for six weeks or two months after the 15th of August. I have asked Howe if he wants it when he comes on about the 15th; I have not heard from him, and it may be that I shall be there alone, and you can put your car in the garage and the baby in Hastings's room etc. I am very glad you are going to be East this winter. No time for more now. I envy you the trip and the good time.

Ever yours,
Alf

[1] Editor of the *Atlantic Monthly*.
[2] Harcourt's wife and son.
[3] At Arlington, Vermont.

[1919]

Lewis and his wife drove East by way of Tennessee and Virginia, stopping off to see James Branch Cabell in Virginia. They arrived at West Chester, Pennsylvania, on August 29th.

c/o Joseph Hergesheimer
West Chester, Pa.
Wednesday, September 3

Dear Alf:

As I telephoned you from Phila yesterday, the whole business of the serial publication of the end of the book is unusual. I was at Lorimer's,[1] and when he asked me what the deuce I'd been doing all these weeks, and I told him, he, not I, suggested my showing him the new part—hence the hasty wire to you. He immediately accepted it, with enthusiasm, and it seemed criminal to miss the good money in hand. But I was more worried than you will believe about the matter of book publication. As a matter of fact, with the difficulties of make-up, I was afraid that he'd demand a postponement of publication till way into November; was afraid I might have to refuse the serial publication. When I saw him yesterday, I went into that first of all, and I think he's more than decent to rush it through so soon.

But of course that doesn't help you any. I wonder if this will be of any value—let the bookdealers know, by word of mouth thru Gehrs, what is the exact truth—that Lorimer liked the new part so much he simply had to have it, which certainly ought to increase their interest in it. Let them know that a lot of readers have been clamoring for more *Free Air*, and they get it in the book. Something like that?

This new part will be published (in the Post) under the title *Danger —Run Slow*. Lorimer gives October 20 definitely as the release date. He's not even setting galley proofs but getting it right into pages.

I hope to God this works out all right. I think I've given enough previous proofs of my interest in your success so you may be sure that, while craftily grabbing off this money, I also devote a whole lot of thought and worry to you, and hope and pray that I haven't been either inconsiderate or foolish in this.

I wonder if some time I can't get Lorimer and you together. I can't tell you how much I admire Lorimer, both for his ability and his incredible niceness in his dealings with authors.

We have a house here, but we don't get into it till about the 15th. Meantime we're at a hotel, but you can address me care of Hergesheimer.

I'm terribly disappointed in the pictures we got on the trip. The ones I'm sending are the best. With them are some pictures of James

---

[1] George Horace Lorimer. Editor-in-chief of the *Saturday Evening Post*.

Branch Cabell and myself, taken in the Virginia mountains. His new book *Jurgen* will be published by McBride this fall.

As ever,
Sinclair Lewis

September 5

Dear Lewis:

We are so infernally busy that I haven't time to do more than acknowledge yours of September 3rd. It is only truthful to say that we hate to postpone *Free Air*, but there is comfort enough in knowing that it is a favor to you and in having our enthusiasm confirmed by Lorimer's making two serials of one story and thinking so much of the ending that he is standing on his head to get it into the Post. Of course booksellers will be afraid that complete serialization in the Post will blanket the market, and this may affect advance orders, but I don't believe it will affect the total sale. Good luck always!

Ever yours,
Alf

Burlington Hotel
Washington, D.C.
Tuesday

Dear Alf:

I've been down here house-hunting (with not much success yet). We decided that West Chester would bore us—and Washington we like tremendously. Don't know when we'll be where, but chances are we'll be here at the Burlington for several days to come.

Sincerely,
SL

1814 16th Street, N.W.
Washington, D.C.
Monday

Dear Alf:

Above is our new address—and we really *will* keep that one all winter! Even after an arduous week of house-hunting, we adore Washington—it has all the stimulus that we found little gray West Chester to lack, yet also a clean quietude that New York lacks. We have a small but comfortable house, into which we move next Friday.

If Howe has come, give him my greetings, please.

Sincerely,
Sinclair Lewis

September 25

Dear Lewis:

It is good to think of you as settled in Washington. The advertising suggestions are good. Send more along as they occur to you. I don't agree, however, about advertising in motor journals. I think we can get a good deal of free publicity from that crowd, but when people look at those journals, they are looking for accessories, not books. We want to give away copies liberally in that field.

It looks as if the 8000 copies we are having bound will just fill the advance orders and leave us enough to see how the cat is going to jump. Not bad, I think.

Ever yours,
Alf

Washington, October 6

Dear Alf:

Your catalogue came this morning, and I think that it is remarkably impressive, especially for a first one. It ought to make an interesting stir.

There is just one criticism, but I think that is important. And it's my fault, seeing that it's based on something I did. . . . The *Free Air* description sounds too much as though this were a typical Munsey-Popular Magazine outdoor adventure romance. It seems to me the line we must stress is that here is romance with dignity and realism—that Milt, in his garage, in his adventuring, is as true to life as though this were a drab story of manners instead of a romance. And there is no hint of the Seattle experiences—one who had read the first part in the Post would have no way of knowing there was anything in the book not found in that first part in the magazine.

Please—PLEASE—think very carefully about giving the keynote of the book in future ads and descriptions, so that it may stand out from the typical Zane Grey ads.

As ever,
Sinclair Lewis

P.S. Send me 20 copies of *Free Air* as soon as you have them. I shall use several for furtherance of selling.

October 7

Dear Lewis:

Thanks for your recent letters. I have been just too busy to answer them. This thing is growing like the green bay tree. You know the first of the quotation. Don and I have been here until 10:30 almost every night.

Twenty copies of *Free Air* have been sent to you. We have sent copies with a special note from me to Harry Korner and John Kidd.[1] We sent out about 130 to sales people, and on most of those either Gehrs or I wrote a personal word. Be dead sure you don't give any of the 20 copies to anybody who will go into a bookstore before the 23rd of October and say "The book *is* published; I know it is published; I've seen a copy" etc. I'd really rather you kept them under your pillow until the 18th. Advance copies outside of the trade raise the very dickens sometimes.

Haven't heard a word from Hoyns. I ought to run into him at a Publishers' Luncheon soon.

We're putting another 3000 *Free Air* to press. Have orders for 5200 without Baker & Taylor or N.Y.City except Amer News which takes 1000. Expect advance of 8-9000.

Yours,
Alf

October 20

Dear Lewis:

Free Air looks so promising that I'm going to suggest a joint gamble. We are spending (besides $500 on window displays, dealers' letters, etc.) $1000 (10¢ a copy on the first 10,000) in regular advertising to give it an initial push. Do you want to say you will accept a 10% royalty on the first 10,000 if we will spend the 5% you forego on a further splurge in advertising and also spend a like sum ourselves? If you want to say you'll make it 10% to 15,000 we will, as soon as we've sold 10,000 outright, appropriate a further $1000 to keep up the push. Now, do just as you please about this. I think it will pay us both. We may get this book over into really large figures; every copy we sell now starts talk and means that many more advance orders for *Main Street*. I'd like to spend a considerable part of the extra money on Chicago and the West.

Let me know how this strikes you. I ought to hear almost by return mail, for it looks as if I'd sail for London on the 28th and there is much to do.

Yours ever,
A.H.

[1] Cleveland and Cincinnati booksellers.

[1919]

Washington, October 22—Wednesday

Dear Alf:

I received your letter at 7:30 this morning, and about 9:30 telegraphed, "Yes, gladly agree to reduction to 10% up to 15,000 copies for extra advertising appropriation." In other words I quite agree with all the suggestions in your letter—that I forego 5% of royalty, on condition that it be used, with a like sum supplied by you, for further advertising; and I agree to do so not only on the first 10,000, but on the 5000 after that. And maybe later—we'll see.

As you say, it will be well to use some of this new fund on advertising west of Chicago—particularly, I should think, in Minneapolis, St. Paul, and Seattle.

Let me know anything else I can do, and if there's a quick answer necessary, I'll telegraph. I don't suppose there's any necessity of our getting together before you go away, and I have no plans to visit New York for Gawd knows how long, but if you should really need to see me, I can always be in NY in five or six hours.

It may be that, before you ever get *Main Street*, you'll have another novel of mine that ought to have twice the sale of *Free Air*, but will be in some degree of the same general character—the story of a young couple bucking society in a city like Minneapolis; a story of that never yet adequately described but extremely important phase of American life—middle-class existence in an American cross between town and city, in Minneapolis, Omaha, Binghamton, and all the rest. I am planning such a story, with a lot of drama and unexpectedness but also complete reality, as a serial for Sat Even Post, and I may do it before I go on with *Main St*—which will almost certainly NOT go as a serial. I may call the new story either *Cobra in the Dark* or *The Dark Alley*. Do you like either title?

I think that's all!

As ever,
sl

October 23

Dear Lewis:

Thanks very much, old man, for your telegram and your letter falling in so heartily with our plans. I have real hopes they will pay us both. We are attempting to follow every suggestion you are making and others which occur to us. Spingarn [1] has the matter in hand, and he and Miss Eayrs will follow it up, as I expect to sail on the *Adriatic* Saturday noon.

[1] J. E. Spingarn (later referred to as Joel or JES). Author and critic and a director of the new firm.

Send suggestions just as freely to them as you would to me. I have gone over the whole scheme with Spingarn and it will sail smoothly. Good luck!

I like the novel which may precede *Main Street* except that I don't like either of your titles.

Sincerely yours,
A.H.

Washington, November 2

Dear Mr. Spingarn:

Let me take this opportunity to greet you and to express my pleasure in having heard from Harcourt that you are on the bridge while he is away. . . . As it's he who's on the ocean that seems to be a rotten metaphor, but metaphors we must have, at all cost.

Let me know anything I can do.

Sincerely yours,
Sinclair Lewis

Washington, November 12

Dear Ellen:

You're a corker to take all the trouble with *Free Air* and to write me the family details about the firm. I enormously like hearing them—all of them. I hope I'm not overdoing suggestions about publicity—I shall always expect you or A.H. firmly to turn down any you don't like.

Note the underlined lines in the enclosed clipping. Would it be perfectly insane and egotistic to suggest that you or Mr. Spingarn send a copy of the book to the prize committee, suggesting that the dern thing is a study in "the wholesome atmosphere of American life" etc.?[1] I think a letter with the book would be necessary, in order that the committee might not hastily conclude—as some reviewers seem to be concluding—that because it is a romance with a motor car, therefore it has no serious study of factualities. Please *don't* follow this up unless it seems advisable. It would be a gamble in any case.

As ever,
sl

During Harcourt's absence in Europe, Lewis corresponded with the office from Washington about details concerning the publication of Free Air.

[1] Lewis was referring to the Pulitzer Prize Committee.

[1919]

Washington, Monday, December 15

Dear Alf:

You ought to be getting back to the office at about the time of the arrival of this letter, so its purpose is both to welcome you back and to give you some news. I have now written about 70,000 words of *Main Street* and am going right ahead with it, instead of doing the dangerous thing of again putting it off while I write a Post serial! I have no idea that it will make a serial, and I have every hope that it will be ready for publication in the spring—certainly for early fall, possibly last week in August. You mustn't suppose that 70,000 means it's almost done though. I'm afraid I shall be doing well (there's such an enormous and complicated field to cover) if I keep it down to 180,000 words, even after cutting first draft. But I'll keep it down as much as I can.

If it takes long enough, I may have to stop once or twice to write short stories for the Post, but if so, I'll go right on again. Whether it's good or not of course I can't tell, but there is this fact usually indicative of some excellence: I'm enormously enjoying writing it, and unusually interested in it—indeed I'm not thinking of much else.

Not only have I written 70,000, but also, for a starter, I have rewritten all of the 30,000 words I had written last summer before I broke off to finish *Free Air*, and I know the new version is much better. It will be a great deal better than *The Job* and I hope that it will give you the chance for a big campaign and perhaps a big sale. (Tho I don't expect it to sell to lovers of Harold Bell Wright. It's pretty out-and-out.)

How does the *Free Air* situation frame up, now that Xmas is approaching? Do you feel anything like satisfied with the sale? I am more than satisfied with your efforts and Miss Eayrs's and those of all the rest, and my only reaction to the whole thing is a hope that you have made some money on it and that it forms a good introduction to *Main Street*.

There is one thing we must keep in mind from the first: Whether because *Free Air* came out in the Post, or because of the wording of the advertisements, or the wording of the jacket, almost all reviewers (the NYTimes almost the only exception) have concluded that not only is this merely a light adventure novel, but that it lacks all factuality, all "seriousness"; so they have not bothered to read it at all, but, god damn them, have merely given fake reviews. This feeling of theirs must NOT extend to *Main Street*. We must be very careful about ads, advance notices, jacket note,* everything, or we shall have them not reading the book. And yet, same time, we mustn't in those descriptions of the book convey the impression that it is too heavy and lugubrious and "highbrow." I think one thing we might do is to send a letter to about a dozen reviewers (Francis Hackett, Mencken, Burton Rascoe, etc.) telling them frankly that we know *Free Air* and *Innocents* were light, but in *Main Street* this brilliant young author far beats his justly celebrated *The Job*, etc. I have such a letter ready, and we might send it out a month in advance of publication to a carefully culled list.

I give this long drool so far in advance that we may all be prepared. I'll NEVER do a novel more carefully planned and thought out and more eagerly written than *Main Street*, and I hope to see it go for years, as *Jean-Christophe* goes. If it does, it will be fine for all of us. So let's not spare any pains—and an important part of this will be planning the *keynote* of all ads, announcements, etc.

You could, if you wanted, begin to let hints of the coming chef duffer leak out any time, now that the novel's so well under way. And now, with apologies for so long a letter so soon after your return, back to writing the novel!

As ever,
Sinclair Lewis

* I'll be glad to write as many of these as you want, tho I couldn't with *Free Air*.

December 17

Dear Lewis:

The fact that I have just read your letter of the 15th to Alf is responsible for starting me on this letter. I know Miss Eayrs has been giving you the news, and I have been so busy since Alf has been away that I have not had a chance to do anything I didn't absolutely have to. *Free Air* is not doing what we hoped it would. I cannot see that we have done or left undone anything that would be responsible for this, and the thing that comes back to us from every source is the Post serialization, especially the second one. We have sold about 8000 copies. I am sure we have done everything we can before Christmas, and we shall see what more we can do after.

I am delighted that you are getting along so well with *Main Street*. Alf is on the *Baltic* which should have been in yesterday, but will probably not be here until tomorrow or Friday. Of course he will write you as soon as he gets a chance after his return.

Sincerely yours,
Don

December 22

Dear Lewis:

This is just a stop-gap, Merry Christmas note to say that I got home Saturday, after a wild voyage of two weeks, with a trunkful of new

[1919]

books. The Britishers opened their arms to the new business in a way that astonished me.

Of course the best part of your letter is that you are really at work on *Main Street*, and you are dead right in what you say about the atmosphere in which the book must be launched. I think the most important element in creating that atmosphere is that it shall not be serialized in the Post. I don't know the details of what has happened to *Free Air*. It hasn't done all that we hoped for, but on the other hand there is a re-order for 50 copies from Los Angeles in the mail this morning.

No time for more today. Aren't you going to get up here before long?

Ever yours,
Alf

Washington, December 24

Dear Alf:

Much merry Christmas and a great New Year. You bet—*Main Street* will NOT be serialized in the Post; almost certainly it will not be serialized in ANY magazine. I don't think I shall even send a copy to any magazine for consideration. I'm booming ahead with it, tho I've had to stop for about a week because my father and mother are here, on their way to Florida. December 26 I'll be into it again.

Harry B. Smith is at last making the musical comedy out of *Hobohemia*—I've seen the first act, and it ought to go. There ought to be a little money to back me while I do novels. It's a joy not to be writing for magazines always.

About *Free Air:* my only hope is that its not going big will not discourage you. You remember that at first I advised against its publication in book form at all. While I'm not, of course, entirely indifferent to it, all my thoughts and planning are centered in *Main Street*—which may, perhaps, be the real beginning of my career as a writer.

I wonder if about six months before the novel is to come out—when you have the ms—it might not begin to create great interest to publish an advance announcement—not as a publicity note but as an ad, in Times, Tribune, Boston Transcript, Pub Weekly and one or two others. Say it's to come out August 25 of next year—publish on March 15 or April 15 just a one- or two-inch ad in each paper to the effect that:

Harcourt, Brace and Howe announce that five months from now, on August 25, they will publish a novel of extraordinary importance as a realistic picture of American life—*Main Street* by Sinclair Lewis. (The book will *not* appear as a magazine serial.)

(Only probably flash up the title more—get it fixed in people's minds so that they will be ready, and possibly eager, for it. If you get any reaction, republish it once a month.)

Or, more simply:

MAIN STREET
Sinclair Lewis
will be published next August.
A book of importance—a genuinely
realistic picture of American life.

I don't think this long-advance announcement has ever been done and ought to affect book-dealers & readers.

Look, Alf, and heed. Through all my letters, the next few months, there will probably be suggestions, sometimes just one sentence, for *Main Street* publicity, etc. Why don't you have all of the suggestions of any possible importance copied and kept together, for future use. OTHERWISE THEY'RE ALMOST CERTAIN TO GET LOST, and to be forgotten by both you and me—and it'll be a bore, later, to have to dig them out of the files.

I hope to God you have made at least a little money out of *Free Air*. Don't worry about me.

And now on with the job (I'm stealing two hours from showing Dad about, today) and a Great New Year for All of Us, and a hell of a success for all of us with *Main St* and everything else. My very best to your wife, the boy, Ellen, Don, Gus, and all.

As ever,
sl

P.S.: I'll be glad to make a contract on *Main St* so that I put part of my royalty into advertising (possibly up to 25,000 copies), as on *Free Air*.

[1920]
January 13

Dear Lewis:

We have been and are as busy as can be with some 50 books (mighty few lemons in the lot too) to publish by the first of April. We'll have a list of them off to you soon. You bet we'll keep all your *Main Street* suggestions together. Sure, we have made some money out of *Free Air*, and I think you will have something over a thousand dollars coming to you out of it.

I have just read *Jurgen*. It's a humdinger; the man gets away with murder, but it's as able a job as I've seen for a long time. I think you are by way of knowing the author pretty well. Is he our sort, and are we his'n? I don't think the chances are in favor of his being comfortable where he is very long. If you haven't read *Jurgen*, please stop and do it before you do anything more about it; if you have and decide to get after Cabell in our behalf, go to it.

Ever yours,
Alf

Washington, Thursday

Dear Alf:

Here's a copy of the letter I am sending today to Cabell. Yes, I have read *Jurgen*, and admire it enormously. In the last *Nation* is an ad quoting me about it. Yes, you would like Cabell, very much.

Working hard on *Main Street*—and doing nothing else. Going to be one grand book. I should think we might plan it for very early next fall. Probably won't have it done till April—anyway, too late for spring publication.

I wonder if we couldn't sell some *Free Air*'s in the spring, late spring, when people are thinking about and planning coming motor tours? Would it be worth while to advertise it then as the one guide and inspiration for such trips? These recent motor articles of mine in the Post (three of them, called "Adventures in Automobumming") have aroused considerable attention and brought me a lot of letters. See them? Pictures of me.

Regards to Don and Ellen and Gus and the several Harcourts.

Sincerely,
sl

[*Enclosure*]

Washington, January 15

My dear Cabell:

I heard from Alfred Harcourt of Harcourt, Brace and Howe, lately, and I find that he is extremely interested in *Jurgen*. If you ever get in the least dissatisfied with McBride, I do wish you would think of Harcourt as your publisher. As I told you last summer, I chose him from among a lot of publishers who were after *Free Air* because, though at that time the firm wasn't yet really in existence at all, I have known Harcourt long and intimately. When he was general manager at Holt, I saw him, at different times, from the standpoint of author, book reviewer, and fellow publisher, and in each capacity I had more admiration for him than for any other publisher in the country.

He is a remarkable combination of sound business man and sound critic, and he does not seem to be afraid to advertise books—or to keep on continuing to push them even at that time when the ink on their pages is beginning to dry, and, therefore, most publishers hate to go on selling them.

His partners are also extremely able, and I hear that he is going to have a splendid list this spring. As he is still young in the game, and as he seems to believe in you, he would be an awfully good man to be connected with. Won't you think him over seriously? Of course I know nothing of your relations with McBride, but if they are at all unsatisfactory, why don't you write to Harcourt and see what he will say? I'd like to have you captured by the same firm which holds me in amiable serfdom.

As ever,
Sinclair Lewis

February 6

Dear Lewis:

I have been going over the figures of the money we spent in advertising *Free Air* to determine the exact number of copies on which we were to pay you a royalty of 10%. As so much of it was spent with dealers on a fifty-fifty basis—some of them sent us bills, and some of them deducted the amount from their remittances—it is a very considerable task. I am convinced that it would save us a couple of days work and considerable correspondence, and save you twenty-five or thirty dollars, if we agreed to pay you 10% on all we sold last year and 15% on sales beginning January first. Will you be satisfied with this rough-and-ready approximation, or are you curious to have us make a complete report? I hope you aren't.

I am spending a little money on it now in Chicago. We are getting re-orders from the Middle West, and now that the travelers are out there, there may be a considerable revival.

I enclose our spring list which I think will stir you. It is weak on fiction, but next fall we shall have *Main Street*, a new Dorothy Canfield novel,[1] an Elias Tobenkin,[2] and four bang-up English novels at least. The Keynes book[3] is selling like the dickens. We printed and bound 4000. These are all gone and now we are selling them faster than we can print them.

Ever yours,
Alf

---

[1] *The Brimming Cup*, but not published until March 1921.
[2] *The Road*, published January 1922.
[3] John Maynard Keynes: *Economic Consequences of the Peace*, January 1920.

[1920]

Washington, February 8

Dear Alf:

A year ago today, first night of *Hobohemia*, and you and I went!

Sure: I quite agree to the approximation of which you write—10% to Jan. 1st, and 15% for this year. Don't take time to figure it all out & make complete report.

Aren't I the darndest best author to deal with? But it's all camouflage so that I can be frightfully emotional and demanding over *Main Street* by and by. My hope is that you're going to have that for your big book for next fall, and possibly as a big seller for some seasons after. I believe that it will be the real beginning of my writing. No book and no number of short stories I've ever done have ever meant a quarter of what this does to me. I'm working on it 24 hours a day—whether I'm writing or playing.

Grand spring list. Great beginning, old man! Saw Heywood Broun down here last night, and told him what a grand publisher you are. I agree with him, and against you, about the title of his book; *Seeing Things at Night* has more charm to it than *Things Seen at Night*.[1] I'm sicking Fred Howe onto you with a new book he's writing.[2] *If* you two get together, and if his book goes, you can take over his earlier Scribner books.

Don't forget that if you decide to take over my Harper's books, you better do it before next fall and *Main Street*—but as that gives you many months, no hurry about it.

As ever,
Sinclair Lewis

We must announce *Main Street* early enough to keep the *title* cinched.

Washington, Thursday

Dear Alf:

Isn't Laski's review of Keynes in the last Nation a wonder? And perfect for quoting in ads.

Oh. Lay off Cabell. Not a chance to get him. He's absolutely tied up, by his own desire, to Guy Holt of McBride's. I saw Holt here this week and he's a wonder—intelligent, energetic, and broadly trained in publishing, and enthusiastic about you. Be a fine man for you to get hold of, if ever possible.

As ever,
Lewis

[1] Published as *Seeing Things at Night*, HB&Co., 1921.
[2] Frederic C. Howe: *Denmark: A Cooperative Commonwealth*, HB&Co., 1921.

With the exception of one short trip to New York in April, Lewis remained in Washington during this period, working on Main Street. *His correspondence with the office continued, but was mainly about business details.*

Washington, Friday

Dear Alf:

Gosh I'm rusty on writing advertising, and gosh but it's hard to describe a long realistic novel. But I've made the effort and am enclosing, as the Boss commands, two accounts, one about a hundred, and one about two hundred words long; and a third about the people. If nothing else, I hope they'll give you a basis for stuff of your own. I'm also writing Grace (who won't be back here till Apr. 26) to try a couple accts of the novel, as she's read it all.

I'm doing absolutely nothing but work on *Main Street*. Before June 1st I'll be able to give you an exact estimate of the length of the whole thing, together with, say, 100,000 words to start setting; and be able to give you all the rest by June 15th, or earlier.

I'm cutting immensely—never cutting for the sake of cutting, but invariably removing any paragraph or sentence that doesn't carry weight. I *think* it will come down to somewhere around 170,000 words. Why don't you announce the thing in Pub Weekly at least? Say, fella, you better send me copy of *Nonpartisan League*. Don't forget I'm the father and mother of that book—who suggested it? Heh? (If it doesn't sell, my Heh may not be so loud. . . .)

As ever,
sl

April 17

Dear Lewis:

Special thanks for coming back so promptly with the descriptive material. We are glad you are sticking to the novel. Aside from making dummies, a piece of it isn't much good to us until we have it all. In the present congestion in manufacture, you have to speak ahead for linotype machines and be sure that you have enough to keep them going on a job when you start them on it. But you are doing finely. Keep it up!

How is Grace? I know that anybody who tries to live with you would need a rest every so often.

We'll announce *Main Street* the first week in May.

Sincerely yours,
Alf

May 5

Dear Lewis:

You will be glad to know we have just sold 1000 *Free Air* to Australia. The price is only 52 cents a copy, but there is a hundred odd dollars in it for you and it means the beginning of your market there.

I hope nothing is hindering *Main Street*.

Sincerely yours,
Alf

Washington, May 8

Dear Alf:

Mighty glad to hear of the Australian sale. No; nothing is hindering *Main Street*. For example, yesterday, when I drove 190 miles to Berryville, Va. and back, was the first day I'd taken off in eleven days; even last Sunday I worked till 5:30 P.M. I'm revising with the most minute care and, I fancy, with success.

Why shouldn't *Main Street*, as an unusually factual picture of American life, go well in England? thus both increasing our return and getting that important come-back from England which seems so much to impress America? I wish you'd plan to send over proofs for consideration by English publishers as soon as you have them. I haven't the contract here in my office, but you and I share on English rights, don't we? If we don't, go ahead and we *will* share 'em, anyway.

There is a little, uh, a small matter . . . do I seem once or twice to have murmured of a certain matter—a man named Hoyns, connected, if I remember, with a firm of waste-paper dealers in Franklin Square, who has the paper-rights to certain earlier compendia of mine? Do you seem to—— Oh the hell you don't.

As ever,
sl

May 10

Dear Lewis:

We have been trying *Free Air* in England and Herbert Jenkins just offers us $316 for a duplicate set of plates for the British market outside of Canada, free from royalty. The one Australian order is worth more than that, and I expect we shall tell them to go to. We'll see what they say to *Main Street*.

Hoyns is in England. I'll get to him before we publish *Main Street*.

Sincerely yours,
Alf

Washington, Friday
Dear Alf:
Yes, I think I should tell Jenkins to go to the devil with his offer of $316. Perhaps after *Main Street* we can do better.

When you get to Hoyns and talking buying books, don't you think it would be much better to *leave out The Innocents*—not take it over at all or, if you have to take it with the rest, not republish it? The general opinion seems to be very strongly that it is too sentimental to be in agreement with the other books, and republishing it might do more harm than good.

I had lunch with Fred Howe, the Heywood Brouns, and the Gilson Gardners today. Mrs. Gardner is, you probably know, one of the three proprietors of the excellent small Wayfarers' Bookshop here. She is *more* than disposed to be friendly to all Harcourt books. They have sold more than 400 Keynes. She volunteered—quite without the slightest suggestion from anybody else—this important criticism. I think I can give it pretty nearly in her words: "There's one thing that HBH must do—they must vary the jackets of their serious books more. Using that same gray and the same general sort of make-up, they all look alike."

I remember as a book reviewer having the same feeling about the jackets of non-fiction books of Putnam and Macmillan—their similarity, whereby no new interest was, at first glimpse, aroused by a new book. Lay out a bunch of your non-fiction books and look at em together and think this over. Mrs. G. is fairly intelligent and may be rite.

SL

May 17
Dear Lewis:
Thanks for yours of Friday. As to *Main Street:* Gehrs and Don are crying for material for a dummy, and I guess you had better let us have something. Do you see it with a picture jacket, or a serious-looking one like a Bennett or Wells novel, or a cross between the two, whatever that may be? I confess it hasn't come clear in my mind, and I'd like your suggestions. We could do a line drawing somewhere on it.

As to jackets in general: there is a gap between the Knopf splashes and our two or three sorts for non-fiction. There is an advantage in having a book of ours generally recognized for its jacket the way Macmillan's and Doran's are. There is a great advantage, when paper orders are accepted subject to three months' delay, in being able to buy considerable supplies of jacket paper, rather than having to hunt around for odd quantities of odd colors. We shall treat each novel differently, at any rate, and of course we shall not be publishing quite so damn much non-fiction after we have hit the public in the eye with this spring's bunch.

All right, we won't buy *The Innocents* unless it won't cost us any more to get it than to leave it out.

Sincerely yours,
Alf

Washington, May 19
Dear Alf:

For *Main Street* jacket, I think perhaps a type-jacket, with a small pen-and-ink sidewise-panel picture of a real Middlewestern Main Street would be best. It must not be humorous or cartoon-y. I enclose a layout for one, with text and make-up; and also enclose a memo for the artist.

I'm not satisfied with the text as I give it on the jacket. Change it as much as you wish, or can it entirely—or use it if you *do* like it. I've tried to get into it an idea of the book as a dignified and serious production, with reality & drama both in it.

I am working right up to my final limit; and I am doing nothing but *Main Street*. But even so I'm not at all sure that I shall have it entirely done before July 1st. It's a damn long and detailed job, and requires unending care. I can however let you have 100,000 words all ready to print by June 1st, if you need it.

As ever,
sl

May 21
Dear Lewis:

I am going to answer your letter about jacket, etc. since these matters fall within my particular province. We should like to go ahead at once to prepare a thin dummy. For this we shall want enough manuscript to set up 32 pages—10,000 words should be enough for this.

We had a session this morning over the jacket. What we are chiefly interested in is a jacket that will sell the book to the limit, but none of us feels that your layout is the best we can do from this point of view. Of course we want the book to look dignified and serious, but not too dignified and serious. We do not want to suggest that it has something to do with travel or that it is a small-town study. The main emphasis, I think, should be on the story—something quite different from *Free Air*. I haven't a plan in mind that is concrete enough to sketch out, but I would like to talk the thing over with an artist and let him make some sketches and see what happens. The material you have sent will certainly be helpful. My hope is that among us all we may evolve a jacket that will be a wonder.

Faithfully yours,
Don

Washington, May 22

Dear Don:

In reply to yours of yesterday, I am sending herewith 90 pages—about 27,000 words—of the *Main Street* ms, together with the introductory matter. It's all ready to print. The estimate for the entire length of the book is 176,000 words, and this has been made very carefully—*ought to* be pretty close.

About the jacket—go to it! Change my plan as much as you like, or can it entirely. One idea for picture would be the girl staring in despair at stupid village street, of the straight, harsh, Midwestern kind I speak of in my memo for artist. Or she might be facing, rather scared by, a group of stodgy, stupid, small-town people—ready to struggle against them. But it MUST NOT be a love-story-romance-pretty-girl typical jacket, or it will lose the appeal to precisely the people most likely to be interested in *this* novel. How about a decoration rather than a straight picture—an effective Franklin Booth pen-and-ink, or the kind of decorations this chap Guernsey Moore often does for articles in the Sat Even Post? Anyway, good luck!

Sinclair Lewis

Washington, Saturday

Dear Alf:

In a few days you—or her as takes in packages—will receive a huge bundle from me, by express. It contains manuscripts and magazine-copies of short stories I have written. I have been holding them against the day when I should be ready to select from them for one or more books of short stories.

Would it be improper to ask you to store that bundle away somewhere till we're both ready (if ever!) to think about the matter of a book of short stories? There's so many of them now that I can't carry them round any longer, and if I stored them in an ordinary way, it would be hard to get hold of them if we did want them.

Zever,
sl

The lease was up June 1st on the house the Lewises had rented. Lewis moved to a new address in Washington where he planned to stay until the book was done, while Mrs. Lewis went to Virginia.

> (New address, June 1 to July 1:)
> 1127 Seventeenth Street, N.W.,
> Washington, D.C.
> Monday, May 31

Dear Don:

Both Grace and I are wildly enthusiastic about the sketch for the jacket. It's just right; I'm sure it's just the thing to sell the book; both dignified and interesting. And we like the shelf-back as much as the front.

I can't tell what the artist plans to do with the figure. If it weren't for the position of the girl's feet, I'd think she was back-to-us, looking at the street. And why wouldn't that be a good, and somewhat original, way to have her—instead of having her face us, have her back to us, as she looks at the street, and possibly instead of working out any details or costume, *have her in complete silhouette.*

The figure should be slender and smart, as now. But she should not have the little purse she now carries. Carol would not have one. She would either have nothing in her hand—or she might be carrying an overnight bag, which would indicate that she had just come from the train and was having her first glimpse of Main Street, thus suggesting the story.

I can't tell but I think the artist means to have Roseb Movie on the sign on the right—as a part of the sign Rosebud Movie Palace. But it also looks like Rose*s* Movie. It should be Roseb or Rosebud.

I'm very much excited about the jacket, and very much pleased. In letter-press on back or flap you mite use the subtitle, "The Story of Carol Kennicott," to give hint that this *is* a *story*, & possibly use w. my name, "Author of *The Job.*" Please give my congratulations to the artist—don't know who he is.

S Lewis

> June 1

Dear Lewis:

I am delighted with your enthusiasm about the jacket. I think it is an unusually striking composition of color and design. The fact that you couldn't tell whether the girl was coming or going reflects her hesitation on that point. She was waiting in the sketch for us to make up our mind. The artist will go ahead and place her back to the audience. She mustn't carry an overnight bag, however, because she went from the station in an automobile and went out afterwards to see the town. You see I have read the part of the manuscript you sent on, although I realized this was an unconventional thing for me to do.

Faithfully yours,
Don

Washington, Tuesday

Dear Alf:
Terribly glad you like the first 90 pages. Of one thing I am dead sure, both from my own revising and from Grace's remarks: the book steadily gets better as it goes on, and the last 200 pages will be much the best of all, which is, I think a good thing—people are attracted by the first part but they are *held*, they are made to commend a book, by the last part.

sl

Washington, Wednesday

Dear Alf:
Here's another note—characteristically modest! It is NOT intended to run as-is, but to form the basis for one or two or three publicity notes or advertising or catalogue spiels.

It probably would best be broken into two different notes: one about this-here author and how he got his material (and to that can be added matter about *The Job, Our Mr. Wrenn*, etc), and the other a challenging, attention-rousing, tho possibly trouble-making suggestion that Mr. Lewis does not find all beautiful and perfect in Red-blooded Small-town Americanism. I don't think it would hurt to let a hint of this critical attitude slip out; it would stir more eagerness than a supposition that (like all the rest save Sherwood Anderson) Mr. Lewis purrs over the American village as being God's own particular residence. Just as it is Keynes's *criticism* that makes his book go.

Grace is also writing some notes, which I'll send when I getum.

Zever,
sl

Washington, Wednesday, July 7

Dear Alf:
Thanks a lot for sending me the new P.W. (Publishers' Weekly) ad —much impressed and delighted by it. . . . Wouldn't it be a good thing

in future ads to mention fact that the book will NOT be, in any part, in any magazine, or will the travelers sufficiently convey that?

I'll be all through and shoot you in the complete ms in eight or ten days. Since I last saw you, in April wasn't it, I haven't stopped for a minute—been doing nothing but work on *Main Street*. Last night I worked till ten minutes after midnight! Grace is down country, but I've stayed here soz to work uninterrupted. My Gawd how much work there has been—how it has gone on, even tho I've tried to hurry. Done my damndest to get it down before but cdn't without scamping the work. But now —week or week and a half more is all, and I'm at it night and day.

Hope you will be in NY middle and end of next week so you'll get it. Will try to come up so that we can take up together any changes *if* any changes or cuts *should* be necessary. If you're out of NY but not too far away cd perhaps come to you.

I'm going to ask you for an advance of $500. Working on this so long—about eight solid months *—with prices what they have been, I'm almost entirely broke.

In haste,
sl

* 8 months since mid of last November, to say nothing of 2 or 3 months in previous years & efforts to get started.

July 8

Dear Lewis:

After I saw the advertisement in print in the Publishers' Weekly, I wished I had said that the book had not been offered for serialization anywhere, but the travelers are pounding that fact, and we shall say it in the next ad.

Your suggestion is just what I had hoped for, that we could have a day or two together after the manuscript is finished. I would like twenty-four quiet hours with it before I talk to you about it. I expect to be here right along. Hastings is off to camp, my mother off to the country, and we have room for you in the house at Mount Vernon.

Here is the check for $500. You deserve it.

Ever yours,
Alf

Washington, Friday

Dear Alf:

You're a *wonder!* That check so quickly! See you P.D.Q.
sl

Lewis came to New York from Washington on Saturday, July 17th, with the complete manuscript. Harcourt read it over the weekend and they discussed changes and deletions at his home in Mount Vernon. The discussions ended to their complete satisfaction, with Lewis making only minor alterations.

Kennebago Lake House,
Kennebago Lake, Maine
July 27

Dear Don:

Here she is—the last thirty pages of *Main Street*—thank the Lord. Now to go fishing! It's about perfect here—lakes, pines, birches, mountains, cold nights.

Will you please tell Miss Eayrs that I'll be writing her some publicity notes P.D.Q.? And will you please ask her if she hasn't that photograph showing me sitting at a table with typewriter, cigarettes, etc. In some ways it's the best one I've ever had.

As ever,
Sinclair Lewis

Kennebago Lake, August 11

Dear Alf:

There's several things I've been thinking of that I want to take up with you.

Claude Washburn

I spoke to you about a new novel, *Order*, by Claude Washburn, published by Duffield. Washburn has ability and should grow considerably. He's really on the job now after some years of rather taking it easy in Italy. I have here a letter from him in which he expresses dissatisfaction with Duffield. He has finished about 2/3 of a new novel,[1] apparently much his biggest one. Will you do this: write him inviting him to send in what he has done (this is his suggestion). This looks to me like the *possibility* of annexing a real fiction writer, and you won't be tying yourself up at all.

Letter to critics

I've thought (and rather worried) a lot about the problem of the *real* critics assuming that *Main Street* is another *Free Air* and not really reading it, or giving it to assistants. I wish that in a week or two you would write to some or all of the following a letter (form letter with a personal paragraph, perhaps) something to this effect: The last two novels

[1] *The Lonely Warrior*, HB&Co., 1922.

by Lewis, *Innocents* and *Free Air*, have been but interludes during the planning of *Main Street*, and the actual work on it has taken most of the last two years. I presume that you like his *The Job*. Well, this is *much* bigger than *The Job*—just as true and much better done. It is almost the first book which really pictures American small-town life. It has *not* been pub. in or offered to any magazine. I'm writing you about it beforehand in the hope that when it comes you will be able to give it your personal attention. *Something* like that to: Henry Mencken, Hackett or Lippmann on New Republic, Van Wyck Brooks on the Freeman, Floyd Dell on the Liberator, Heywood Broun on N.Y. Tribune, Mrs. Dawson on the Globe, Benét on NYEvening Post, Franklin P. Adams on Tribune (BE SURE SEND HIM A COPY), Christopher Morley on NYEvening Post, O.O.McIntyre, who does a colyum syndicated thru US, Wilson Follett, Lawrence Gilman, William Lyon Phelps, Stuart Sherman. AND any other really important critics you can think of.

I think that such a letter—a short, tactful one, interesting yet devoid of superlatives—would be of importance in counteracting the danger of this being neglected as another magaziney tale. Couldn't Spingarn—if he reads the proofs and likes the book—write some of these letters to the critics and sign them himself, perhaps?

Publicity Notes

Why don't you save yourself and Miss Eayrs the task of writing publicity notes (and occasionally Planting a Story) by having some trained publicity man or woman do it on the side? *And it does take special training such as having been on a newspaper.* Most publishers fall down in doing publicity because, however fine and full their training as publishers, they've never had that newspaper experience which is the one basis of getting publicity. Thass all!

As ever,
s.l.

August 14
Dear Lewis:

Thanks for yours of the 11th. I am glad to notice that you date it. I had to go back through your letters the other day to look up something. Something like "Thursday" is all you indulge in. Of course I am interested in Claude Washburn. I have written to him. Thank you.

The sort of letter you mention for critics will go, of course, except that I have made a point of running into a number of them, and doing part of it by word of mouth. I know I have Heywood Broun and the Post folks primed for it in that way.

We do have some trained people to do special publicity. You know I don't believe much in the John-Hobank-has-stubbed-his-third-toe-and-so-can't-finish-his-new-novel-until-Thursday sort of publicity, and thank heaven you don't either.

Have you become an earnest fisherman?

Ever yours,
Alf

(*Undated*)

Dear Alf:

I *think* the title of the next gt. realistic not-to-be-serialized nov. by Mr. Sinclair Lewis, which'll be the story of the Tired Business Man, of the man in the Pullman smoker, of our American ruler, of the man playing golf at the country club at Minneapolis, Omaha, Atlanta, Rochester, will be the name of the central character, and that name, and title, will be (I think): PUMPHREY. How does it strike you? Doesn't it delineate the man to you? And titles that are names are rather successful in sticking in mind, for example: *Clayhanger, Mary Olivier, Kipps, McTeague, Ethan Frome, Adam Bede, Silas Marner, Nicholas Nickleby, David Copperfield, Mlle. Maupin, Madame Bovary*, pretty good precedents, don't you think. G. T. Pumphrey, of Monarch City. . . .

Like it?

And it will be done—

Oh, Gawd!

As ever,
sl

Lewis and his wife stayed at Kennebago Lake through September 9th, arriving in New York on Friday, the 10th. For several weeks they remained in New York at the Manhattan Square Hotel. Mrs. Lewis, however, went to Washington house-hunting and rejoined Lewis in New York for about a week before their departure for Washington on October 17th. Main Street was published on the 23rd.

TWO

Publication and Success

[1920]
1639 19th St., NW.
Washington, D.C.
Thursday Oct. 21

Dear Alf:

Lord it's beautiful—the three, to date, F.P.A. boosts, and the Broun review! I'm terribly glad. Bully letter from Cabell—seems to like the book a lot and says he's proud to be in the dedication.[1]

And, with just-recd check from Post for story sold while I was in NY, Lorimer has raised my price per story from $900 to $1000, so everything flourishes.

I snook secretively into Brentano's here yesterday and noted they still had a pile of about 15 *Free Airs*. Hope to Gawd they get rid of them, and hope there's not many other stores still heavily stocked therewith, or naturally it'll cramp their enthusiasm for *Main Street*. Perhaps *M St* will also start up *Free Air* again. In fact: @$"?%*"(#;;)$*-/%**—$. as Guy Pollock so well says in that brilliant new book *Main Street*, which you really must read.

sl

In the early days Harcourt often wrote to Lewis by hand or from home, and there are no copies of many of his letters. However, Lewis's references to them often supply continuity.

Washington, October 25

Dear Alf:

You know how glad I am of the news that calls for *M St* have been such that you've had to reprint. Have you ever talked to Robert Benchley about it, for the World?

[1] Lewis dedicated *Main Street* to James Branch Cabell and Joseph Hergesheimer.

This letter is about three possible Harcourt authors:

Arthur Bullard

Author of *A Man's World* and *Comrade Yetta* (both admirable novels), *The Stranger*, recent and pretty good: books on Morocco, Panama, and Russia, all published by Macmillan. He lives here in Washington, and I was sounding him out the other day. He is, I'm sorry to say, of the Cadet faction regarding Russia, which shows poor judgment; and certainly his recent novel hasn't shown any increased skill. So he's by no means a certain bet.

Arthur D. Call

Brother-in-law of George Soule. Secretary of the American Peace Society, Washington, and editor of The Advocate of Peace. He has a series of ten articles on the idea that the recent war has not destroyed the peace movement which would make a book at least worth considering.

Gene McComas

There is, in California, a girl who, if she would, could write as well as Joe Hergesheimer: Mrs. Francis McComas, wife of a water-colorist well known on the Pacific Coast. She's young—probably 32; father editor of an Oakland, Calif. paper; when he died, she had to leave art school and go to work on Oakland paper; since her marriage has gone back to painting. That's why she hasn't written more—has taken it out in painting. But like many others—Hergesheimer, Yeats, Robt Chambers—I expect her to turn from one kind of color to the other some day.

I judge her great ability by her letters. Ordinarily of course that's a deceptive basis of judgment but so remarkable is her sense of color in words, so brilliant her phrasing, so distinguished her taste, so illuminating her bits of scenes, so fascinated her interest in everything from smart parties at Del Monte to Jap fisher boats wrecked on the beach, that I know what she can do. She declares that she has no sense of plot; I've given her hell many times but with no result. I'm quite sure that a letter from the great publisher would stir her where I couldn't.

So!

Sinclair Lewis

Washington, Wednesday, October 27

Dear Alf:

Letter this morning from John Peter Toohey, theatrical press agent who writes many stories for Sat Even Post, but a man I've never met or had correspondence with or know anything about. He says, among other things: "I lay in bed this morning until 1:15 reading *Main Street* and if it isn't the best novel written in these United States in a decade I'll eat my hat. I've just written Harry Mencken to go out and grab a copy instanter and I'm calling Booth Tarkington's attention to it in a letter which I am sending him."

I've thanked him and suggested that perhaps you may call him up. My idea is this: *Perhaps*, IF Tark likes it, you can get, through Mr. Toohey, a boost from Tark quotable in ads. Mencken we'd better let alone—he'll be getting touchy.

Hope all goes gloriously.

As ever,
sl

Have qualms about name Pumphrey now—too English and mite be thought humorous. But I think I shall use for next novel's title a man's name, standing alone—Pumphrey or some other name.

October 27

Dear Lewis:

I enclose the Heywood Broun part of this morning's Tribune. It is intensely interesting, and of course a good thing from every point of view.[1] This letter is to say it is my judgment that you would be very unwise to answer it yourself. Somebody else will, and the thing to do is to get as many people as possible passing it back and forth, without your coming in to settle it. Forgive all this present tense, imperative mode about what is after all your business.

Yours,
Alf

Washington, Thur. Oct 28

Dear Alf:

Your special delivery letter came last evening. No indeed, I shan't answer the Floyd Dell comments in the Tribune—shan't even comment. The Dell discussion is stimulating & I'm glad of it.

As ever,
SL

[1] Refers to a controversy in the New York *Tribune* in which Heywood Broun answered Floyd Dell's attack on *Main Street*.

October 29

Dear Lewis:

The letters from Toohey and Flandrau are bully and very useful. Pass on anything else of the sort you get. I am using them in a letter to the trade, and if they pile up enough, we can get permission to use them in public advertising.

We have orders for a thousand out of the next edition which will be in the first of the week.

Sincerely yours,
Alf

Washington, October 30

Dear Alf:

Wonderful letter from Philip Curtiss! Thank you very much for sending it to me. Doesn't Curtiss live in Hartford, at least part of the time? Couldn't you get him to review *M St* for Hartford paper? Would be marvelous to quote.

Mencken likes it. John Peter Toohey writes me that Mencken wrote him, "I have read *Main Street* from end to end and with great joy. It is, as you say, a fine piece of work. It seems to me that his quotations from the Gopher Prairie Dauntless are even better than his conversations." Then, today, comes a voluntary letter from Mencken to me saying, "I hasten to offer my congratulations. *Main Street* is a sound and excellent piece of work—*the best thing of its sort that has been done so far*. More, I believe it will sell. I'll review it in the January Smart Set, the first issue still open."

Luck!

As ever,
sl

Washington, Monday Nov. 1

Dear Alf:

Delighted to know of orders against second printing. Like your letter to the trade extremely. My only criticism is that I'd quote the Flandrau letter differently—in case you use it again. There may some time be a place for the longer version, and it's good to get in the "no volume has gone deeper"—unless it's *too* superlative. I'd quote most of the last paragraph in Curtiss's letter—about "may not seem of calibre of *Anna Karenina*, but I know of no more delicate scene in literature" etc.

Do you know anybody who is in touch with W. L. George? He's beginning to air his newly formed opinions on American novels. Wouldn't it be highly advisable to get a *Main Street* through to him in some personal sort of way, and get him to read it while he's lecturing and being interviewed all round?

As ever,
sl

November 4

Dear Lewis:

I have seen Mr. Call. Nothing in it for us yet. I shan't bother about Arthur Bullard or Gene McComas. Bullard has gone too far without really doing anything, and life is too short for the other.

I like the idea of "a man's name" for the next novel, but not any queer-sounding name like Pumphrey. Get a name like *Main Street*.

Henry Forman has been in and given us some winged words that we can quote. Note the fit that Lewisohn throws in this week's Nation, and even the respectful consideration in the Weekly Review.

Sincerely yours,
Alf

Nov. 6

Dear Lewis:

Philadelphia North American had a decent review this morning, and Chicago Daily News a perfunctory one last Wednesday. It's curious that the sophisticated Tribune folks, and a real critic like Lewisohn see the greatness of the book while the provinces like it but lack the nerve or the sense. Not so curious after all, just too bad. Not that these reviews are in any sense slams. I suppose I want everybody on his hind legs about it and nothing less.

Yours,
A.H.

November 6

Dear Lewis:

I am sending you an advance copy of Jacob Wassermann's *The World's Illusion*. Since Spingarn has read *Main Street*, he is not so sure that *The World's Illusion* is the most distinguished work we are publishing. What do you think?

Yours,
Alf

Washington, November 11

Dear Alf:

The Nation review is tremendous! Did you see Robert Benchley's review in the NY World for Monday?

About the next novel. We ought to be thinking of it before too long. Mustn't let too long a time elapse between *M St* and next. The principal problem will be to finance it. About that we'll know more by next May, say; but I wish you'd keep it in mind. . . . I'm busy making many notes for it.

Pumphrey, you say, is too freakish a name. I don't think, tho, that the title name ought to be too common—like Jones, Smith, Robertson, Thompson, Brown, Johnson—for the reason that then people will associate the name not with the novel but with their numerous acquaintances who have that common name. What do you think of the following: BURGESS—BABBITT—HORNBY—or some name of that type—normal, yet not too common?

A New Haven friend writes me that Prof. Billy Phelps is enthusiastic. Did you send a copy to Prof. Stuart Sherman? *Might* be worth while?

As ever,
sl

Nov. 11

Dear Lewis:

I wish we could have another hefty novel next fall, but I'd rather have it much later than not to have it of real heft, and of course so would you. "Burgess" is a good name.

I've just read Zona Gale's *Lulu Bett;* it's a clean tight job, should interest you for the sheer economy of words to get the effect, but it doesn't hold a candle to *Main Street.*

Yours much,
Alf

[1920]

Washington, Nov. 11

Dear Alf:

Would it maybe be wise to send a copy of the Nation review to H. G. Wells, Bernard Shaw, Galsworthy, Conrad, Geo Moore, Walpole, Compton Mackenzie, W. L. George, Arnold Bennett, Edmund Gosse, Leonard Merrick, Thomas Hardy, Edith Wharton, with a letter:

> We fancy that you are interested in the advance of American fiction. Doesn't the enclosed review indicate to you the rise of a new and authentic interpreter of America? The New York Nation, under its present eager and international-minded editorship, is of somewhat more than respectable judgment—and it has never, so far as we know, shown quite such enthusiasm for a novel as it has for *Main Street*.
>
> Have you a copy of the book? Would you like one? If you will send us a Yes on a card, we shall hasten to send you one. We believe that in it you will find expressed, honestly, observantly, without the tabu of the old tribal formulae, the real America of today—Middlewestern villages and farms, business men, restless women.
>
> We admit that we have a crafty hope that you may perhaps be moved to send us a sentence of approbation, inasmuch as your verdict means so very much to America, but we promise not to pursue you with further requests for such an opinion unless you feel really like volunteering it.

Would you like a copy?

Might something like that flush a covey, possibly? I dunno. *If* you got anything, could also be used in selling edition to England. I include WLGeorge and Walpole with the bunch, despite the fact that they've had copies, because I suspect they're getting American novels in piles, and tend not to read 'em. For Edith Wharton, being American, partly American maybe, the letter might have to be changed—but not so much, not so much!

Thrilled over the tidings of the melting of the second printing. Could you get Mencken to give you one quotable sentence in anticipation of his review? If you happened to run into him, you might be able diplomatically to approach the matter.

As ever,
sl

P.S. IF you want to do this, and IF any of the authors do send for the book, I think you could properly, despite promise not to pursue them, send *with the book* a note to remind them of what we want:

> As we promised, we shall not pursue you for an opinion on *Main Street*, but if you do by any chance feel moved to send us one voluntarily, it will be of invaluable assistance in our none-too-easy task of persuading America that this is a book worthy of its earnest interest.

P.P.S. I suggest sending the Nation review, instead of a book, first, because thus, if they do answer, you can be sure of some interest on their parts when the book arrives. And copies of the Nation are cheaper than books for the experiment—as experiment it would be.

Washington, Nov. 12

Dear Alf:

You speak of your wish for hefty novel next fall. God, I wish so, too! It's purely a matter of financing. If I had the money I'd be working on it right now—tho indeed I am making notes, lots of them daily. The devil of it is that it will take about one full year from the time I start the actual writing of the book to the time when, with proofs and manufacture all over, it can actually be published. I don't see how I can begin that writing till next spring, at the earliest, which means publication in spring of 1922, at the earliest. And, double damn it, with the need of getting ahead, I don't even know that I can start it next spring. But of course there are three possibilities for financing aside from H.B.&H. making me a guarantee. Those are: *Main Street* may really make some money. "Willow Walk"[1] may go as a movie. The musical comedy may go over.—We'll probably have to postpone Europe some more!

When I do the next one, it will be at least as good as *Main Street*. I think it will be better. I think the central character will bulk larger than Carol. And all details will be done with at least equal care. And it will NOT be serialized—at least not in any magazine with a large circulation, and probably not in any at all.

Some time this winter I'm going to some Midwestern city—say Cincinnati or Dayton or Milwaukee—and complete the material for the next novel which I made a good beginning of gathering in Minneapolis, St. Paul, Seattle, San Francisco, New Haven, Washington. . . . I want to make my city of 300,000 just as real and definitive in the novel as I made, or tried to make, Gopher Prairie.

sl

Wash'n, Nov. 13

Dear Alf:

Hope orders have now justified printing of 3d edition. Some blowout in the Tribune yesterday. Isn't it getting to be time that somebody gently answered Floyd Dell, or everybody will be saying that I've been unfair. I shan't answer, but I wonder if you couldn't get somebody to—

[1] Short story by Lewis published in the *Saturday Evening Post*, August 10, 1918.

[1920]

say John Peter Toohey, Philip Curtiss, or somebody you know personally? If so, couldn't you send 'em a copy of the following, announcing that you do NOT wish to influence unduly, but that it does represent our attitude:

Why this controversy as to the attitudes of Felix Fay in *Moon-Calf* and Carol in *Main Street* toward small towns—toward American life? The answer is so simple! Felix really is Floyd Dell, and therefore, since Mr. Dell is a genius, since he is introspective and creative, would be about equally happy or unhappy on Main Street or in the Quartier Latin. Whereas Carol Kennicott distinctly is not Sinclair Lewis. She is, as Mr. Lewis specifically states, a small-town woman, differing from other small-town women only in being more sensitive and articulate. Another thing: Felix is young, detached, and he is a male. He can work in factories, go to beer-flowing picnics, be ardent at socialist locals. But Carol, wife of the country doctor, watched, criticized, could do none of those things without a courage so extraordinary that it would make her not a small-town woman but an Ellen Key.[1] Indeed in one paragraph she is presented as wishing that she could do just the sort of thing Felix does—work in the mill. Finally, though he is born in a village, Felix spends years in a town of 30,000, with half a dozen philosophers and poets. Half a dozen confidants are as good as half a thousand. But in her prairie town of 3000, Carol hasn't even one—and it may be said that there are ten or twenty thousand Carols in this country who would be amply content, for all their lives, if they could have merely the half dozen that Felix does have.

Wouldn't that be worth while—if you can ethically and worthily plant it? It is, if I am not mistaken, both true and pertinent.

As ever,
sl

Washington, Nov. 17
Dear Alf:

I strolled through Brentano's, Pearlman's, and Ballantyne's, this afternoon. I couldn't, of course, examine minutely, but I looked about pretty well, and the *Main Street* jacket does beautifully stand out. Well, I couldn't see a single copy in either Ballantyne's or Pearlman's, and in Brentano's only two copies, which were stuck away on a shelf *under a counter*. Of course you can tell more in one minute from order sheets than I could from a hundred snooping trips. I know there's nothing these damned authors do oftener than complain that their bally masterpieces aren't being done-right-by in local bookstores, and I make this report for what little value it may have.

[1] Swedish feminist and writer.

Thanks a lot for copy of letter to Columbia *re* Pulitzer Prize, for having thought of submitting *M St* for the prize, and for note about 3d printing. I don't see how a publisher could possibly get behind a book more actively and more intelligently than H B & H have behind *M St!*
As ever,
sl

November 18

Dear Lewis:
We thought there had probably been enough stir in Washington by this time. They'll get the reaction from New York presently, surely by the first of December when Congress assembles. The book is really selling in New York City. Baker and Taylor take another thousand, which just cleans out the second printing. In fact, we are not filling the entire order at once so as to be sure to have stock until we get the third lot next week. We have bought a piece of paper which will print 6000 more as soon as the third lot is off press. When that paper is used up, it will mean a total of 26,000. All this gives us some real money to spend on our advertising scheme.
Yours,
Alf

·Washington, Nov. 19

Dear Alf:
Prof. Wm Lyon Phelps lectured here last night. He says that he is going to speak extensively of *Main Street* in his lectures in Philadelphia, Bridgeport, and New Haven, and that he will urge his audiences (which run about 800, largely women) to *buy* the book. Gus might tell this to buyers from those three cities, if he sees them or is writing them. Prof. Phelps said to me, "1920 is an extraordinary year in American fiction. There hasn't been another with so many good novels for many, many years. And the three outstanding books—the three on which I shall specialize in lectures—are *The Age of Innocence, Main Street* & *Miss Lulu Bett.*

I enclose letter from George Doran. As *The Young Visiters*[1] was presented here in play form this week, and was excellent, I wrote him about it suggesting publicity stunts, hence his letter. (Also I think that

---

[1] A novel by Daisy Ashford, a nine-year-old English girl, which caused a sensation when J. M. Barrie, who had written the introduction, was accused of being the author.

[1920]

any pleasant relations between HBH and GHD are worth while, and I contribute as a humble member of the firm of HBH.)

So!
sl

Washington, Nov. 20

Dear Alf:

Bully ad, the big one for the Times for a week from now. Have bought *Miss Lulu Bett* and will read it. My first impression is of the horribleness of the jacket. Mighty glad you insisted on full picture for front of *Main St* jacket.

The name of the next novel will be, I think: FITCH. The name of the central character will be Jefferson Fitch. I believe it combines normality with sufficient distinctiveness to be remembered; it sounds as American as John Brown. How do you like it—especially after a day or two?

sl

Washington, November 24

Dear Alf:

If you wanted to, I think you could get a line from Edna Ferber about *M St*—nice letter from her but nothing that can be detached for quotation. Same about Charles G. Norris, author of *Salt*.

Carl Van Doren writes me that he heard a Columbia instructor or professor "arguing with a whole gang of men at luncheon that *Main Street* is the most truthful novel ever written." If you run into Van Doren, or call him up, why don't you find out who said that; possibly get said unknown to write twenty words to that effect—though of course he may not yet be sufficiently advanced on the academic ladder so that the Dear Readers will listen to him.

Zasall!
sl

Washington, November 26

Dear Alf:

CHEERS! An unsolicited letter from Galsworthy, apparently out west lecturing. It runs as follows: ". . . I am an ignorant person, but it seems to me that so wholesome and faithful a satiric attitude of mind has been rather conspicuously absent from American thought and literature. . . . It's altogether a brilliant piece of work and characterisation. My hearty congratulations. Every country, of course, has its Main Streets, all richly deserving of diagnosis, but America is lucky to have found in you so poignant and just and stimulating a diagnostician. . . ."

I should imagine from the friendliness of this that you might be able to get him to write for you something to be used in advertising etc., or get him to let you use sentences from the letter, or both. It does seem to me that Galsworthy's undoubted fame and reputation for sheer honesty would make this worth while.

Lewis Galantiere, an intelligent chap I know here in Washington, friend to Sherwood Anderson, Guy Holt, Burton Rascoe, et al., is going to France, to be stationed there on a business mission. He insists that *Main Street* must be translated into French. He seems to know something of French publishers and of the proper approach. He is a fine lad and I have given him a card to Spingarn so that he may talk over this with him.

Corking, 17,000 already. We'll get that 100,000.

Thaznuff
sl

Washington, November 27

Dear Alf:

Here's something possibly even better than the John Galsworthy letter—the enclosed editorial on *Main Street* by William Allen White because Middle America knows White and knows that he knows the Middlewest. It can't be said of him, as it might of Galsworthy, "but he is no judge of Main Street." In his letter Mr. White says: "Mrs. White and I, reading aloud, have just finished *Main Street*, and I hasten to tell you what a noble thing you have done. . . . With all my heart I thank you for Will Kennicott and Sam Clark; they are the Gold Dust Twins of common sense. I don't know where in literature you will find a better American, or more typical, than Dr. Will Kennicott. . . . If I were a millionaire, I should buy a thousand of those books and send them to my friends and then I would go and bribe the legislature of Kansas to make *Main Street* compulsory reading in the public schools. *No American has done a greater service for his country in any sort of literature than you have done.*"

Mr. White says he wants to send out a number of *M St*'s to various friends with my name in them. For this, he sends a blank check to be sent to you and by you filled out. (My God, what trust!) He says, "I want to use your book for a Christmas present."

Wouldn't a copy of White's editorial and one of Galsworthy's letter be very valuable things to send to the proper persons regarding the

Pulitzer Novel Prize—in addition to the clippings which, in your letter to some Columbia professor, you said you were sending? White is known as a fine upstanding American of great intelligence.

And wouldn't a copy of Galsworthy's letter be of value for trying to sell a respectably large edition to the English publishers?

I am glad of the beautiful break on 2nd and 3rd printings. Do you know, I think we ought all now to be expecting to sell not 40,000 alone but actually 100,000! And I think we can do it! The book has just *begun* to percolate outside of NY, and 15,000 are gone. Give us a year and a quarter of pushing, and we ought to see 100,000 sale *anyway*—which would enable SL to write his next novel with clear sailing and then some, and would, I hope, with costs slightly diminishing, give HBH a little money to spare. Won't you talk that over with Gus, Don, et al. and see if they don't think with me that there's a fine sailing wind for 100,000, and reasons for working toward it? If this proves true, if the 3rd and 4th printings go as the second have, pretty soon you'll have to begin to print 10,000 at a clip, don't you think?

In all the above I say "we" not "you," because I expect to do anything and everything I can to help. For one thing: As you remember, our contract arrangement is that I am to receive 10% as long as active advertising goes on, then 15%. Well, I should quite serenely see myself receiving only 10% all the way up to 100,000 if continued advertising will help the sale of the book.

And if it's any help I'll keep up these profuse epistles, tho God knoweth—even to my naive authorship it occurs—it may be that the one thing I could do to help would be to relieve you of all this flood save perhaps such items as the Galsworthy letter! But till I get beaten up, I go on trustingly writing at length.

By the way, doesn't the Galsworthy letter suggest some merit in my recently at-length-outlined scheme to try to get comments from Wells, Shaw, George, et al.? You might well quote to them from the Galsworthy letter!!

So! Off for 100,000! Alf, we've got 'em all by the ears! Harcourt, Boni, Knopf, Huebsch will dominate the publishing world and me—oh hell, I'll go home and read a book about real estate as preparation for

FITCH
by the author of *Main Street*
First printing:
50,000

sl

November 27

Dear Lewis:

The Galsworthy letter is perfectly fine. The printings now ordered total 32,000. It is not a question of printing 5000 or 10,000 according to the sales you expect in quite the fashion which used to prevail when you were in the publishing business. The way the paper market is, it is a question of picking up what you can find of the right size and weight, and the odd numbers mean so many books according to the piece of paper. As the paper market is falling a little, we don't want to load up with heavy supplies at the top price, but keep just far enough ahead so that we can surely keep our books in stock. Knopf is out of *Moon-Calf* for two weeks.

The letters went to the English authors with the Nation review, so it is too late to send them a quotation from Galsworthy.

As you know, we thought of raising the price after the first edition. Gus and Don and I have discussed it a good deal, have said 100,000 to ourselves before you did, and don't feel like monkeying with the price at least until the book gets all the legs under it that it will; say sometime next year. What we are out to do on this book is to make you as an author. We'll get a contribution to our overhead now and can take profits next time or the time after that.

I suppose you realize the change that has come over your position as a novelist because of the success this book has had and is going to have. It is something like the change that has come over me as a publisher in the last year because of the success this business has had, and I must give you a tip out of my experience. There were a great many people who had all the good wishes in the world for this enterprise, and to whom I could spill my hopes and aspirations as frankly and freely as to you or to Don. With success, that changes somewhat, and one has to stop wearing his heart on his sleeve and play with the cards closer to his belt. I should think that with an author whose fortune seems sometimes to depend a good deal on the whim of the public, the jealousies that grow up are apt to be even more acute. You have now made a great success, and it is going to be a good deal bigger, and so very early in the game when there is no particular reason for saying it as far as you are concerned, I am giving you this little lead out of my own experience with a warning to watch your step in your letters, and perhaps most of all, watch from whom you accept any favors.

Ever yours,
Alf

Washington, November 29

Dear Alf:

The *Main Street* ad in the Sunday Times of yesterday is magnificent —simply leaps out of the page, indeed, leaps out of that whole magazine-review-section, at the reader. It's one of the best book ads I've ever seen; one of the best examples of use of white space.

Bully letter, yours of Saturday. Your tip about not wearing my heart on my sleeve, about being careful of letters and of alliances, is excellent and shall be kept in mind. I'm glad you gave it to me. It's the sort of point of view to which, if it were not early suggested, one might win slowly and by experience none too pleasant. I'm awfully glad you-all see a possible 100,000, as I do. I think you must know how much I appreciate your faith—and all the damn, straining, hustling attention to details you have to give.

As ever,
sl

Washington, November 30

Dear Alf:

I had hoped to be able to keep from doing it, but I'm afraid I shall have to ask you to let me have another $500 on *Main Street* royalties, and P.D.Q. I received, this morning, a rejection of a story from the Post, and on that story I had considerably counted to keep me going and a little more. I shall send story to Harper's, but I can't bank on it, and meantime the bank account is down to almost nothing.

I am, frankly, having a hell of a time in trying at once to turn myself back into the successful S.E.P. writer I was a year ago—and yet do for them nothing but stories so honest that they will in no way get me back into magazine trickiness nor injure the *M St.* furore. And so, three weeks ago, I destroyed 60,000 words of just-finished copy which, with a couple weeks revising, I'm quite sure I could have sold to the Post for four or five thousand dollars, but which was so shallow, so unreal, so sentimental that (featured as they do feature a serial, even a short one) it would have been very bad for *Main Street*. God knows I don't expect you to bear the responsibility for this, which may have been foolhardy. I relate it only to prove how vigorously I have been attacking this problem.

This torn up, I started the story they have just rejected. I tried to make it a real story of business, and probably I fell between two stools. Fortunately the third story, which I shall send the Post in a few days, is of a romantic type, honestly written yet by its "go" almost certain to attract them. But meanwhile I need five hundred a good deal—damn it—

had been hoping to leave *all* my royalties with you for use in the immediate needs of your business.

Of course one thing that complicates my magazine writing is that *all* my keenest eagerest thought tends to sneak off into my plans, thoughts, notes about *Fitch*—which will, I believe, correct any faults of "exterior vision," of sacrifice of personality to types and environment, which in his New Republic review Francis Hackett finds in *Main Street*.

Oh, I'll get along all right, without, I hope, too much leaning on you. We're going to do, together, Alf, the biggest job of novelizing in the country, and that I suppose naturally takes a little more sweat and worry than smoothly issuing neat books. I'm going, of course, to go on plugging at the Post, but I don't believe I shall ever again be the facile Post trickster I by God was—for which, doubtless, we shall in the long run be glad.

Nice note from Fannie Hurst, whom I've never met nor corresponded with: "I am so deeply glad that *Main Street* has been *said* (and in what masterly fashion!) that the impulse to write you simply will not be gainsaid."

Heh-cha-cha, them kind words is all dissimilar to this morning's note from Lorimer politely but firmly placing my short story back in papa's hands b God.

sl

December 1

Dear Lewis:

Here is the check for $500 you ask for. Don & Spingarn and I have talked the whole matter over, and your letter and our talk, and what has happened to *Main Street* lead us to make the following proposal: Actual sales of *Main Street* are within four or five hundred copies of 20,000. We have contracted for within $300 of the advertising appropriation earned by 20,000 copies, and copy I am sending off today will eat that up. You know as well as we how good the prospects are for large sales the rest of this year and on into next year. If you will consider the enclosed $500 check to cover January, we will agree to pay you out of royalties earned $500 a month during 1921. I think we are running very little risk, but I want to get the records clear. I hope that a balance will be built up so that this arrangement or a modification of it will continue for a long time and you can go ahead and write the novels that you ought to and want to, but we are making the proposal only for the year 1921, and you mustn't have any hard feelings if it should turn out to be for only 1921.

What I hope is that you can get a short story or two ahead of the game during December and that our guarantee will enable you to plan your next year's life and work as you want to as a novelist. Let me know what you think of all this.

Ever yours,
Alf

Washington, Dec. 3

Dear Alf:

I am, of course, immensely pleased by your offer of a guarantee of $500 a month during 1921 (the $500 received to cover January), and I am glad to accept it—with the prayer and hope that it will be much more than covered by the royalties, and that you will be taking no risk. . . . If *Main Street* doesn't go the 100,000 we hope, it will, I think, go forty or fifty thousand for a minimum.

What I plan to do is this: Keep plugging at short stories till some time in, say, March, getting four or five or six thousand ahead over and above the guarantee. But of this time I expect to spend say from about January 15 to March 15 in Cincinnati or other Midwestern cities completing my ideas, notes, and facts for FITCH. I'll be writing short stories part of the day but circulatin' the rest. Then about April 1st I can begin the actual writing of *Fitch*, and possibly before that—particularly if I sell movie rights of "Willow Walk," which I have directed my agent to sell if he can get a renewal of the offer of $2500 previously made.

Fitch, then, will be ready for publication either spring or fall of 1922—I don't believe it will hurt a bit to have a year and a half or two years elapse between *Main Street* and *Fitch*, and I can't, doing the job I want to, get it ready before.

I may, after next April, with my material all ready, go to England for the actual writing of it—both because of the joy and benefit of that experience, and because it will actually be cheaper to live in Europe than to live here.

Like all my plans always (and yours occasionally, b' God!) the above is subject to change, but that's about how it maps out now. I shall certainly finish *Fitch* at the earliest possible moment consistent with proper work; I shall certainly not serialize it; and we will—or shall! certainly have expectant interest from critics, bookstores, and private boosters.

I'm glad to say the story rejected by SEP which caused me to write you has just been accepted by Harper's—they pay only $500, half of what SEP would, but this will relieve the stress, and in many ways it is better to be writing for Harper's than for SEP—leaves me free-er and introduces me to better book-buying audience. And last nite I finished and sent off to Post a story which, if they don't take, Harper's certainly will. So I'm already getting ahead the surplus which, for safety, I ought to have above the guarantee.

I more than understand your limiting the first offer of guarantee to 1921, with renewal probable but not at all assured, and I shan't be hurt if it proves inadvisable to go on with it after '21.

I am right now working on *Fitch*. Not a day goes by, literally, that I don't add many notes to my plans for it, and when I get to Cincinnati or somewhere, I'll be piling them up—to be digested, selected, discarded, expanded. This, of course, I can do nicely while plugging at short stories. But when I start the actual writing, I shall do nothing, think nothing, eat nothing but *Fitch*, whether I'm here or in England.

Good letter—at last—from Hergesheimer. He says, among others, "*Main Street* is a courageous, a lovely, and quite a heart-breaking book. The detail and labor are stupendous and the felicity open to no question." So!

As ever, or more so,
sl

December 7

Dear Lewis:

Just a line reporting progress. Baker and Taylor re-ordered 2500 last Saturday; McClurg 250; Macy 500, which is about the way it is going—like the dickens in New York City, and only beginning to catch on in the provinces. We have ordered another 5000 to press, which makes total printings of about 38,000. We have broken joints on every edition so far, so that we have not been out of it at all either here or at Rahway where it is bound. I think sales are about 23,000. We'd print 10,000 now, but that takes two weeks instead of ten days, and we want to be sure to have the last 5000 available on the 16th for the business that may come that weekend. A telegram for 100 from Pittsburgh this morning; 25 to Albany; 25 to Montclair, etc.

Howe is pulling out, probably the first of January. The difference between academic and business life was too great, and the connection did not mean on either side what we had both hoped for, so it seemed best to sever it before it went on any longer. His withdrawal isn't going to mean any change in the resources or policies of the business; it is merely incidental to our proper growth.[1]

Ever yours,
Alf

[1] The firm name was shortly changed to Harcourt, Brace and Company.

[1920]

Washington—Dec. 10
Dear Alf:
Entranced to hear of latest figures you've sent me. Sorry to hear Will Howe is planning to pull out.

An aeroplane just came along into a nice open piece of sky right before my window and casually did five loops. How much simpler to loaf around in the sky than to write books for Alf to publish for Gus to sell for the bookstores to get rid of for poor devils to read!

As ever,
sl

December 16
Dear Lewis:
I have just sold an edition of 2000 sheets (of *Main Street*) to Hodder and Stoughton for British publication. We are a little behind in our records, but I think it is a safe guess that we have sold 35,000, not counting this British sale. We have printed 43,000, and another 7500 goes on press tomorrow. Telegram orders this morning show that it is really getting its legs in the Middle West. Too bad they were so slow about it for Christmas business, but it means the sure carry-over to next year. I hear it is to be the book-of-the-month in February Hearst's, which is also an assistance in that direction, and perhaps an intimation that you are on the verge of a flirtation with the Cosmopolitan Book Company. Rumor is that they have just paid Joe Lincoln $75,000 for book and serial on his next.

Yours,
Alf

Washington, Thursday, December 16
Dear Alf:
I've got to draw my five hundred for next February. Can you send it to me as soon as you get this? The last five hundred you sent me was almost wiped out by my last installment of $358 on income tax, paid on the 14th. I have $42 in the bank, and forty in cash, and on Saturday Dec. 18 I have to pay $200 in rent; on Monday $35 in office rent; on December 27th $125 insurance premium; along with a few incidentals such as food.

Harper's have now owed me $500 for a story for two weeks. In Wells's[1] letter of acceptance he said he was having "the voucher put through right away." Ten days ago I wrote him saying I'd love to have the check in a few days. Day before yesterday I *telegraphed* him asking

[1] Thomas B. Wells, editor of *Harper's Magazine*.

him to get it in the Tuesday mail. Not only have I not had it but I have had no answer whatever from him. Meantime he is—or is supposed to be—considering a second story, one that I regard as the best I have done for a long time, but rejected by the Post. Also Siddall [1] is considering one finished a week ago for the American, and I finish another for the American tomorrow. Also my movie agent says, in letter received today, that he is almost certain he can sell "Willow Walk" movie rights—and for *more* than $2500. And while all these beautiful things go on—I have $80 to meet about $600 worth of expenses which will have to be met before January first . . . and Grace has been going cold evenings because we can't afford to send $125 to Jaeckel to get out her fur coat, which had to be repaired. . . .

It's all coming—I'll be all right once the American and Harper checks begin coming, but meantime—I turn to you again, Alf—and I give all the above depressing data not for the joy of whining (not hitherto a sport necessary to me) but that you may know I do not turn lightly. This new $500 should, of course, count as the February check.

sl

Washington, Friday, December 17
Dear Alf:

It begins to break right again! Letter this morning from Siddall of the American, taking story done last week for $750 and promising check soon. As this is a very short story, only 4500 words, as against the 9000 or 10,000 words I usually do for the Post, it is at a much higher rate than the Post's $1000 per story. And Siddall is very anxious for a number of others—one of which I'll finish today or tomorrow. So, despite the fact that I *still* haven't heard from Harper's, this makes everything start right. I'll do six or eight stories for Siddall (they take less than a week apiece) and so be way ahead before I start the next novel—be enough ahead so that, with this lump in addition to your guarantee, I shan't have to worry again till late spring of 1922, at least.

The sale is glorious! 35,000! And a start in England! Hope you may be able to use the Galsworthy letter in connection with that. Mary Austin writes me she is sending some copies abroad. That probably means H. G. Wells among others, as she is a correspondent of his, and this may help in England. Want to ask her to send one to him?

So you think the Cosmopolitan Book people may get after me—may offer me vast and indecent sums? Alf, they don't make enough money to

[1] John M. Siddall, editor of the *American Magazine*.

get me off'n Harcourt, Brace and Howe. Entirely aside from all questions of friendship and decent appreciation of the magnificent way in which you've handled *Main Street*, I am quite sure that as a cold business matter, no one could do so well by my books as Harcourt. When the Hearst people get after me—*if* they do—I'll tell them to go to hell—as I have once already told them, a year ago, apropos of short stories.

Gaw, I hope we can keep *Main Street* going all next year. I suppose we'll have to do a little advertising next year, and a lot of keeping after the dealers who get slack on stock, but it really seems now as tho there was enough discussion to keep it going. Frinstance, t'other evening I met Jane Addams and the wife of an editor on the Manchester Guardian, and they both knew all about it. Same with Norman Hapgood.

Now to work. I feel much cheerier today—feel as tho the immense immobility, for the last week symbolized by Harper's, is giving way. Siddall is very keen for my stuff, and ready to pay. And every day the notes for the next novel go down in the book.

By the way, I've changed the name again, from FITCH to BABBITT. Fitch, I realized, would to so many critics carry a connotation of Clyde Fitch, dead tho he is. The name now for my man is George F. Babbitt, which, I think, sounds commonplace yet will be remembered, and two years from now we'll have them talking of Babbittry (not at all the same thing as Potterism).[1]

As ever,
sl

Washington, Tuesday, Dec. 21
Dear Alf:

Wrote gloomily to you on Thursday, acceptance from American on Friday, check from you on Saturday, check from American on Monday for $750, check from Harper's—the long-delayed one—today; $1750 in three days, so that I'm able to meet all the bills and work again in a beautiful security. And Harper's and the American are both now considering other stories. And, after spending all this week on notes about *Babbitt*, the next novel, I'll do another American story next week.

Next, and very interesting, is the fact that Vachel Lindsay has constituted himself a committee to make the *whole* of Springfield, Ill., and the surrounding Sangamon County, with 100,000 population, read *M St*. (This is confidential, but he says that he has a secret Machiavellian plan to make them read it as a preparation to reading his own *Golden Book of Springfield*. Really, he is making this a perfectly definite campaign!)

[1] An expression made popular by Rose Macaulay's satirical novel *Potterism*.

He asks (1) that you send a review copy to his friend Frank Waller Allen, Springfield. Allen will lecture about the book, says Lindsay, all over Central Illinois. (2) Send a large bunch of *M St*'s on consignment to Coe Brothers, after winning Mr. Coe's consent thereto. (3) Try to get H. E. Barker Art Store to take another consignment.

Now may I suggest that (4) tho I am writing myself to Lindsay you also write to him, thanking him. Really I think from his letter that he is prepared to campaign for *M St* as tho it were his job, and at the very least, he will make the book talkd of. Doubtless much of Springfield regard their poet as quite mad, but doubtless also there's a few hundred people who regard him as inspired—as I most certainly do! Lindsay's friendship for me is based not only on his own liking for *M St* but also on my having quoted and praised a poem of his in *Free Air*—and that quote in the S.E.P., said he, meant more to his benighted townsmen than hundreds of pages in the Nation et al.!! Will you then please suggest to him your gladness to co-operate.

Gawd this has been a long and meaty letter, and I pity you, having to plug thru it, but I hope all the details may be of value. Oh. I'm getting after Al Woods and his interest in dramatic rites on *M St* through Giffen, my agent.

As I may not write you more than six or eight more times before Dec. 25—

                 Merry Christmas!
                    sl

                     December 23
Dear Lewis:

We shall attend carefully to the Vachel Lindsay—Springfield Illinois suggestion, but not until next week because the booksellers there will merely be cleaning up from their Christmas trade and taking inventory, and not wanting to see any more stock until after the first of January. We are writing to Lindsay at once, as you suggest.

For a book and its publishers to have created a demand for 50,000 since October 23rd is going some, and as far as *Main Street* is concerned, we are all entitled to a very Merry Christmas. I think I said in a longhand note the other day that we wouldn't stop to figure up the advertising appropriation until I got the actual bills on the third of January. I know we have enough so that I am ordering January advertising. I think we'll have something like $3000 to spend after the first of January earned by sales to the first of January. If the figures work out that way, I'd be inclined to propose that the 15% royalty begin with sales after January first and that we use up the balance of the money earned on fall sales on the spring advertising.

Ever yours,
Alf

Washington, Tuesday, December 28

Dear Alf:

Bully ad, the rooster crowing over *Main Street* sale. And I hope all of you are now somewhat recovered from the rush of the last few days before Christmas, which must have been terrific.

Interesting note about *Babbitt*, yours on the edge of the ad—"hidden undercurrents of loves, work, training, friends, associates, shaping an ambitious man's career." Only it isn't the *ambitiousness* of Babbitt which is emphasized. He is ambitious, very much so, but "ambition" gives an idea of a man who climbs very high, whereas Babbitt never becomes more than a ten-thousand-a-year real estate man. He is the typical T.B.M., the man you hear drooling in the Pullman smoker; but having once so seen him, I want utterly to develop him so that he will seem not just typical but an individual. I want the novel to be the G.A.N. in so far as it crystallizes and makes real the Average Capable American. No one has done it, I think; no one has even *touched* it except Booth Tarkington in *Turmoil* and *Magnificent Ambersons;* and he romanticizes away all bigness. Babbitt is a little like Will Kennicott but bigger, with a bigger field to work on, more sensations, more perceptions. . . . He is all of us Americans at 46, prosperous but worried, wanting—passionately—to seize something more than motor cars and a house *before it's too late.* Yet, utterly unlike Carol, it never even occurs to him that he might live in Europe, might like poetry, might be a senator; he is content to live and work in the city of Zenith, which is, as everybody knows, the best little ole city in the world. But he would like for once the flare of romantic love, the satisfaction of having left a mark on the city, and a let-up in his constant warring on competitors, and when his beloved friend Riesling commits suicide, he suddenly says, "Oh hell, what's the use of the cautious labor to which I've given everything"—only for a little while is he discontented, though. . . . I want to make Babbitt big in his real-ness, in his relation to all of us, not in the least exceptional, yet dramatic, passionate, struggling.

Why don't you lay plans to have *Main Street* translated into the Scandinavian tongues? So many of the characters are Scandinavians, and so great is the interest in America in Scandinavia, that it ought to go there. But I wouldn't think of speaking about it to a man like Bjorkman, to whom nothing good is done unless it is by a man named Edwin.

Another *most* friendly letter from John Galsworthy, from Santa Barbara, California; speaks of our meeting in Washington, winds up "may we soon have from you another book baked as thoroughly (in this half-baked age) as *Main Street*." Have you got in touch with him yet? Want me to write & ask Galsworthy to do a quotable opinion & use his letter?

My agent is apparently still negotiating with Al Woods about *Main Street* stage and movie rights—don't know whether anything will come of it or not. Meantime I write short stories and make millions of notes about *Babbitt*. And incidentally an occasional note about the eleven other novels for which I have more or less vague plans!

Happy New Year, and a prosperous one!

As ever,
sl

Do as seems wisest to you about the 15% royalty. I'm more than willing to go ahead on 10% as long as it's useful to do lots of advertising.

[1 9 2 1]
Jan. 4

Dear Lewis:

I've been so darned busy this afternoon I didn't get time to dictate this letter to you, and now all the stenogs have gone home and here it is only a quarter to seven—so I'm typing myself, one finger of each hand, to say:

Some time ago I talked to The American Play Company about picture rights of *Main Street*, and told them to go to it and see what they could do. This morning they phoned that they had someone interested in the dramatic rights. I told them to take the matter up with you direct. The dramatic rights would, they tell me, include movie rights, and movie production would naturally wait till after the play and would be correspondingly more valuable. If there is anything you want me to do to help along, let me know.

Can't keep this up any longer—ends of fingers getting sore. Started 13,000 *M.S.* printing today.

Yours,
Alf

It is not evident from the correspondence whether Lewis came to New York or whether negotiations were conducted by telephone. However, arrangements were made through Elisabeth Marbury of American Play Company for the dramatization of Main Street *by Harvey O'Higgins and Harriet Ford for the Shubert Brothers.*

[1921]

Washington, Sat Jan 15

Dear Alf:

I enclose a pompous official statement of your share in play and movie rights.

Friend writes from NY that she met a bunch of Swede and Norwegian professors (presumably in Lutheran-American colleges in US) and they all talked *Main Street* and said it was better than Knut Hamsun's *Hunger*, which won the Nobel Prize. This friend is Mrs. Frank P. Nohowel of Islip, Long Island. She is the type of cultured, musical, polylingual German-American with lots of money who is as used to Europe as to America, and she's not a close enough personal friend to be too prejudiced. Why don't you write to her, get from her the names of three or four of the profs who best combine influence with enthusiasm for *M St.*, get in touch with them, and have them send copies of *M St* to the Ole Country, both to arouse general interest in it there (as a novel and as a picture of Scandinavians in US) and to see if there may not be one chance in 50,000 that we'd get the Nobel prize on *M St* or a later novel. They are likely to know, and write to, Scandinavian publishers, and possibly even to the committee that gives decision on the Nobel prize. I pass this buck to you because I couldn't speak of it to Mrs. Nohowel without seeming egotisticaller 'n hell.

Probably be in NY about a week from now—end of next week—for a day or so on the play, with O'Higgins and Miss Ford, then immediately duck west, but I'll see you.

As ever,
sl

[*Enclosure*]

January 15, 1921

Gentlemen:

As you know, there are now afoot negotiations for the dramatization of my novel *Main Street*, published by you, with a probability that following the stage version, there will be a motion picture made of the book. My contracts are not yet signed but the probabilities are strong enough to make it now proper to present the following offer.

Though there is in my *Main Street* contract no mention of stage or motion picture rights, and though I could claim all sums accruing from dramatic presentation, it is my feeling that your efforts as publishers have so far enhanced the commercial value of the book that you have an ethical right to participation in all gains from such presentations which amounts to something more than a mere legal right.

I therefore, in accordance with our recent conversations, propose (and this may be taken as an official addition to the contract) that Harcourt, Brace and Howe shall be entitled to twenty (20) per cent of whatever sums I may make from the stage presentation over and above the first $7500 (seven thousand, five hundred dollars), with the proviso that unless I make such sum of $7500 for my share, they shall be entitled to nothing; and that out of the motion picture earnings, they shall be entitled to twenty (20) per cent of my share after I shall have made $5000 (five thousand dollars), but be entitled to nothing unless I make at least that $5000.

Let me add that it seems to me that in this arrangement I am really giving you a very small share, and that this smallness is justified only by the fact that by having money ahead, and my time thus kept clear, I shall be able to continue with other novels from which, I hope, we shall all profit.

If by any chance the present negotiations, with Shubert Brothers, through Miss Elisabeth Marbury, should fall through, and later another theatrical arrangement should be made, the terms outlined above are still to stand.

Let me sum up your share more briefly: Harcourt, Brace and Howe to have 20% of my net earnings on the stage play from *Main Street* over and above $7500, which I am to have clear; and 20% on my net motion picture earnings over and above $5000, which I am to have clear.

Sincerely yours,
Sinclair Lewis

Washington, Wednesday January 19
Dear Alf:
I'll reach NY tomorrow afternoon and be there till Friday or Saturday evening. I may call you up tomorrow afternoon, but please don't wait in for me—if I'm tied up with O'Higgins and Ford I'll see you Friday.

In the Baltimore Evening Sun for Jan 3, H. L. Mencken has a good second review of *M St* very amusing. Percy Hammond says in the Chicago Tribune: "As an antidote to the brag, bluster, boosting, 'Watch Us Grow' green sickness still epidemic in the nation, *Main Street* has not its equal in American fiction."

sl

By this time the success of Main Street *was assured, and when Lewis arrived in New York on the 20th, his monthly guarantee payment was increased from $500 to $1000.*

[1921]

          Double Duck Farm
          Martinsville, New Jersey
          Sat Jan 29
Dear Alf:
 How's the book been going this past week? Play goes fine—we'll finish by end of next week—then I'll have coupla days in N.Y. & start West—see you before I go.
 Have you sent to England Galsworthy's letters (both of 'em) & news of how the book is going? They ought to be ordering more than 2000.
              Greetings!
              SL

          Martinsville, N.J., Jan 31
Dear Alf:
 If you want it—& it's rawther good—F. Scott Fitzgerald says: "After a third reading I want to say that *Main Street* has displaced *Theron Ware* [1] in my favor as *the best American novel*."
              SL

          Queen City Club
          Cincinnati, O.
          Feb. 16
Dear Alf:
 Off to Chicago this evening—3 lectures there. Back here Feb. 21st or 22nd. Drop me a line & let me know how book has been going since I saw you—on the 8th. Examine enclosed Toronto clipping with care (it's a corker) & see if you can't somehow use it to make those hellhounds in Canada sell a few copies.
 Note: Sam Margolies writes me that a relative of his met the great Gordon Selfridge [2] of London, who proved to be much interested in *M. St.* Why don't you call up Sam about this & send the news over to Hodder Stoughton. He mite be the cause of several thousand selling in London.
 Bully time, met lots of people, really getting the feeling of life here. Fine for *Babbitt*. . . .
              As ever,
              SL

[1] *Damnation of Theron Ware* by Harold Frederic.
[2] Harry Gordon Selfridge. Born in America, he founded Selfridge and Company, Ltd., London, one of the largest department stores in Europe.

Sunday 20th (address Queen City Club, Cincinnati)
Dear Gus:
Will have made 6 talks in Chicago & North Shore suburbs before I return to Cincin, Tuesday. Notably that under the auspices of Booksellers' League, on the 18th, with a lot of the trade present. They seemed to like it a lot, & *Main St.* is selling fast all over town. So wouldn't this be a good time to try to get McClurg's to take 5000? They were out, several days. Carson Pirie had a big *M St* window.

About Sears-Roebuck. Not only was the Book & Play lecture @ Julius Rosenwald's [1] house, but he'd read *Main St* himself & professed to be crazy about it—he used many excellent adjectives! Also he seemed to like me & wanted to show me thru Sears-Roebuck. Can't you somehow use his personal interest to get S-R to take an order? I *think* that if their buyer talked with Rosenwald he'd recommend it. (And R. was delighted by fact that S-R were mentioned.)

I've called on several bookshops, including McClurg's, Marshall Field, Kroch, & become chummy. So this field will, I hope, be more favorable than ever.

Sincerely,
Sinclair Lewis

Cincinnati, February 25
Dear Alf:
Because it is so out and out can't you use Octavus Roy Cohen's statement, "I consider *Main Street* by far the greatest American novel ever written"? You have noticed, of course, how *Zell, Seeds of the Sun* and *Sisters-in-law* are all being advertised as better than *Main Street!* It would be a very fresh, but might it not be an effective ad to say,

THANKS FOR THE COMPLIMENT!

Three big books of the spring season are all being advertised as "Better than *Main Street*." This admission that during the four months since it was published, *Main Street* has become the standard for comparison is received with gratitude.

I shall lecture in Pittsburgh on March 3rd, and in Milwaukee on March 17th, and you might warn the bookshops in those two towns to be ready for an invasion. You can truthfully say to them that both in Chicago and Cincinnati the added interest due to my coming was sufficient to cause bookshops to run out of stock.

[1] Merchant and philanthropist; President of Sears-Roebuck and Company. In 1917 he created the Rosenwald Fund for the well-being of mankind.

[1921]

Between Walpole, Galsworthy, and Laski, we ought to get some serious critical attention in England, and I hope that Hodder & Stoughton know about all of them.

As ever,
SL

Cincinnati, March 5
Dear Alf:
March check, for $1000, received this morning—thanks. But why so brief and curt? Why don't you say howdy? And how is the book doing now? Pittsburgh lecture, Thursday, seemed a great success; and I was introduced to the bookstore men. . . . Asinine story about me in last McClurg's Bulletin—you *know* I never said "My word" or "deuced." Still, at that, it's probably good publicity.

I'll be here till the tenth, then, via Bradford, Pa., to Chicago.

As ever,
SL

Cincinnati, Mar 7
Dear Alf:
Lectures coming (if you want to inform booksellers): Mar. 11— Bradford, Pa.—The Literary Club; Mar. 15—Milwaukee—College Club, @ Athenaeum; Mar. 19—Winnetka Ill. (write Evanston stores??); Mar. 21— Sinai Social Center, Chi; Mar. 29—Town Hall, N.Y.; Apr. 1 or 2: Princeton, N.J.—before a student organization. That will be about my last lecture. Then—thank Gawd—I cut 'em out!

I have your letter of Mar. 5. Glad of the 130,000.[1] *Good luck, old man!*

As ever,
SL

Cincin
Dear Alf:
Off for Bradford, Pa., then Chi, tonight. Gave a lil talk for John Kidd @ Pogue's auditorium yesterday & he sold about 70 copies afterward, just for a starter.

I'm to lecture for the College Club, Detroit, on April 11; & some woman's club in Harrisburg, Pa., April 2. Both places will boost the show,

[1] Sales of *Main Street*.

& I think you ought to be able to sell books in anticipation. Also Women's Canadian Club, Hamilton, Ontario, April 13.

As ever,
SL

Chicago, Mar. 19

Dear Alf:

I'll be back in Washington on March 23, & stay there several days before lecture in N.Y. on the 29th.

About the second serialization. I wired you yesterday that I wish you'd talk to several bookmen—e.g. Fred Hood [1] & Melcher [2] of the Publishers' Weekly—before deciding about this. I wouldn't take any chance of injuring the sale, which ought to keep up all this year; & 2nd serial rights may, possibly, be worth as much next year as this, *particularly if the play goes well next fall.* Or would the 2nd serial help the sale? I want to leave the decision to you but, with our perfectly good chance of a sale of 100,000 from June to December this year, for the love of Mike be careful & take counsel. I back you up in whatever you may finally decide—but don't be tempted by ready serial-money if it's going to be bad in the long run. . . . Isn't *Four Horsemen of Apocalypse* being serialized *now*, 100 years after publication? Or wasn't it recently? . . . Wonder how much they got for it? . . . In any case I certainly shouldn't release before June 15. Do be careful—this may involve thirty or forty thousand dollars. But, I repeat, I'm with you when you finally *do* decide what will be best in the long run.

Do you think it would be wise for me to autograph books @ the new bookshop of which you speak? *Wouldn't it make the other shops sore?* I'm afraid of it. But if you're quite sure there's no danger of that, I'd just as soon. It would have to be on March 29th, I think.

I don't seem to agree with *nothin'* in this letter, but let's be *sure* about both these propositions. I hate to tinker with a good market.

As ever,
SL

Apr. 8 (On the train between
Urbana & Galesburg, Ill.)

Dear Alf:

U of Ill lecture seemed great success. They've all been frantically discussing *Main St.* Met a *lot* of the English faculty—Zeitlin, Miss Rinaker,

---

[1] Fred R. Hood, vice-president of the Baker & Taylor Company.
[2] Frederic G. Melcher, co-editor of *Publishers' Weekly.*

[1921]

Scott, et al, & made a hit with most of them, I think. I *know* Stuart Sherman liked me. Stayed @ his house. Smoker of Eng. instructors after the lecture; then, from 12 to 2 AM, the Shermans & I sat & talked, me giving a hand to H.B.&Co. For all his Spingarn-Mencken complex Sherman is a fine solid fellow. See you late next week.

As ever,
SL

Lewis arrived in New York the end of the following week and left almost immediately for Washington, from where there is a letter dated April 18th pertaining to various business matters he discussed with Harcourt while he was in New York.

Washington, Thursday, April 28

Dear Alf:

I'll probably see you next Monday. We leave here Saturday morning, and go right thru to Forest Hills, L.I.—we'll stay at the Forest Hills Inn till we sail.

I think I've bullied the Wayfarers Shop here enough about their small orders so that Gus might be able to sell them a hundred if he dropped them a note. Introduced myself at last to Sid Avery of Brentano's and he was more than cordial.

Are you following up translations into Swedish, Danish, French, etc.?

See you Monday!
SL

Lewis was in personal touch with the office while he was at Forest Hills until his departure with his family for England in May. The first word from him after his arrival on the other side was a letter dated June 4th.

BABBITT

THREE
Creation Abroad

[1921]
Cadogan Hotel
Sloane Street, London, S.W.1
June 4

(Address % Guaranty Trust Co., 50 Pall Mall,
as before—no cottage yet—too much London!)

Dear Alf:

A bully time! Mostly bumming about London, dining and having tea. Saw Jonathan Cape [1] about the second day. Called on Geoffrey Williams [2] and he took me to lunch at the Savile (where I encountered W. L. George and had a long talk—of course about American Wimmin) and had me made honorary member for a month; will also have me made temporary member for a year if I want. Nice chap. Tea with Harold Laski, whom both Gracie and I like immensely and of whom I expect to see a lot. Lunch at Hodder-Williams' [3] house yesterday, with Pinker [4] there, all very pleasant. Have a feeling he never will sell any *Main St* but I'm going to try to suggest a few methods. Seen Pawling [5] a lot of times—he's a corker. . . . Then we've lunched and dined with an assortment of people, and begin to have some feeling of London. Went up to Sonning to look for a house—otherwise we've shystered on that important duty! Luck!

As ever,
sl

[1] English publisher who had recently started his own firm.
[2] Of Williams and Norgate, British publishers.
[3] Sir Ernest Hodder-Williams, chairman of Hodder & Stoughton.
[4] Of James B. Pinker and Son, English literary agents.
[5] Sydney S. Pawling, partner in William Heinemann, Publishers.

London, June 15

Dear Alf:

Good, awfully good, to get your long letter written at home. I'll write a personal letter to Don today. Hope he is all right now. Terribly sorry to hear of his sickness. He is one of the finest—as well as most efficient—of human beings. Glad you're able to take over the whole house at One West 47; that ought to add greatly to ease of working. You ought to have a coop all to yourself, and off the ground floor. How many *M Sts* have sold now, and how goes the second serial campaign of Aley?[1]

I am now just beginning to feel that itch which means that I want to get back to writing, and after about three weeks more I shall start. I'll do just one short story, to get my hand in (it will take only about a week) and then get right at *Babbitt*. . . . I think it will have been a good thing, this long long loaf, and will have quite cleared out the long accumulated weariness of writing almost without cessation for years.

Our plans? We'd hoped to find a country house into which we could move July 1st, but the only one we've liked enough to want to spend quite a time in is not free to August 1st. We've just taken that, after a long hunt and an examination of many other houses—which, though it didn't produce a home, did give us many hikes, by motor and train, thru country we mightn't have seen, and did give us an excuse to butt rather intimately into a number of houses. . . . Yesterday, for example, we drove all over Surrey—the Hindhead moor, Dorking, Reigate, etc.—flats, then rolling hilly moors all gorse and heather, then suave farming country; and we looked at several houses. And last week we flirted with a twelfth (really) century manor house near Oxford, and spent a couple days sightseeing at Oxford (and lunching, tell Spingarn, with his cordial friend, Percy Simpson, a don).

The house we've finally settled on is an early sixteenth century one with marvelous old beams and half-timbering—excellent bath room and furnishing, however, with perhaps half an acre of tennis lawns, garden, etc., right on the common (so Wells[2] can play with village boys and have his nose instructively punched) in the tiny old village of Bearsted, near Maidstone, in the heart of Kent farming country—hops and wheat. The village is in a valley and beyond the old gables across the common rise smooth hills. Quelque platz!

Meantime, we'll spend ten days or two weeks more in London, go for July down to a hotel in, say, Cornwall or Devon, with the sea for a

---

[1] Maxwell Aley, manager of Century Newspaper Service.
[2] Wells Lewis, born July 26, 1917, was the only child of Grace and Sinclair Lewis.

contrast to Kent, and after a week or two sightseeing, with probably some walking, I'll get on the job.

Look. Here's something to remember. In case I should ever need money suddenly, I'd cable you (say) "Cable one thousand," and what I wish you'd do is take the money to the Guaranty Trust and have them cable it to my account here on Pall Mall. Probably I shall never need this, but we'd better have it understood.

I've blown in a reasonable amount of money, including several grateful quids on gins and bitters, Asti Gran Spuma(n?)ti, Chablis, and long Scotch and sodas; and after letting my wardrobe become practically nonexistent, I've bought some clothes, but I don't think we've been particularly extravagant. We still have a whale of a lot of money left, and shall not need to start the thousand a month again for quite a time.

English hotel prices, just now, are quite as high as America, and so is food at such hotels as the Savoy, but otherwise things are very much cheaper. I'm getting a suit for twenty-two guineas at one of the best tailors in town. It's true that at one time it would have cost only about fifteen guineas here, but for a suit of like material and workmanship I'd be paying right now, in U.S., about $135 (bein' as it has an extra pair of pants with it). I paid one pound for a hat at Heath's which would cost eight or ten dollars in the States. Our country place in Kent would, for that sort of place so near to N.Y., cost at least $250 a month, and we get it for nine guineas a week including silver and linen—say one hundred and seventy a month. Servants still get very small wages—from thirty-five to fifty pounds a year and found. On the whole prices seem to be enormously higher than they were five years ago, but still only about two-thirds of what they are in America. I'm quite sure that my American accent adds a bob here and a quid there but I haven't been here long enough yet to be able to tell.

Of the coal strike there are curiously few traces. Nobody mentions it. Really if it weren't for the dry-fact stories about it in my Times and the fact that railroad service is about cut in half I'd never know there was a strike.

I know one thing, now, I think—I'd never want to live in England. It's fun, I do get some contrasts by which I see America more clearly, but—oh, it's a dying land. No eagerness. The aristocracy absolutely as firmly ruling as ever. I'd been told that everywhere, since the war, I'd find a rude and resentful servant class. Nonsense. They're as meek as ever. As in the old days, the Derby, the Ascot, the prospects of autumn hunting, and the minor incidents of the visit of the Prince of Wales to Cardiff are so incomparably more important than any strike, any book, any educational news, any reform, any business news, that one feels only the nobility and the hunting set really exist. . . . I had dinner with Oliver Onions and his wife Berta Ruck the other evening, and they spent all the time praising the aristocracy and cursing any force that might imperil its splendor—the coal strikers are horned and hoofed fiends and W. L. George, for very mildly sympathizing with the Bolsheviks, is some kind of a degenerate.

We dine with W. L. George this evening, by the way, and lunch with Walpole tomorrow, then have dinner with Margaret Wycherley, and on Sunday we dine with the Harold Laskis. Last week Hodder-Williams gave us a reception, very nice, tho Frank Swinnerton was the only one present who much excited me. Others there were E. Phillips Oppenheim, William Robertson Nicoll, Berta Ruck, Ruby Ayres (!), Clement Shorter, Mrs. Belloc Lowndes, and so on.

Lots of good luck, old man. I think I shall have to start writing a book called, if I remember rightly, *Babbitt*.

Zever,
sl

London, June 21

Dear Alf:

Haven't encountered any new writers whom I've wanted to grab yet; everything is, of course, pretty quiet because of the printing situation.

Been having a good time. Be here for nine days more, then go to Cornwall for a month at a hotel at Mullion, then to Kent for two months. I shall start *Babbitt* in Cornwall. Had dinner and talked to some students at Laski's, taken yesterday by Laski to lunch of Nation editors—Brailsford, Massingham, Hirst, Nevinson, et al there. AND so on, with some sightseeing and last Sunday a wild lunch at Claude Grahame-White's country place, much booze and tennis and Ethel Levy and Marc Klaw, and the Duncan Sisters.

Last night dined with Hodder-Williams (or rather, had him at an agreeable but hellishly expensive dinner at Claridge's, with Clemenceau at the next table, bein' over here to get his D.C.L. from Oxford) and as delicately as possible suggested that I'd love to have him sell some *Main Streets*. He said he could do a whole lot more if he had a lower price on sheets and I promised to hint as much to you, and here I am hinting and of course you never could guess that I'd promised Sir Ernest to write you. . . . Seriously, if it can be made to go over here, I think it might be a good thing in the matter of kudos. Whether he's getting sheets at so high a price that he can't make any money on them, I don't know; and naturally I shall not butt in nor ever recommend any price to him that will not allow you at least a little profit. But this I can say: He seems strongly in favor of the Lewises, and I'd keep after him, and politely, if I were you. I think my being over here will somewhat help the English sale. Hodder-Williams has really been awfully nice—lunch and reception, which last resulted in an account in the News which I haven't seen, in the British Weekly thing by Robertson Nicoll, etc.

I want you to read with considerable care the enclosed letter from Edith Summers Kelley—an old friend of mine, former secretary of Upton Sinclair, first wife of Allan Updegraff, now married to a man who is, I should judge tho I have never met him, a charming companion with artistic leanings. It sounds to me as tho she had a novel here, as tho she had grown from the poetic yearnings she had fifteen years ago when I knew her best to real stuff for a good American novel. She knows the Kentucky background of which she speaks; her husband and she farmed there for several years. Why don't you write her expressing willingness to see some ms?

We're to meet H.G.Wells and Rebecca West this week, and to dine with Hugh Walpole, Frank Swinnerton, Rose Macaulay. But after another nine days of dinners and the like, it will be good to get to the sea, to Cornish villages, to walking—and to work!

Zever,
sl

Poldhu Hotel
Mullion, S. Cornwall
July 1

Dear Alf:

Thursday morning we left London for here—a delightful and easy journey thru Wiltshire, Devon, and so on; hills wooded or patched with colored fields, and a few glimpses of a radiant sea.

Since writing you the most interesting person I've met has been Rebecca West. If she proves not to be too tied up to Century I may try to pinch her off. Same with Norman Angell. These are the only authors I've met who seemed worth much for us—and with both of them I have merely sung the praises of HB&Co. and delicately suggested that if they should ever have a hiatus in their American publishing plans, I know that the esteemed Mr. Harcourt would be interested in them. . . .

Sorry to say I have not met Strachey yet. Did have lunch with James Whitall just before leaving, and liked him a lot. . . . I feel (and it's important if my feeling is right) that tho the Young British Authors of the Walpole-Mackenzie type have been of great importance, there is just now quite as much literary energy breaking loose in America as over here; I feel that the Britishers are rather settling down to a great smug contentment with their clever selves; and if this is true, our future as publishers will be, as largely it has been, with the Americans rather than with the Britishers. . . . Some day I ought to go out and make a young-author-visiting trip for HB&Co in America. . . . Good luck with Strachey.[1]

This hotel is on a cliff, overlooking the most glorious vista of sea and out-reaching cliffs along the shore—one sees clear down to Mount St. Michael. We shall have some good walks. The hotel itself is second rate and the people look duller than hell—Main Street's respectables vacationing. All of which is to the good because it means that I shall at once get busy on *Babbitt;* working daily till midafternoon, then tramping and a little swimming. London is really too exciting to do much work in. Smorning I sat on the edge of my bed thinking about *Babbitt* for half an hour when I was supposed to be dressing.

We'll be here till July 29, then to October 1st, at our blinkin' Elizabethan cottage in Bearsted. Now to *Babbitt!*

As ever,
sl

P.S. Also N.B. I still have about £340 in England, even after buying a helluva lot of clothes, and the expensive London visit (down here it costs us only about half as much as in London), and paying in advance for half the rent of the Kent house which we shall have for nine weeks. That will last me about two months more. But I guess I'd better be sure of plenty of money here, and I want to keep my N.Y. account well ahead. So will you please have Don deposit $3500 to my account at the Guaranty Trust Co.? This should last me till mid-December—indeed if the play goes well, I may not have to call on you for any more money at all till way long next year. Is it convenient for you to pay out this $3500 now? If not, make it less—say $2000. And can you let me know, roughly, how much money is coming to me from H.B.&Co. *after* deducting this $3500 (or $2000)? I'm getting balled up.

SL

July 5
Dear Lewis:
I Coronaed you a note from home yesterday saying how Don was and that sort of thing.

Hodder-Williams. We have had two transactions with Sir Ernest in the last eight months: *Main Street* and *The World's Illusion,* and it is the

[1] Harcourt, Brace had just published, on June 10th, Lytton Strachey's *Queen Victoria.*

most glowing example of negotiations after a contract is signed that I have seen in a rather long experience. It isn't as if he had been "stuck," but he bought two good books at moderate prices. He pays 50 cents a copy in flat sheets, including royalty, for *Main Street*. He should have set the book and paid us 100 pounds advance. I let him take sheets as a favor and because both you and I were anxious for the kudos that would come from prompt British publication. I'll show you all the documents when you come home.

I am glad you hooked up with the Laskis. He is a smart young man.

Yours,
Alf

Cornwall, July 12

Dear Alf:

He's started—*Babbitt*—and I think he's going to be a corker. I've been working on him for a week now, mostly, of course, turning notes into a final plan, but also writing a little, and I find him coming out firm and real.

I think that Babbitt is the best name for him—and the best title for the book as well. One remembers name-titles really better than apparently more striking titles, and it so causes the public to remember the name of the central character that he is more likely to be discussed. I haven't yet thought of any other satisfactory titles. The following are the only ones I've thought of: POPULATION, 300,000—GOOD BUSINESS—SOUND BUSINESS —A GOOD PRACTICAL MAN—A HE-MAN—THE BOOSTER—A SOLID CITIZEN —ZENITH—and none of them satisfy me. Are there any of the above which you like better than *Babbitt?*

I have your letter of June 22nd. Write me often. You and Ellen are really the only people who keep me in touch with things in the States. Terribly glad Don can be in the office again. Make him go up to Maine for a month this summer. I recommend Kennebago Lake.

Your use of the (much appreciated) Robert Morss Lovett letter in an advertisement is a corker and should be of value. But I don't like so much the phrase "remarkably well-written tale" in the last part of the ad—sounds somewhat as though you were saying wonderingly, "Why, this book isn't badly written—for a best-seller!"

This is (and I think Kent will also be) a fine place for work. I have a room to myself; I get on the job immejit after breakfast: work thru to tea time, then go for a walk or a swim or both, and read or talk in the evenings. Not much doing here in the way of gaiety, which is much better for me. Walking interesting—beautiful cliffs and sandy coves along the sea, and in the interior, charming old villages with churches of about

1450 and thatched cottages. I'm in fine shape & at once seeing real England, keeping husky, and getting a lot of work done. Cheers!

Harriet Ford writes me that *Main Street* the play is to go into rehearsal in NY about July 14, and rehearse three or four weeks. I do wish you'd see a rehearsal after a week or two, both so that you might let me know how it is going, and because you might have some good suggestions to make to Harvey and Harriet.

Good luck!
SL

Cornwall, July twentieth

Dear Miss Eayrs:

I am writing you as my husband's English secretary: The chances are we shall be in England not later than October first, so it hardly seems worth while to establish a cable address. I rather think we shall go to Italy in the autumn.

Will you be so good as to call at Brentano's and see what they have in the way of books on house plans, big and little, houses, Georgian, Dutch Colonial, and other suburban kinds? Country Life, House Beautiful, House and Garden probably get out such books collected from designs issued in their magazines. Hal [1] needs them for his real estate developments in the new novel, and there are a lot of technical terms he does not know. Have the books as up to date as possible. Use your own judgment as to the most helpful. Thanks a million times.

Cornwall is as enchanting as ever, but the people are as dull as any we ever found on Main Street. We leave next week with delight at being in our own home, if only for two months. I am in the throes of finding a governess for Wells. Fancy forty-four applicants in two days.

I am sorry to bother you about the suburban house books, but if Hal *will* write books of accurate realism——

Sincerely and gratefully,
Grace Lewis

Cornwall, July twentieth

Dear Mr. Harcourt:

Hal is *Babbitt*-ing away furiously in another room, and so I am answering for him your letter of the third, which came yesterday. Our

---

[1] Grace Lewis was accustomed to addressing her husband as Hal, though he was known among his friends as Red and sometimes Harry. Not to be confused with Harrison Smith, also called Hal.

chief answer is congratulation on your great success—not *Main Street* alone, but on your incredible achievements of the last two years. It is wonderful for us to feel that you are OUR FIRM as well as our publishers.

I hope you like Kennebago as much as we like Cornwall. I wonder which of the three cottages we lived in is now yours. We used to get so tired of the "chops, steak, ham, bacon or eggs," but how we should love to have a waitress say that to us now. Soggy bacon, undrinkable coffee, everlasting unseasoned joints, junkets and stewed fruits, all served to an accompaniment of formal clothing and formal speech. The only redeeming culinary feature is the shameless bar which crowds our table, and beloved bottles of some of Heinz's 57, which we traveled ten miles to get. On the other hand, the scenery is as lovely as anything around Kennebago, plus the enchanting thatched villages with fourteenth-century churches upon which one is always stumbling, or fishing villages snug in deep coves, with ample teas of thick cream and jam and "splits."

Hal works all morning and an hour or so in the afternoon. Then we walk or drive or swim, all the time talking *Babbitt*. We have just finished struggling over the names of the other male characters. And Hal has made the most astonishingly complete series of maps of Zenith, so that the city, the suburbs, the state, are as clear as clear in Hal's mind. We had such fun making the plans of and furnishing Babbitt's house.

Our very best Maine—and Cornwall—love to you three.

Grace Lewis

Cornwall, July 27

Dear Ellen:

Tomorrow evening we leave here for Kent. I am, with enough walks and swims to keep in beautiful shape, working all the time now on the next novel, *Babbitt*. It seems to be going beautifully.

Hoppé, the English photographer who was over in America last spring and who photographed a lot of American authors, has been trying to get hold of me both for his own collection and for the English Bookman. Just before I left London he snapped me. I am sending you some prints of the result. I doubt if I am likely to get anywhere a much better picture for newspaper use than the one with the tortoise spectacles. If Harcourt and you agree on this, why don't you hold this one and *use it for the Babbitt publicity next year?* Certainly I like it much better than the other two poses—the standing one and the one with face between hands.

If you use the one with face between hands, don't use it except with some very highbrow or new-thoughty sort of magazine as, tho it *is* interesting, the well-known young author looks quite mad in it.

I do most awfully hope you're not getting too bored having to do things for me (for *us!*). *Babbitt* and I have only you, and H.B.&Co. in general to depend on while we're abroad. Yes, I want some other things!

Grace wrote you a few days ago asking you to get me one or more books giving plans, pictures, technical terms, etc. regarding the kinds of houses which Babbitt would be likely to buy and sell in suburbs and in residential sections far out in cities. There's also several other things I need, and which I wish you could send me as quickly as possible: (1): The last copy of System; (2): The last American; (3): The last two or three Saturday Evening Posts (you'll probably be able to get only the very last); (4): The last three or four copies of Printer's Ink.

5 & 6 are trickier: I'd like one or more of these pompous pamphlets or books which big N.Y. advertising agencies get out telling in phrases of pseudo psychology about their magnificent service. The more highfalutin "psychology" in them, the better. You might be able to get these by writing to several ad agencies asking them for whatever literature they are publishing about their service, etc.

(6): There is published, I think in N.Y. by the Realty Records Company, a thing called the Record and Guide, containing not only records of mortgages etc. but also real estate gossip and tips, which is what I want. If there is one, with such gossip, and it isn't too bulky, please send me a copy or two, probly two.

Please thank Mr. Harcourt for his two letters received in last few days. This will have to serve as letter to him, this week. At least it will show that I'm alive and kicking, and good and busy with *Babbitt*. Tell him I quite understand his opinion of Sir Ernest. Terribly glad you now have quieter office on second floor. Lots of luck!

As ever,
S.L.

The Bell House
Bearsted, Nr. Maidstone
Kent
August 3

Dear Alf:

It was bully to have your letter from Kennebago. Lord I'm glad you had the rest there! We're more than happy here—charming house, perfect English maids, lovely old village and country—lanes, woods, fields of hops and wheat, pastures, and the slopes of the North Downs for climbing and for views. I'm really working hard—from about 9 A.M. to 4:30, then tea brought into the gracious drawing room by the deftest and prettiest of maids, then off for a good tramp. So far I've been planning —planning—planning, in the greatest detail—none of it wasted—and in about two more days I'll start the actual writing, and be all finished, ms ready to deliver, before the first of next April, even with a bit of traveling in between. I've written just a little of the actual text, and both it and the plans seem corking.

If I meet Katherine Mansfield of whom you write I'll make love to her for you, but I'm really of extraordinarily little use to you here—I'm seeing, in Cornwall and Kent, nothing of literary people or publishers; and while I may encounter some here, I rather doubt it—and *Babbitt* won't let me run up to London very often, if at all.

I'm more than rejoiced to hear that you will be coming over, and think you are very wise to plan to see more of writers than of publishers. About meeting you:——*Probably*, tho not necessarily, we'll go to Italy when we leave here, about October 1st, and, after a week of Paris and a week of Venice, settle down at Lake Maggiore, and stay firmly put till I finish the book. (That place appeals both because of its beauty and because Claude Washburn will be there and would be useful to us, as he knows Italian and knows people, and is more than eager to do anything he can for us.) I don't suppose you'd be coming till after that. Well, I'd join you in London, or in Paris. But why wouldn't it be nice for you to come down to Maggiore where, in more leisure than we'd ever have in a city, we'd talk, walk, look over *Babbitt* plans and ms and every evening get reasonably mellow on Italian wines and MANY small brandies? We'd have a corking time—and one to the advantage of *Babbitt*. What yuh think?

Apparently *Main Street* the play is going to go. You probably know by now that it was tried out by Stuart Walker's stock company in Indianapolis. I send clippings. But it's better than the clippings because, judging by Harriet Ford's letter received this morning, the company had only abt four rehearsals before putting it on. Lee Shubert went out to see it and seemed enthusiastic.[1]

You got right! England *does* make good Americans of us—or rather, not England but the thick English.

I'm awfully glad you're going to be able to be more to yourself, in the new office, and keep yourself for bigger things.

Zever,
SL

[1] The dramatization of *Main Street* by Harvey O'Higgins and Harriet Ford was presented by the Messrs. Shubert at New York's National Theater October 5, 1921.

Bearsted, Kent, August 16th

Dear Alf:

A letter or two from you since I last wrote, and one from Don. No special news, I think, except that we like this placid old house and village immensely, that I'm hard at it on *Babbitt*, and that last week I sneaked off to Paris for three days with Harold Stearns! Great time—pure but wet. Watched Stearns with care, and he isn't half so shaky and drunken as we said. He's a curious, solid, enduring person, for all his dissipating, and I think he will have an ever widening future. I'm for him.

Fine letter from Edith Wharton. I wrote to her congratulating her on the Pulitzer Prize and telling her of my long and deep enthusiasm for her books, and she answers charmingly, with a rather more than good word for *Main Street*. She's living near Paris, and we'll see her when we go thru in early October.

As ever,
Red

Sunday morning, ten-thirty,
September fourth.
Church bells jangling beautifully out of tune.

Grace Lewis is writing this time, because after two days of playing with Mr. Brace, Hal is working to catch up.

I think Mr. Brace was rather a lonely man that first day at the Cecil. So it was a blessedly fortunate thing that he came down to us that very afternoon, to a home and friends and quiet sleeping and a brisk autumn day for our motor to Canterbury (which is the fourteenth century untouched), and just enough sight-seeing, and the final excitement of meeting George Bernard Shaw.

No other English notable has so gloriously come up—and over—our expectations. Every word he said was quotable, and Hal and I fairly squirmed with joy over his wit. Mr. Brace will give you, I fancy, all the details, and perhaps tell you of Hal's astonishing resemblance to Shaw—not at all striking until you begin to compare them feature by feature, even to the two deep lines on either cheek, like sabre cuts when they smile. I know Hal will sooner or later buy a fluffy white beard and eyebrows, and a mephistophelian moustache and a foolish little hat like a child's beach hat, and give an imitation, tho he can't do the soft English voice with an Irish lilt.

All the laborious, fatiguing, time-exhausting planning of *Babbitt* is over and Hal's Corona rattles away all morning in the room above me.

He seems beautifully sure of what he is doing, and I save him time and distraction by attending to as much of the mail as possible.

All good wishes,
G.L.

Bearsted, Kent, Sept. 5

Dear Alf:

Two good letters from you just come. "Shall we say 15% after 60,000 and give us $2000 more to spend on ads till spring?" says you. SURE! And still more for ads, if you want it—let's try to keep her going —maybe after the smoke from the Porter-Harold Bell-Lincoln-Curwood et al. battle, of this early fall,[1] has cleared away, they'll find us marching right on, and I'm for constant insertions thru into spring. So count on me for any co-operation you wish.

Grace wrote you about Don, etc. He hadn't a devil of a lot of strength yet, tired easily after much walking, but seemed quite happy and sound, and increasingly glad to be here. I think he was a little lonely when he first landed, but we had him down for a couple of days and that, I think, made him feel at home and eager to go on seeing things. I know how he was at first—first time I ever landed in England, years ago, I was lonely and scared. I'll see him before the week is over; and we'll soon have him down here again.

I'm working like the devil on *Babbitt*, and it seems to be going fine.

Far as I can figure out, there was about $52,000 coming to me from Harcourt, Brace and Co. on August 26. Is that right? I still think you'd better hold all this to my credit, as formerly; and I shan't draw out any more this year unless it should prove necessary for expenses of running— and that ought not to be more than one thousand dollars—if indeed, with play royalties probable, I shall take *any* more from you this year. Next year or the year after—or both—I'll do some more investing in bonds etc. —I think I'll wait till I get back to America and talk it over with Jes and you before I do that.

Our very best! You gotta come over this winter, and come see us in Italy, and have—*a*—DRINK——two drinks———

As ever, and in some haste, & some grubbiness of having worked all day,
SL

[1] Lewis was referring to the publication in one season of Gene Stratton Porter's *Her Father's Daughter*, Doubleday; Harold Bell Wright's *Helen of the Old House*, Appleton; Joseph Lincoln's *Galusha the Magnificent*, Appleton; and James Oliver Curwood's *God's Country*, Cosmopolitan Book Corporation.

Grace forgot to tell you that I talked to Mary Austin (who took us from Canterbury over to Herne Bay to see Bernard Shaw) about her showing H.B.&Co. a novel some day. Houghton has her really original and different work, and she's much dissatisfied. She says she will; it's left in the air but with a nice twist toward you-all and you not bound to nuthin![1]

Bearsted, Kent, Sept. 10

Dear Alf:

Spent day and a half with Don in town this week. I think he really enjoyed a bat—we sat about Café Royal, me drinking strong waters while he had just a mouthful of muscatel and listened in on my lurid conversation with Nevinson the artist and his Lady Friends. He'll come down to us for a day and a half or two days early next week. He's probably written about Keynes. I'm sorry for any poor dollar-chaser who has to do business with these money-scorning artists and scholars!

The chief point of this letter is: I enclose a letter from Evelyn Scott, which please read with attention, then write to her. I have, as you know, a great admiration for *The Narrow House*, and while you won't necessarily share that, you must understand how really big is her promise. She will, I think, do novels ten times as good as *Narrow House*, her first book; she is, I think, precisely the kind of American youngster with promise on whom we want to build our fiction list.[2] Luck!

As ever,

SL

When the Lewises left Bearsted October first they spent time in London and Paris before going to Italy. There was no correspondence while they were en route.

Hotel Eden
Pallanza, Italy
October 18

Dear Alf:

This place is easily the most beautiful I have ever seen. We have four big rooms, each with good balcony, on top floor; and on all sides look on amazingly varied vistas of lake, cliff, mountain, island, and towns

---

[1] In the following year Harcourt, Brace published Mary Austin's *The American Rhythm*.

[2] Harcourt, Brace published Evelyn Scott's *Narcissus* in 1922 and took over *The Narrow House* at the same time.

either on the lake or fascinatingly perched halfway up mountains. I shall be back on the job day after tomorrow, and from then on——

This two and a half weeks' lay-off has been good for *Babbitt*—not only because of the change but also because I've thought out some good things about it during the period—made those valuable readjustments in the general plan which one doesn't always make if he keeps too close to it for too long. Shall be glad to get back on it.

In Paris I made overtures to Wilbur Daniel Steele for the novels he is more or less planning. He may some day come over to the true and righteous party. Hope so. He has big things.[1]

Luck!
SL

Pallanza, October 26

Dear Alf:

We're really settled down here; we've had some good hikes, and I've been at work for several days. For a start I've been reading over minutely the 70,000 or so words I had written of *Babbitt*, and it strikes me as the real thing, with a good thick texture. As always it needs cutting—and will get it! I hope Don will have brought you good reports of it; personally I think it is, tho very different, as good as *Main Street;* and usually I can get some idea of whether there's anything there when I re-read. At least it's *real*, seems to me.

We're marvelously situated here. The service is perfect, the food bully; and tho not as cheap as it might be, last week for everything (including hotel and food, tips, taxis, several boats including a motor boat a number of miles down the lake, some cables, extra teas for visitors, this for *four* of us) it cost 3000 life, or about $120!

We went up Monte Mottarone with the Washburns last Monday—and just across the bay are the Ward-Browns—W-B is an architect whom we knew in Washington. So we have enough to keep from feeling lonely. We have delightful walks, boat rides, and four times a week a lesson in Italian. And WORK!

Many thanks for your cable on *M St*'s birthday. I cabled you Saturday asking for news about the play—if it was still on—and haven't heard yet (Wednesday 9 A.M.). I suppose that's about the ordinary rate of transmission of cables here now—even in Paris, a man told me, it took him four days to get an answer to a cable!

Did you read Carl Van Doren's summary of myself and other novel-

[1] In 1925 Harcourt, Brace published Wilbur Daniel Steele's novel *Taboo*, and in 1926 his volume of short stories *Urkey Island*.

ists in recent *Nation?* I have written him, personally, a friendly but strenuous protest against his two assumptions: (1), that I am merely a disciple of Edgar Lee Masters in writing *M.St.*—somewhat humorous in view of the fact that I have never sat down and read *Spoon River Anthology,* but merely heard parts of it read aloud, and this not till 1917, whereas I first began to plan *M St* 1905; and (2) that I have always been a writer of "bright amusing chatter to be read at a brisk pace." I asked him if he had read *The Job* or *Our Mr. Wrenn* or *Trail of the Hawk,* or certain short stories which I enumerated; and I hinted, if I did not say directly, that if he hadn't read these, he had one devil of a nerve, and he was one devil of a bad critic, to dare to sum me up thus. . . . You or Spingarn might follow this up by sending him a copy of *The Job* and making him read it. . . . As this rotten article of his is one of the first which pretends to sum up all my work, as the Nation is a journal of some importance, and as Van Doren regards himself as a serious critic, I think he ought to do something about it. I think he ought to do an entirely new article about me in the Nation. Think you could get him to? It would really give him a nice chance to cry "mea culpa" very prettily . . . and certainly he must change this if he's going to publish these articles in book form.

In criticizing his criticism, I most carefully and repeatedly said that I was not maintaining that *The Job* etc. were necessarily in the least *good;* but that they were serious work and not "bright amusing chatter"; and that whether I have been and am a damn bad writer or not, certainly I have NOT been a tinkling chatterer who was by the mighty powers of Mr. Masters miraculously converted to seriousness. God! You who went with me thru plans of *The Job* and all the rest—you know. Get after Van Doren politely, if you think well.

As I had had some nice polite correspondence with Van Doren before, and been complimentary, I was able to write this protest without impropriety, I think. . . .

On the job!

Our best!
sl

Why don't you close with one of the German offers & gamble in the marks—let 'em pile up there. Like to have it published in Germany.

Pallanza, November 5

Dear Alf and Don:

Your two letters came at once today, and much joy was had thereby. . . . First, before I forget it: Don't send any more mail to Pallanza. Send it again c/o Guaranty Trust Co., London, until you receive a cable from me. Then start sending to Rome—as that will, I hope, be my address for several months. You see it will begin to be pretty cold up here in a few weeks, and we probably shan't stay after December 1st. We'll go to Rome and stay there till *Babbitt* is done and I'm ready to start home—that is, if we like Rome; otherwise we'll probably go to Capri. . . . It may even be possible—as there are not many people here—that the hotel will close before December 1st, in which case we'll go to Rome as soon as it does close.

Been working very hard on *Babbitt*. I've now finished about 95,000 words of the first draft, besides reading over, doing a little revision on, and making a lot of later-to-be-taken-up suggestions on, the first 70,000 words. My guess now is that when finished, it will be between 120,000 and 150,000 words long—i.e. from 60,000 to 30,000 words shorter than *Main Street*. I think it's going to be good. It is satiric, rather more than *Main Street;* and for that reason I think—I hope—that the novel after *Babbitt* will be definitely non-satiric—except, of course, for occasional passages.

Hope you will have received safely my letter asking you to deposit for me in Guaranty Trust a new $1500. I haven't yet received any money from the play; and tho I still have almost two hundred and fifty pounds sterling on this side of the water, I don't want to be caught short. I suppose I shan't get any play money for a little time yet.

Weather bully here—warm days, cold nights; tho it's dusty, the mountains are glorious, the lake ever changing, the sunsets as wonderful as on the prairies. We've had some good walks, one long bicycle ride—we found ourselves quite at home in the saddle, tho it's six years since we've ridden. And one afternoon Claude Washburn and I tramped up a mountain and had dinner by ourselves afterward.

Confidentially, I don't think C.W. will go much farther than he has now. He'll keep up to present level. But he lacks a passionate reaction to daily life.

Letter from Edith Summers Kelley saying that she has actually started her novel—written 20,000 words.

We're all awfully well and happy. We miss only Don's presence, which we were lucky enough to have in Eng and Paris. We'd like to show him two or three of the lovely islands in the lake here. . . . Do write often—it's incomparably my best glimpse of home, your letters. . . . Our very best!!!!!

SL

Rome, November 18
Dear Don:
All right sir, I'll give you enough pages to make a dummy right away, soon as I can get them done. I enclose hints for the artist who is to do the jacket picture. For I decidedly think that, as we did with *Main Street*, we better have a picture on front and, for first several editions, text all over the back.

I doubt if I'd have the *Babbitt* jacket in exactly the same color scheme as *Main Street*. Would look as if we were doing just the same thing all over again. But *I do believe I'd have the actual cloth binding exactly the same*—we'll try to begin to make lines of books, all in that blue and orange, across library shelves. I know I like to have all my Conrads in same binding.

About the title: Certainly nothing better than *Babbitt* has occurred to any of us. Personally, I like it. It's short, fairly keen: and nothing has been more successful than names for titles.

Yes, Pallanza proved glorious—beautiful, bracing, fine. Algernon Blackwood was crazy to knock it, in Kent. I think perhaps he had it balled up with some other place—or else he stayed at one of the dull little hotels down in the town itself, instead of at ours, a half-mile out, on a lovely point.

Terribly sorry to hear about Mrs. Harcourt. How are you feeling, yourself? Luck!

As ever,
SL

Grand Hotel de Russie, Rome
November 18
Dear Alf:
I'm most terribly sorry to hear, from Don's letter of the first, that Mrs. Harcourt has been having a rotten time with infected teeth. Will you please give her my love? Of course she may say that as a soother of nerves and of teeth my love is a poor specific, but assure her that she is wrong—that it is being eagerly applied for by Russian princesses (now keeping restaurants), Fascisti leaders (now keeping quiet), and rich young American ladies come here to study singing or tatting (now keeping parrots).

Edna St. Vincent Millay is here, and I'm trying to decide whether, as an agent of the firm, I want to tie her up with a contract. I may be cabling you about her, before you get this letter, and I may not be. Her poetry is splendid, and much worth having, and she is planning a novel.

But the devil of it is that she quite definitely plans to make this a novel that would be sure to be suppressed—and she wants enough advance to live on for four months while writing it! I'm afraid that, not as a pure author but as a crass publisher, that doesn't attract me so much as it might.

Luck!
sl

Rome, Dec. 1st

Dear Alf and Don:

Have your recent good letters sent to Pallanza. No news except working hard. Like Rome immensely—glorious city, good hotel, enough people we know. I'll write @ more length when the revision is off my chest. . . . I'm doing it, by the way, with extreme carefulness—it may get itself read with some thoroughness. . . . I'm dedicating the book to Edith Wharton—have written her so, & she seems delighted.

Till soon—
Red

You're publishing Piccoli's *Croce?* [1] He's here, & I like him—& admire him—immensely. . . . Have talked more to Edna Millay *re* novel, but she's a Tartar—thinks VERY well of herself—sweet, young, pretty, & loves Edna. . . .

December 13

Dear Sinclair:

Wonderful stuff—your letter of November 18th and its enclosures! We all gathered round and read over shoulders, in silence except for frequent outbursts of "Jeezz, that's great," "Just listen to this," and so on. Really, your descriptions are beyond praise. My memory of what I read makes me appreciate them especially. Everybody is enthusiastic—only your presence could make us more so!

As for the title, *Babbitt* suits everybody. Melville Cane [2] says why don't we call it *George F. Babbitt.* That *is* pretty good. The "George" and especially the "F" mean an awful lot. But I've decided they mean too much. Just *Babbitt* is better because it can mean Babbitts everywhere, the Babbitt kind of thing, rather than just a character. So it's *Babbitt.*

This is the last week of the play in New York. It's going on the road for a long tour of smaller cities. Don't know details. Have been trying to get hold of Harvey O'Higgins, without success so far. The theatrical

[1] *Benedetto Croce* by Rafaello Piccoli, HB&Co., 1922.
[2] Legal adviser to the firm and on the board of directors.

people are clams as far as giving up any real information is concerned. An American Play Company man told me they had refused an offer of $25,000 for movie rights. I don't know whether it's like Caesar and the Crown. Ellen's written you about the German rights sale. I'm holding their check for 20,000 marks. When it came, it amounted to about $94.00. Today it's something like $120.00. Hope you don't mind my gambling with your money! The worst of it is that the results are so modest in proportion to the number of marks.

All good wishes,
Don

Rome, Dec. 13

Dear Alf:
   Day before yesterday I mailed you 57 pp., & front matter, of *Babbitt;* hope you get it all right. Reading over part of *Bab* written at Pallanza, I see where I shall have to cut it a good deal; & I see that, being inherently more satiric than *Main St.*, *Babbitt* must not be anything like so long, or it will be tedious. Indeed, I *may* keep it down to 100,000 or 110,000 words.
   I think I shall make my next novel after *Babbitt* not satiric at all; rebellious as ever, perhaps, but the central character *heroic*. I'm already getting gleams for it; I see it as the biggest thing I've tackled. . . . We'll talk it over next spring.
   Good letters in yesterday from you & from the office. Merry Xmas!

Ever!
SL

Rome, December 26

Dear Alf:
   A good Xmas—party @ studio with reasonable amounts of drinks & dancing & nice Americans & Italians on Xmas Eve; toys for the kid yesterday—an Italian train; a Sicilian wheat cart with oxen; in the bright afternoon, a long hike thru the Borghese gardens.
   All goes well—plenty of people but not too many. Don's brother Ernest (Brace) arrives here in 2 days, & I've found a pension for him. We see more of Raffaello Piccoli than of anyone else. He's a corker— charming, intelligent (very!), amusing. You're publishing his Croce book. *Please give it an extra big boost for me.*
   Judging by cables, *M. St.* movie rights are to be sold for $40,000, out of which I'll get about $9640 & you about $1160. (Rem. Amer. Play

[1921]

Co. get 10% on all—drat 'em!) Play receipts to date have been about $1660, for my own share *including* the $1000 advance of last spring. I see b' the papers play is closing in NY & I don't yet know if it's going on the road.

Hope to God Sue is better. D' you know, she and Hastings wd enjoy a month at this hotel some winter.

Babbitt goes marching on. Hope that by now you'll have rec'd the 57 pages sent you on Dec. 11. Grace has been reading the ms, all to date, & seems enthusiastic.

Look! Please send Gene Debs, in Atlanta Prison, a *Main Street* with a note saying I asked you to send it to him, & that I hope he will like Miles Bjornstam.

Awfully glad you've received & liked catalog stuff, etc. of *Babbitt*. Happy New Year. God bless you all!

SL

Rome, Dec. 26
Letter #2

Dear Alf & Don:

Second letter today—yr 2 just came in. Two fine packages of books came via Baker Taylor. Many thanks.

Nothing more doing *re* Edna Millay's novel; she'd already offered it to Liveright, & he probly accepted.

The enclosed is from some South American paper—Chile, I believe. Very laudatory. What about a Spanish translation, *especially for So. America?* Look into it. *Might* be done in Argentine rather than Spain.

I'd change that "so honest & so interesting" ad line now. How about "most discussed book of the last twenty years—and now looks as though it might be the most discussed book of the next twenty!" And how about a freak ad quoting German, French, Spanish et al. comments *in the original languages?* And This

MAIN STREET
M.D.B.
(—still the Most Discussed Book)
M.D.B.

Slove!
SL

Rome, Tuesday December 27

Dear Alf:

Today came a letter from Dawson Johnson[1] about material for French articles on me. I've sent him a little extra material. Numerous other requests for biographical material made me suggest to Don, in England, that some time shortly after the appearance of *Babbitt*, there ought to be a pamphlet devoted to SL—like those good little books Doran got out on Walpole, Swinnerton, et al.

It should contain a thorough biographical sketch of SL, written (and signed) by somebody like George Soule, perhaps, based on material I'll give him when I return to America; brief accounts of books before *Main Street;* extracts from the best reviews etc. of *Main Street;* some acct of the circulation of that book, of controversies over it, of the burlesques on it and the translations of it. Then take up *Babbitt*—what it is, etc., and hold pamphlet long enough to get in the first good reviews of *Babbitt*. Then shoot it out to bookstores, women's clubs, etc. and use it when clubwomen who want to write papers inquire for data. It might suggest, in small separate article, the study of both *M.S.* and *Babbitt* by clubs, schools, colleges, etc. Would be illustrated with several snapshots of me and fambly, and Hoppé portrait.

We'll talk this over next spring; see if it's advisable. One important thing is to get just the right person to do the book. Bill Benet, Updegraff, and Soule are all possible. Or perhaps it should be someone who does *not* know me personally.

Now for this book we ought to have certain material. I foolishly haven't kept either *Jane Street* or *Ptomaine Street*. And one of the interesting things about the pamphlet would be an account of the *Main Street* literature which is already growing up. Later it will be impossible to get hold of some of these. So will you please get now, and hold in the office for this purpose the following: *Jane Street, Ptomaine Street,* Meredith Nicholson's *Man in the Street* (is that the title?) with its article "Let Main Street Alone," Donald Stewart's *Parody Outline of History* with its excellent *M St* burlesque, the Swedish and German translations of *M.S.* when they come along, and any others. And later books with important references to *M.S.* And we might quote from several of the burlesques, to compare them—of course besides those in separate books there's several appeared in papers and mags. But for heaven's sake gather and hold the above-mentioned books before they disappear—as most of them will!!!!

[1] Director of the American Library in Paris.

We might have part of the stuff, especially the biography, run in the Bookman or some other magazine, during the coming *Babbitt* interest, before using it in pamphlet. Heh?

Love,
SL

On January third Lewis cabled from Rome that he was returning to America, but that he might stay in London a couple of weeks.

[1922]
Georgian House
10 Bury Street
London, S.W.
January 8

Dear Alf:

You must have been wondering what the devil! I found just because I *do* like Rome, and Italy in general, so darn well, and because it was so agreeable to go on long loafing jaunts that, though I was still working steadily, I was more than likely to get lazy. Some day I'm going back to Italy and do nothing but loaf and play and dream, but I can't afford to now till the book is done, so I suddenly decided to jump north, get some cold and good gray energetic days, either in London or New York.

I half planned to catch the *Aquitania* from England on January 28, but now that I'm here, I like it so much, feel so energetic, and have found at the above address so bully a service flat, that I may stay on here till late April. One of the several good things about it—I haven't wasted any time in coming up here because I'm now just one stage from New York.

I didn't see any reason why Gracie and Wells should come north, both because they're so well off there, because G is studying Italian, and because it may, perhaps, be just as well for me to be alone during the rest of the time I'm working on the book. She may come home with me in the spring, she may stay over and me rejoin them in Italy. We haven't decided about that yet. But meantime, here I am in a charming sitting-room-bedroom-bath with good service, on a quiet yet convenient street, and though I got to London only day before yesterday, I'm already all unpacked, settled, and on the job. Is there anything I can do for you in London? Let me know.

Well, here I be, back next door to you, and I'll see you-all before many months, at least.

SL

London, Jan 15

Dear Alf:

Grieved to hear of Hastings's illness. Hope that by now he's splendidly well again. Gawd what a year you've had, between successes & illnesses!

I'm working beautifully here—just the right place—quiet and charming little flat, & plenty of people after tea time. Have seen Galsworthy, Walpole, Drinkwater, Geo. Moore, May Sinclair (I dine with her on Tuesday), John Cournos, Beatrice Harraden, Wm. Archer, Rebecca West—who is to make me 'quainted with H. G. Wells,[1] when he returns, in about six weeks. Doran here—haven't seen him yet, but I lunch with him today. Seen Liveright several times; he's hustling like the devil, & hints he will bring home some big authors of older firms. Waiting to hear your reaction to 1st 57 pp.—hope to God you have rec'd them all right—tho I have complete carbon.

Ever!
SL

January 20

Dear Lewis:

Just have yours of January 8th from London. Thinking that you might be sailing almost any day has been something of an inhibition about writing to you. When we first got word that you had gone to London and might come home, of course we speculated on the reason for your changed plans, but Don and I agreed that it would be just what you say it is. Bless your heart for your conscience about your work. If the second-raters who wonder why they don't get first-rate rewards would only realize the blood and tears that go into a first-rate job.

When I got back from Florida a week ago, I read at once the first part of *Babbitt* which you sent over. It is sure enough good as gold. In fact, I think it is the best thing you have done so far—the first chapter even better than the Prologue you have made out of Babbitt's speech. I wonder a little about giving away as much of your point of view as that speech does rather than having it grow out of the development of the characters as the reader goes along. But we'll get to all that when we have the whole book and when you are over here.

Sales of *Main Street* the last six months of last year were 104,000. It's a comfort to have somebody suggest some new way of advertising

[1] Apparently the meeting with Wells which Lewis expected to have the previous June had not come off.

Main Street. In the course of the last eighteen months, it has been advertised in every size of every font of type.

I am endlessly glad you are so comfortably fixed in London. I know just where Bury Street is.

I wonder if anyone has thought to tell you that Harrison Smith is working for us. He started the first of January; he is responsible for the preliminary clean-up of the flood of manuscripts that comes in and is helping me on the advertising. He is an awfully nice chap; I think he will be happy here and a great comfort.

Ever yours,
Alf

London, January 20

Dear Alf and Don:

Don's letter announcing arrival of first 57 pages just came in, via Rome, this morning. About cutting the Introduction, we'll see later, when you-all have read the book as a whole. I have already cut it a little, and as it so completely sums up certain things in all contemporary Babbitts, I'd want to be pretty sure before cutting it much more. . . . I think perhaps you're wrong to omit, in the dummy, the dedication to Edith Wharton, however, because it might arouse interest. But it's an unimportant matter.

I like it here, am working well, and may stay two or three months before coming home.

The enclosed two stories from the (American) Smart Set Henry Mencken sent to me with the comment, "I lately unearthed a girl in Iowa, by name Ruth Suckow, who seems to me to be superb. She follows after Dreiser and Anderson, but she is also a genuine original. *She is now at work on a novel.*" I agree with Mencken that Ruth's work as shown in the stories enclosed is remarkable—lucid, remarkably real, firm, jammed with promise. I should certainly hasten to query Mencken about her, get her address, and write to her about the coming novel, in the hope of getting ahead of Knopf.

Jan. 21, A.M.

Cable this morning from Ray Long.[1] "If you have not closed agreement for serial rights next novel would like to negotiate with you." I'm answering: "Sorry serial rights not for sale."

Oh. Had lunch and an afternoon with Geo Doran. He was at his most charming—and you know how charming he can be. Liked him a

[1] Editor of *Hearst's International Magazine.*

lot and, best of all, he made no efforts to grab my next novel, thus saving me a refusal.
On the job!

Luck!
Red.

February 4
Dear Lewis:

Your good letter came this morning. I have read Ruth Suckow's stories and am writing to her. They are clear and tight. So few of the new people write well. I wonder what she is writing a novel about.

I have a letter from Cape saying he would like very much to have *Babbitt* in England, and that you have intimated that would please you. It would please us too. I am inclined, however, not to make a definite commitment now. I should not give the new book to Hodder. He has been cantankerous about the price, though Lord knows he got it cheaply enough; after he saw the book was going, he should have taken our suggestion of buying a set of plates and printing in England. Cape will probably not pay as much for the new book at the start as some of the older houses, but like ourselves, he doesn't let a book just drop into the hopper, and in the long run he would sell more, I think, than anyone else.

I guessed that Ray Long was cabling you about serial rights from the way he telephoned me asking your address. You may be sacrificing an immediate bunch of money, but I am pretty sure you are not doing so in the long run. I believe, too, that *Babbitt* will be a better novel just because you know it is not to be serialized.

Yours,
Alf

London, February 4
Dear Alf:

Delighted, couple days ago, finally to hear from you your opinion of the part of *Babbitt* sent you.

Alf, why don't you consider making your European trip this spring, while I'm here? There would be several advantages. You would then be free to watch *Babbitt* next fall; second, we could begin to take up *Babbitt* together, third, we could have a good party—you might stay right here in the same house. We could go home together, say in May. Think it over carefully.

As ever.
SL

[1922]

London, Sunday February 12
Dear Alf:
The enclosed clipping further bears out my suggestion of the need for sending out a note about the new novel not being *Zenith* but *Babbitt*. Since people are beginning to want to know about it, we better feed them a *little* information. This suitcase story has also persisted. So you might add something like the following:

A story which has recently appeared in a number of newspapers regarding the author of *Main Street* announces: "Shortly before going abroad, last year, Sinclair Lewis bought a fancy suitcase for his wife. They used it on a weekend trip up the Hudson and it was stolen on the train. And in it was the manuscript of Lewis's new novel! The real punch of the tragedy is that Mr. Lewis did not have a carbon copy."
Aside from the facts that the stolen suitcase was not one but two, that neither of these fancy suitcases—whatever a "fancy" suitcase may be—belonged to Mrs. Lewis but one of them to her mother and the other to Mr. Lewis, that they were not stolen on a train up the Hudson, U.S.A., but at a station in London, that in neither of them was there a single word of manuscript, notes, or any other literary material, that Mr. Lewis always keeps a carbon copy of everything he writes, and that, finally, when the suitcases were stolen he had completed only a small part of his new novel, *Babbitt*, the story is a triumph of correct detail.

I've seen this stolen ms story now about six times, so it must have been used a lot more. Our dear friend Mrs. Dawson referred to it with expectant pleasure the other day. I see she has broken out with frequency lately. We owe her a lot for her advertising.
I've been thinking about your comment that the Introduction to *Babbitt*—his speech—should be queried lest it give away too much of him to the reader at the start. Well, perhaps it should be cut, as being too exhaustingly long, but I'm not afraid about the giving away part: In the first place any sophisticated reader would, even without the Introduction, know pretty much all of Babbitt's ideation before the end of Chapter II; and second where the surprise is going to come in is that, being so standardized, Babbitt yet breaks away from standards, a little, when the time comes. And I do think the Introduction, as is, will attract a lot of attention for its portrait of the mind of a man like Babbitt. I like especially the Chum Frink poem. So let's not be hasty about cutting it. Often, in novels, these apparently tangential things prove to be the things of greatest value.
I hope to have the first draft done in three more days, and I have done some revising. The final draft will be longer than I'd thought—between 120,000 and 145,000 words. Anyway, it will be considerably shorter than *Main Street*, and the part I've recently been writing is much more straight

narrative, much less satiric, than the earlier part, so it can run longer than could all satire.

Will you please send me two books: the Harcourt *Short History of the American Labor Movement* by Mary Beard; and the *Life of Debs*, written, I think, by David Karstner, and published, I believe, by Liveright? With them you might include the Stearns *Civilization* book,[1] and Washburn's novel. I should be very grateful.

Feeling fine, like London, working hard, all's well! Love to all.

SL

Still think it would be a great idea for you to come over here this spring. . . .

London, February 13

Dear Ellen:

Many greetings from London. I write to you surrounded by manuscripts, my sleeves rolled up, my mighty brow beaded with perspiration, struggling through the last sixteen or twenty years of this damned book. The roar of the typewriters resounds from my outer office, my office manager rushes in with stacks of new material. . . . At least, that is the impression you can give to anybody that inquires about it.

Don't you think we had better send to that child out in Italy, Texas, who is going (and very sensibly, too) to deliver a graduation thesis on my life and works, some of the earlier masterpieces? If you have any copies of these earlier books handy you might send them to her—especially *The Job* and *Free Air*. If you have *lots* of them you might send her the whole bunch.

Bully weather here, just cold enough to make it nice for working. I hope you have gotten over being frozen to death in New York.

Sincerely yours,
Sinclair Lewis

February 13

Dear Lewis:

Thanks for your notes. You must surely by now have had my letter saying how much I liked the first part of the book. The first chapter is better, if possible, than Babbitt's Prologue speech. There is no use saying anything more about that speech until I have read the whole book. This is going to be a great book about a man—a living, breathing character. You know that when a novelist has done that, he can quit. If I had to

---

[1] *Civilization in the United States*, edited by Harold E. Stearns, HB&Co., 1922.

decide on what I have seen now, I'd keep the whole book as the story of a man, and let it show what it will about big towns, small towns, or civilization, or any other damn thing. God bless you, and heaven help you! If you were where it was handy to do it, you ought to have your life insured for some round sum until it is finished, both for our sake and that of your family. That's not such a damn fool idea.

Yours much,
Alf

February 21

Dear Red:

I have thought of coming over for some fun and work with you before your return, but the upshot is rather in the direction of not coming unless some further reason arises. We are becoming more and more American publishers; we have a heavy contracted-for list for the rest of the year. Keynes, Strachey, and the other real ones we have from England are sewed up either by contract or sentiment or something and I have been thinking that Don and I would stick to our knitting here this year and let the other boys play abroad. A considerable reason is the development of our textbook business—$10,000 in January, and I'd guess there will be $150,000 or more this year. And that means as much every year for ten years if we didn't publish a new textbook. When we have a quarter million of that we are impregnable.

What I'd say now would be: You come home about April; let me read what is done of *Babbitt* over a weekend; then you and I take my car and drive to Atlantic City or somewhere, just talking it all over loosely as we drive. When we get where we are going, stay a week or two and say all we have to say, lay our plans for advs and for all sorts of things, and get our heads around it all—and incidentally have a damn good time.

Grosset wants *Main Street* for cheap edition in fall. We've said a not too tentative "No." Play opens in Chicago March 5th.

Yours,
Alf

London
Feb 22 and Washington's birthday
but they haven't heard about it here.

Dear Don:

Yes, I think perhaps the type and color-splash jacket is better than a picture would be. I can understand your difficulties in getting a picture that would not limit the appeal. The only other thing would be a portrait of Babbitt, and that would not be attractive. I've been looking at the jacket as you sent it to me, last evening and this morning, and I like it better and better. Let's go . . .

You speak of Strachey and wonder what my impressions. I've met him!—at tea at Lady Colefax's. I thought he was singularly unappetizing, with his watery beard, mild spectacles, and feeble voice. I talked to him two minutes, informed him what hellish good publishers H.B.&Co. were, and went my ways, content for to see him no morrrrrrrre, my love, con-tent for to see-hee him no more! (Try that on your baritone; it sings very nicely.)

I think that between now and May it would be a good stunt to run a full-page ad of *Babbitt* in the Publishers' Weekly, announcing it for publication early in September, and reproducing in one corner our 1st *Main Street* announcement of a year and a half ago. . . . Gawd, a year and a half!

All well. Grace still in Rome—gets a bit lonely sometimes, but has a good time and working hard on Italian and French, and saw the new Pope crowned from a front seat. She says he didn't come down off the sedia and say anything about *Main St*, but otherwise the ceremony went off very well. . . . My plans as to exact date for return are vague, but knowing me I suspect that sometime between now and May 1st I'll suddenly get fed up with London, grab a ticket, cable, and sail, and have Grace join me in US instead of waiting for her here. But meantime the work goes splendidly and otherwise I seem planless.

Best to all.
SL

February 27

Dear Lewis:

Congratulations on the note you wrote declining election to the National Institute of Arts and Letters.

"Said Elmer More to Stuart Sherman,
'Let's clean up these younger vermin.'
'All right, let's; they make me sore,'
Said Stuart Sherman to Elmer More."

Though I think Sherman knows good stuff when he sees it—if his eye isn't cocked over his shoulder at his colleagues when he is deciding whether or not he ought to be let to like it.

Don't think any more than you have or than you may in the most passing fashion about what I said about the speech which is the introduction to *Babbitt*. I attach very little weight to my remarks in that direction as they were based on reading only the 57 or so pages you sent over. My judgment about that sort of thing isn't worth a damn until I have read the whole book, if then. After I have read the whole book, if I have suggestions to make, I'll make them, as I did about the episode you left out of *Main Street*, and then you can be the doctor.

Don't let these literary fellers drain your strength. It's a hell of a hard job to write as good a novel as the one you are at. If you were here, I'd put you to work in a garage for a few days.

I am thinking about your proposal that I should come over before you come home. I'd sure like to see you. Just now it seems to me it would be more fun to drive around here for a week or two together than to be in the thick of things in England.

Ever yours,
Alf

London, March 12

Dear Alf:

You're right about not coming over but seeing me in US, I fancy. But I can't get there in April. I ought to bring you the novel in something like final form. I think I still have the ring of the American voice in my ears all right—you must remember that I encounter a fair number of Americans here—I'm a damn sight more likely to be having a drink with the fine chaps from the Guaranty Trust Co than with the blinkin' English writers.

You may expect me, with ms quite or practically ready to set, about May 16th to 20th, and as soon as you go over it, we'll beat it out to the country and talk it over. Grace will join me here about May 1st. One advantage in her not being here is that I'm working practically undisturbed till dinner time, then get out for a good walk. Another thing about not returning in April is that it's bad to stop before the ms is something like all done, because one relaxes and it's hard to go on. I had that experience rather with *Main Street*, after I came from Washington up to NY then Maine.

I have your note about A.S.M.Hutchinson. I'll see if he knows when his book will be published, and I'll say nothing about mine. . . . You could get *Babbitt* out even before September 14 if you had full ms by May 20th, and if there weren't too many changes, couldn't you? I'll try to hustle out proofs—if necessary come to NY to read them, if I'm in the country at the time.

No, I wouldn't let Grosset have *M St* for cheap edition for a year or

two more, if then. Yes, I'd wait yet awhile before tying up with Cape on *Babbitt*.
See you in two months! Work going fine.

Luck!
Red

March 15

Dear Lewis:

I have just booked passage for Sue and one of our most intimate friends, Mrs. Dr. (Bill) Slaughter, on the *Adriatic* for April 8th. Sue has been gradually coming back to first-rate health, and some time spent abroad with this lovely old friend will put her on her feet. The plan is ten days in London; a week around the part of South Germany where Sue's people came from, near Mannheim; over the Alps and down to Florence; then back to Paris and so home about the middle of June. I have suggested that the girls stay at the Old Metropole while they are in London. I don't know whether they will arrive before you leave or not. Sue will have the latest news from us. I wish I could get away, but we seem to be unbelievably busy. Ellen is just starting for a three-weeks' holiday which she sadly needs, and there are some questions about added stockroom and perhaps moving our quarters and so forth that I hesitate to get far away from.

We just have the Ersten Almanach from the Volksberband der Bucherfreunde, Berlin. It announces *Hauptstrasse aus dem Amerikanischen*, translated by Dr. Baldorolden. There is an extraordinarily interesting two-page discussion of the book.[1]

No time for more today.

Yours,
Alf

London, March 26

Dear Alf:

We shall sail on the *Aquitania* on May 13. I hope to have the ms with me, all done. I shan't write many letters to you these coming six weeks—be rather more than busy revising. What advance sale do you expect on *Babbitt*?

All well! Luck!

Ever,
SL

[1] German edition of *Main Street*.

During this period before sailing there were only brief business notes from Lewis. He and Mrs. Lewis arrived in New York about May 20th, and after spending several weeks there, Lewis bought a car and drove to Sauk Centre to see his father, while Mrs. Lewis went to Fishers Island, New York.

FOUR

A Reputation Established

[1922]
Sauk Centre, Minn., July 9

Dear Alf:

Good trip—*grand* car (4 passenger Cadillac in a fetchin' beige)—find my father well. I'll be here for a week more, then to Chicago via St. Paul. I am meekly bored here—not aggressively. The town far from resenting *M. St.* seems proud of it.

I'm sending for your fall use two pictures made of me in Madison. The one at typewriter seems to me a corker.

Lemme know how things are going.

Luck!
SL

July 19

Dear Sinclair:

In accepting our proposal for *Babbitt*, Cape says: "I think that I shall print a glossary at the end of the book, and very likely ask Hugh Walpole to write a foreword; this will be good advertising. You might let me know what Lewis thinks of these two suggestions."

Cape says, by the way, that he thinks the book stands a very good chance in England, and that we have a good chance of selling almost as many copies as of *Main Street*.

It has been hot and busy in the office since you left. I hope both your father and you have enjoyed your trip.

Faithfully yours,
Don

[1922]

The Blackstone, Chicago
July 22

Dear Don:

Your special delivery t' hand. Yes, I think Cape's idea of a glossary might be a good idea—if he can get a good man to do it. *I'd like to see proof on it before publication.* . . . And bully to have introduction. Tell Cape that if he can't get Walpole, he might try the following: Wells, Galsworthy, May Sinclair, Somerset Maugham, Compton Mackenzie.[1]

I rather doubt our living in either Madison or St. Paul—too cramped, both. Gracie arrives from the East this afternoon & we'll talk it over. I RA-ther think we'll start motoring East next Tuesday.

Lecture @ University of Chicago last evening; afterward a somewhat spirituous party with Ed Morehouse, Brett Stokes [2] & coupla others—very sunny & salubrious. Luck!

Ever,
SL

July 22

Dear Sinclair:

Had a rush visit from your wife yesterday and I hope that by now you are safely reunited. I am sending you copies of some correspondence we've had with the Babbitts. In both cases I have consulted a lawyer before replying. The B. T. Babbitt matter is entirely safe. I think we are in no danger from George F. either, though of course the man can bring an action if he thinks he has cause, but our lawyers think that he would be unable to prove any damage and I hope my reply to his letter will allay his fears. I hope we don't hear from a George F. Babbitt who has a wife called Myra and who is in the real estate business!

I will send you an advance copy of *Babbitt* as soon as you have an address that seems to offer time enough to be sure of its getting into your hands. We are trying to guard the copies carefully.

Faithfully yours,
Don

[1] When the British edition of *Babbitt* appeared it had a three-page introduction by Hugh Walpole and about 125 American expressions "glossarized."
[2] Edward Morehouse, salesman for Harcourt, Brace; Brett Stokes, son of Frederick A. Stokes and salesman for Frederick A. Stokes Company.

Chicago, July 22

Dear Don:

Gracie, just arrived hot and dusty but safe, tells me of the possible trouble with Mr. George F. Babbitt of Boston regarding the name of Our Hero. If you have to do *anything*, why don't you do this: Make him an offer to put in each copy of the book a slip (not attached, simply slipped in) to this effect, say:

> The author and publishers of *Babbitt* regret to learn, just as the printing of the first edition of the book is completed and changes are therefore impossible, that the name George F. Babbitt is the same as that of an important Boston journalist. They both avow that the similarity was unintentional and regret the coincidence. With the millions of people in the world, it is impossible to choose any name for a fictional hero without the chance of its corresponding to the name of some real person, and the author & publishers do most earnestly assert that in choosing the name George F. Babbitt, the author was unfortunately unaware of the identity of the real Mr. Babbitt, a journalist of standing.
>
> (*Signed*) Sinclair Lewis
> Harcourt, Brace and Co.

OR something of the sort, to be OK'd by your lawyer. AND should you make this offer keep more than one copy of the letter for possible use in any suit or injunction hearing.

Look. Gracie and I will be here till some time Tuesday. You should have this before then. Please wire me if there seems to be any difficulty, and lemme know what you want me to do.

Ever,
SL

Chicago, Tue July 25

Dear Don:

I think we'll be off, tomorrow or next day. Here are some thoughts on the GFBabbitt of Boston case, in case it should chance to become serious, which might be of value. You might turn them over to your lawyer:

We can deny that the name of the hero of the novel *is* the same as that of the Boston man! The name of the novel character is given, specifically, emphatically (see chapter near end—scene at Boosters' Club meeting), as George Follansbee Babbitt, whereas the Boston man's name is George F—— (discover his middle name) Babbitt. Furthermore (and this is at least as important in identification as is the name), George Follansbee Babbitt is a real estate man of an imaginary city called Zenith, a city of a type obviously very different from Boston; while George F—— Babbitt is a journalist of Boston.

And suppose the name in the novel were changed to (say) George F. Brown. There probably, there *certainly* are many George F. Browns among the 110,000,000 people of the U.S.—there are two of them in the Chicago phone book alone. Any of these people could then demand that the changed name be changed again, till finally it would be impossible to issue a novel with named characters at all! For there is no possible name for a fiction character which will not have a resemblance, real or imagined, to that of some actual person. Yet certainly all laws and customs, universally, do permit authors to give names to characters, interfering only when it is PROVEN that by INTENT the author means to indicate and INJURE some specific real person. And in this case the proof seems to be that the author is honest in his contention that not only did he *not* mean to refer to the real Mr. George F—— Babbitt of Boston, but that actually he had never heard of that person till this case arose.

Mr. Babbitt of Boston shows prejudice by presupposing that some injury *may* be done to him by the use of this name in the novel: he must PROVE that actual injury HAS been done to him. Actually it might as well be advocated that Mr. Babbitt, of Boston, is likely to receive large advertising and attention which will be of great value to him as a journalist (whereas he is known only locally, the fictional Babbitt will be, indeed is even before publication, known nationally and even internationally!). Therefore the publishers might, with as much reason and justice as Mr. Babbitt of Boston, claim from him payment for this invaluable free advertising!

I'm NOT really worried about this at all, but I do believe that it's just as well to take precautions, to be READY, in case Mr. Babbitt of Boston, obviously an agitatable person, tried to get an injunction or something which would delay the important date of publication.

Ever,
SL

Broadway Inn
Geneva, Ohio
Friday

Dear Don:

East'ard bound! Ran into Geo. Horace Lorimer in Chicago, & again this morning in Toledo. Ast him if offended people whose names happen to be the same as characters in a story often write him. *Frequent*, says he; & he answers with a good *stiff* reply that the circumstances surrounding

the story-hero show clearly that he is not the same as the real person; & this, Lorimer says, usually closes the incident.
Fine easy tug.

Ever,
SL

After exploring the possibility of renting a house in Madison or St. Paul, the Lewises decided on Hartford, Connecticut. Mid-August they found a house near the golf club. While living in Hartford, Lewis visited New York frequently.

25 Belknap Road,
Hartford, Connecticut
September third.

Dear Alfred Harcourt:

After reading the Stuart Sherman essay,[1] I should have kicked off two slippers, except that kicking off one is more effective. As the eight-year-old wife of Sinclair Lewis, I bear witness to the exceptional, and true, understanding of Hal in this article. It is just as right as right can be, except possibly the influence of *Bovary*. I don't think Hal had read *Bovary* until after *Main Street* was finished. But I am not sure. Of course, I love the impressive seriousness with which Mr. Sherman dissects Hal's work.

And how wise of you to get out the booklet at once. Hal may be in your office as you are reading this note. So I shall retain this manuscript. Do come up soon. Come back with Hal, if you can. Aren't you really and truly thrilled about September fourteenth?[2]

On with the dance!

Grace Lewis

September 11

Dear Red:

What news there is is good. Doc Smyth[3] telephoned that he has a fine review from May Sinclair. McLeod[4] has telegraphed for 2500 more *Babbitt* for Canada. I'll have the total of the advance orders the end of the week, and let you know exactly what's the upshot of all the fuss. You know that my guess is 200,000 before New Year's.

[1] *The Significance of Sinclair Lewis*, HB&Co., 1922.
[2] Publication date of *Babbitt*.
[3] Clifford Smyth. Editor of *New York Times Book Review*.
[4] George J. McLeod, Ltd., Canadian agents for Harcourt, Brace.

I had a mean cold and stayed home most of last week after you left. It gave me a chance to read *The Job* at leisure. There is a good deal in it you will never be ashamed of. There are a lot of women who have come on since 1917 who will "love" that book. Except for a little airing of your private views here and there, I didn't let go of it until Chapter XIII. From Chapter XIII the book wants to be pointed a little more toward the job and a little less toward Una's life outside the job and S.L.'s ideas toward life in general.

Hope you like the new home.

Yours,
Alf

September 13

Dear Red:

Yesterday I read some of a manuscript which had rather full references to Disraeli and his political novels, and recalled Henry Adams and his *Democracy*. All this made me realize that there had been no really good serious novel of Washington national and international life for the forty years since *Democracy* was published. How about casting your eye that way for a theme? A real and honest picture. Of course there can be a woman in it with at least a promise of what women may mean in political life. Perhaps the action might be mainly confined to the U. S. Senate. If you don't write that book sometime, Grace will. It would be a great stunt to have that job done right once, and the international audience would be large.

Upton Sinclair sends us a carbon of his Appeal to Reason review. It's bully. Maurice [1] of the Herald phoned that Owen Johnson's review was so good that if I didn't acknowledge it was the best review of *Babbitt* he'd buy me a lunch. It's lining up just right. You'll have them all flopping to get right side up first by next Monday. There has been just enough silence, delay, knocks, soft answers, and enthusiasm to catch the press part just right. Right-o! Stay home, take it easy, and keep quiet.

200,000 before Christmas, Son! It's a damn good book. Nuf sed.

Ever yours,
Alf

Harcourt kept Lewis informed of sales, reviews, etc., in this period immediately following publication of Babbitt, *and there were brief letters in return from Lewis.*

[1] Arthur Bartlett Maurice, literary editor of the *New York Herald*.

Hartford, Sept. 26

Dear Alf:

Herewith important tidings. I enclose authorization for you to close *Babbitt* movie deal at $50,000. If it prove, later, that we can't get this, I'll make out new authorization at a lower sum.

I enclose a letter from Clifford Smyth. I wonder if you couldn't quote this; I think he might consent. And, most important, copy of a letter from H. G. Wells. Do you want to cable asking him to reply collect whether he'd be willing to let us quote it? He might not be—but, à la Galsworthy with *Main Street*, he might be willing to give us a few words to quote. Use your judgment about this, only don't quote without getting permission. I fancy Wells is (very properly) touchy.

I'm very grateful to you for your work on movie rights. Oh. Better send a copy of Wells's letter to Cape. And have you sent him the May Sinclair review from the Times?

I'll be in NY some time about October 8, on my way West to lecture. I don't believe it's really necessary for me to be there to wind up negotiations with Warner Bros., but if you should need me of course I'll come on the jump.

Ever,
SL

Hartford, Sept. 27

Dear Alf:

Here's a chance for a couple of big books. Mrs. W. S. Cowles, of Farmington, Conn., wife of retired Admiral Cowles, and sister of Theodore Roosevelt, has what is probably the most complete collection of Roosevelt letters extant. She seems to have been his favorite sister. The letters extend from before he went to college till within a week of his death. They give a complete view of the man and his times. She is thinking of having them edited (to leave out certain purely personal paragraphs) and published. I'm sure we could get them. She knows and is very fond of Hal Smith—whose uncle, Winchell, lives in Farmington. If you're interested, you'd better send Hal up to see her and make arrangements. She'd probably have unpublished Roosevelt pictures also.

Also, by coincidence she has something else equally interesting—the diary of a little Cowles girl kept from 1797 to 1802, still in her handwriting. It gives a marvelous view of the customs of the day—it's unusually frank. She wrote it in the same house in which the Cowleses now live, a fine old house with lovely rooms, and the book would be illustrated with views of the house and other houses, hills about, etc. as mentioned

[1922]

in the diary. Hal could take care of this also. Talk it over with him. I think it's a double chance.

Ever—
SL

September 27

Dear Red:

Wallace Munro has had me on the phone on and off for the last forty-eight hours on the dramatic rights of *Babbitt*. I have heard of him as the producer of *Faust* and such, and he refers to Winchell Smith. Hal Smith says you can get W. Smith on the telephone at his home in Farmington, or drive out and see him and find out about this man. What shall we do about this sort of thing? You see you have written a great book, and these marginal rights are going to be sought after by folks who recognize what is in the book. The sale of the book is going to head it all up rapidly. It may all get settled before you go off on your lecture. But if it should not, I think it is important that someone easily accessible should be able to do the business.

I am getting a clear notion that there is a chance for *Babbitt* to be an extraordinary success in England. The reports of you have made your name familiar all over the place, and you can be sure the book that has the backing of such people as Wells and May Sinclair—and Cape according to contract with money to spend on it—is apt to get away to whatever market there is for such a book in England. It may be rather large, especially at a time when they realize it is important for them to understand what sort of folks Americans are.

I have not been unmindful of your suggestion that we drive up for a weekend at Hartford. It would be great fun. I have been hoping we could do it, but Ellen Eayrs is on a three-weeks' business trip out West, and we are unbelievably busy. So I can't make promises to get away early on Saturdays. Also I am afraid the trip would be more than Sue is up to just yet, although she is improving. I am not working so killingly hard as a year ago, but while there are so many irons in the fire in so many directions, I find questions every few minutes that only I can answer.

Babbitt re-orders are beginning to come in. We can't tell for sure whether it is a forced sale from the reviews and advertising, and your reputation, etc., or whether there is a spontaneous comeback from people who have read the book and told other folks about it.

Yours,
Alf

Hartford, Thursday Sept 28
Dear Alf:
My feeling is that it's folly to have *Babbitt* dramatized at all, because then the manager, the dramatists, and everybody else who isn't busy robbing someone else dips into the movie rights, and in the long run, as happened with *Main Street*, I actually lose by having the thing dramatized instead of just selling movies from the book. If Munro or anybody else wants to buy drama AND movie rights together for, say, $60,000, cash money, due January 2, 1923, on note signed by financially responsible persons, they can have em. Ask Munro why he doesn't combine with some movie company in making such a gamble. And actually I'd take $50,000 for drama and movie rights combined, and then not have to do any more fussing and rowing about it.

I'm quite willing to stand behind you if you make any reasonable bargain on my behalf—only remember that if the book is to be sold as a play, I will not give up one cent of movie money to the manager or anybody else. About that I'm going to be hoggish. If it's worth anything to them as a play, then there's no reason why they SHOULD have anything on the movies. If it's not worth anything as a play, why should they want it?

I think I'll come down to New York next Monday and stay overnight, and then we can take up together whatever has come up.

I have a note from Hugh Walpole, who is staying at the Waldorf. I'm sure you could get a nice blurb about *Babbitt* from him. In his note, he says merely that he likes it better than *Main Street*. A word from him would be of value now, when he is starting off lecturing. He leaves Saturday, *so nail him quick.*

Luck!
sl

If *Bab* has a chance for English success, Cape ought to buy *M. St. now.* Suggest it.

September 29
Dear Red:
Through some unaccountable quirk of reticence, I don't like just to blow in or write Hugh Walpole for something we can quote about *Babbitt*. He is apt to do so incidentally in an interview or article soon, and then we can quote him that way.

I agree completely that you should keep the dramatic and the movie rights of *Babbitt* separate. I wish you had done it with *Main Street*.

Yours,
Alf

Lewis went to New York on October 2nd, stayed overnight, and returned to Hartford. He left Hartford again in time to keep his first lecture date, which was in Detroit on October 12th. There was no correspondence while he was lecturing, and Lewis's next letter to his publishers was dated November 6th.

Hartford, Nov 6

Dear Alf:

Note Canby's letter enclosed. If you'd like, he'd probably let you quote it—or, better, he'd probably write something more quotable to the same effect—about *Bab* sticking to his ribs some time after reading it.

Walpole writes me that St. John Ervine writes him from London that it looks as though his *Cathedral* and my *Babbitt* would be THE two books of the season in London. As I recall, it's one hell of a time since any American book has been a "the" book in England.

Ever,
SL

Hartford, Nov. 9

Dear Alf:

Gracie has been reading *The Job* & is strongly opposed to our republishing it. First (says she) it is in so many places amateurish that rewriting wouldn't save it, and more important, everything in *The Job* has been said again, & better, in *M. St.* & *Babbitt*—everything except Mother-and-daughter. What you think? I'd hate to have us damned by a fluke here.

SL

Hartford, November 10

Dear Don:

J. Henry! This man Feipel[1] is a wonder—to catch all these after rather unusually careful proofreading not only by myself and my wife but also by two or three professionals at Quinn's! You ought to hire him to go over page proofs. But NOT to make all the corrections he wants to, because he too falls down. It gives me a devilish pleasure, after he has so adequately got the goods on me, to get 'em on him. E.G.—Bertrand Shaw is, of course, an intentional error; and I see no reason why rathskeller should be capitalized, even though it would be, as a noun, in German. (Gawd, Feipel has me nervous about hyphens!)

[1] Louis N. Feipel, of Brooklyn, New York, who made a hobby of proofreading already-published books.

Yes, "areoplane" is facetious and "lisped in blueprints" is all right, though when it gets queried it doesn't sound so DAMN humorous.

There's another correction—the one pointed out in Keith Preston's [1] column—page 121 "I tip my benny to him" is wrong—benny means overcoat. But whatnell is *hat?* Is it kelly? Or kelley? I wish you'd call up F.P.A. about this, and change in accordance with his decision—he's very accurate about slang.

Oh Gawd.

>Yours for light beers and wines,
>Or would Feipel make it yours for beers and light wines, or beer and light wines, or light wines and beer, or light wines and beers, or light wine and beer, or light wine and beers or
>Gawd!
>SL

Hartford, Nov 13

Dear Alf:

I think that, if you wished, Zona Gale would let you quote from her letter, or write you something else to quote.

I wish you'd have Hal Smith take you out with Charlotte Dean to lunch, and see what job you think she'd be qualified for, if she hasn't yet got one since leaving Harper's. She has a corking mind and personality; she ought to be of value; and she knows how to write publicity.

>Ever,
>SL

November 14

Dear Red:

By now you have two sets of our edition of the earlier novels. They look pretty good to me, and when I saw them in a row, I had the clear hunch that the thing to do was to sell what we could of them as is to such as want them. This jibes with Grace's notion that it would be unwise to revamp *The Job*. The crudities in it will not work against your reputation if it is let out onto the market as an earlier book—while your rep will get full credit for the mother and daughter portion and the many other

---

[1] Columnist and critic on the *Chicago Daily News*.

honest pieces in it. Revamping it would mean rewriting it quite seriously, and you could do a new novel with pretty nearly the same amount of effort. The thing for you to do about all these questions is what you are ripe to do and what you want to do. If you want really to rewrite this book, we ought not to let it out any farther than we have to in its present form; if you don't want to, we might as well have what money there is in these earlier books as earlier books. I shouldn't be surprised if we should sell twenty or thirty thousand as they are.

I didn't know that Charlotte Dean was out of Harper's. There isn't a ghost of a chance for her here. We have a big and rather expensive staff now; thank heaven, it deserves to be expensive. It handled $118,000 business last month without a crack which is at the rate of a million and a quarter a year. That means we have too much of a crowd for the inevitable $50,000 months, and we must not expand until we are permanently on something more than a million dollar basis. Also we haven't room for any decent or indecent person to sit in these quarters and we won't have new quarters until next summer.

Yours,
Alf

Hartford, Nov. 15

Dear Alf:

The two sets of your edition of the earlier books have come. They look corking—much better than in original format. Yes, I think I'd better not rewrite any of them; do what you can with them as earlier books. Next spring we might advertise them—just a *little*. Eh?

Ever—
SL

November 17

Dear Red:

Warner, the President of Warner Brothers, is going to Chicago this afternoon, but he has paid $2500 to bind the bargain, and his lawyer and Melville are going ahead to clean up the contract (for *Babbitt*).

So the sale is made. Warner raised the question of dramatic rights yesterday, saying that he might want to buy them also because he was thinking of beginning to produce plays, because he thought there was a good play in this, and because he did not want his large investment in rights and the picture jeopardized by what someone else might do with the play. I told him I thought if he offered a satisfactory contract with some moderate sum down that you would be inclined to play along with him on the understanding that if the play was not produced within two or three years, the rights would revert to you and you would keep the advance.

Yours,
Alf

Hartford, Nov. 22

Dear Alf:

Gracie and I will come down to NY about December 7 and spend a week or ten days in town on a bat, especially theaters and trying to keep HB&Co from getting any work done.

Yuh, I AM thinking about the next novel—a lot—it's ripening slowly but I hope it'll be the real big thing when it belooms.

Ever—
SL

What do you think of a de luxe *M. St.* & *Babbitt* @ $5 for Xmas 1923?

November 23

Dear Red:

Miss Cuff from Don's office has just brought the Harper contracts to me for *Our Mr. Wrenn*, *The Trail of the Hawk*, and *The Job*, asking if the provisions in those contracts are to apply to our editions. It seems to me simpler to propose one new contract for these three books on our form. I would suggest 10% to 10,000 and then 15%. The reason for the 10% is that we are beginning to plan a considerable advertising campaign on the old books in connection with *Babbitt* the first of the year, and this will give us a contribution of a thousand or two thousand dollars toward that expenditure. One thing I think we should certainly want to do would be to reprint about 50,000 of the Sherman pamphlet, of course in somewhat cheaper form, and distribute it widely. There ought to be a good deal of trade and considerable newspaper publicity. I had a talk yesterday with the Ladies Home Journal people about their use of *Babbitt* and *Main Street* as premiums next spring. This should do a good deal toward spreading interest in the old books. Will you let me know what you think of all this?

Yours,
Alf

[1922]

Hartford, Nov. 23 (obviously misdated)
Dear Alf:
Yes, I think it would be well to prepare new contracts for *Job—Wrenn—Hawk*. I should think the proper royalty would be 10% to 25,000 or 35,000, starting at par—that is, as though no copies at all had been sold by Harper's; with movie, dramat & serial rights as in *Babbitt* contract (& maybe radio!! rights on somewhat same basis!). I think 10% only to 10,000 as you suggest wouldn't allow you enough for advertising.

At the proper time, show *Our Mr. Wrenn* to Warner for movie. It has a chance. The "proper time" may not be till next year.

Ever—
SL

In the next month the correspondence between Lewis and the office had to do mainly with closing the Babbitt *motion picture deal with Warner and with the idea that Lewis might write a biographical sketch of himself for publicity purposes. Lewis and his wife came to New York on December 5th and stayed at the Chatham for about a week. Harcourt left before Christmas for a Florida vacation.*

Hartford, December 22
Dear Don:
Alf wanted me to write a sketch of the life of that interesting young writer S. Lewis, to be sent out in answer to requests for material for women's club papers, etc. Here it is.

Alf thought that four printed pages, about 1200 words, would be long enough. In my version it comes out 2600, which is cut from an original 3200 or so. It seems to me that all of it has some interest and that perhaps you'd better use the whole thing. What do you think? You might send it down to Alf. As it will probably be quoted a good deal, Alf and you and Hal Smith ought all to look it over, that nothing *too* indiscreet may get by us in it. If you send it to Alf, explain that it came out this way and I believe it'd better all go. 1200 words is too short to give anything but a few statistics regarding a life of unusual nobility, courage, beauty, tenderness, wit, scholarship, and bunk.

Merry Christmas!

Ever,
SL

I'll hit NY either Jan. 2 or very early on the 3'd—I sail the afternoon of the 4th.

ARROWSMITH

FIVE

The Scientist as a Hero

In December 1922, through a casual meeting in New York with Paul de Kruif, a young man of science, Lewis's old idea, a novel founded on the familiar practitioner of his youth, suddenly grew into a vastly more significant theme. Within twenty-four hours after he had met De Kruif, Lewis had sketched out roughly the outline of his novel. One part was to deal with the conquest of the plague on a tropical island. A trip to the West Indies would furnish a good means of beginning his researches, and Lewis thought that Paul de Kruif, who had recently left the Rockefeller Institute, was the one man to help him. In January 1923, Lewis and De Kruif started for Barbados.

[1923]
S. S. Guiana
Wednesday, Jan. 10

Dear Don:

The hills of St. Thomas (Virgin Islands) are ahead—we'll be in there this noon and I'll mail this letter. We've had perfect weather; not one bad day. Rather dull bunch of passengers, but we haven't minded, for Paul and I have been working like the devil and, I think, with success. *The Barbarian* looks bigger and bigger, better and better (every day nevery way), and Paul and I find we can work together perfectly. Each day I have greater respect for his totally unusual and fine though fiery brain. . . . Btheway, you might add on our contract "novel provisionally called *The Doctor or The Barbarian*." We have worked like the devil every day since we've sailed, and the plan is becoming complete.

I wish Alf and Hal and Gus and you were along—we're sailing through seas of the most tropic blue you can imagine. I doubt if I shall be able to get any mail till we reach England—probably about March first to fifteenth.

God bless you all! You might send this down to Alf, with my love to him and Sue as it goes to you and all the office.

Ever,
SL

Marine Hotel
Barbados, B.W.I.
(*undated*)

Dear Alf and Don:

I leave here today on the *Crynssen* of the Royal Netherlands West India Mail line for a round of the Spanish Main, touching back here on February 21—and I hope to find a lot of mail from you, sent in care of the Marine Hotel—and then on to England, arriving there March 6.

The trip has been perfect; we've seen a lot of lovely islands, met a bunch of interesting people, and the work is going superbly. The novel expands and takes on new life each moment. I am quite sure that it will be much better than either *Main St* or *Babbitt;* the characters have more life to me, more *stir*. De Kruif and I have proved to be able to work together perfectly—he is not only a damn clever man but the Rock of Ages.

I'll send you a few cards along the way. Love and kisses.

Ever,
SL

Hartford, January 16th

Dear Don Brace:

Just received a cable from Hal in The Barbados. It reads thus: "Going around Caribbean. Return Barbados February 21st on way to England. Marine Hotel will hold mail."

This is not entirely unexpected, tho I did not think he would go to England so soon. However Hal wrote *Babbitt* very contentedly in London, and there is no earthly reason why he should not write the new novel there. I have had two other radios from Hal, but no letter since reaching the islands. There should be one any day.

Sincerely,
Grace Lewis

January 19

Dear Grace Lewis:

Don has shown me your letter quoting Hal's last cable. I am not really surprised that he feels they will have exhausted the West Indies before very long, and it probably means that the book is taking more and more definite shape in his mind and that he wants to get at the actual writing of it.

I did have a good time in Florida and a complete let-down. I grew so languid that three meals a day, ten hours' sleep, one rubber of bridge, and a half-mile walk made a full twenty-four hours. But after I had been home a day or two New York air was like a cocktail, and I'm going along again. I do hope you are having a good time and a nice winter.

Sincerely yours,
Alfred Harcourt

January 24

Dear Sinclair:

I have your letter mailed from St. Thomas, and this morning a letter from Grace says that she has received a fat letter from you. From all this, I get a clear impression that you are immensely excited about *The Barbarian* and that it is going splendidly. I am not surprised, but just the same it is fine to know that you and De Kruif are so enthusiastic and busy over it. Your wish that we were all sailing the tropic seas with you comes at just the right time, for as I look out of the window, it is snowing hard and it is chilly and wet and generally unpleasant. Alf came back from Florida last week and is feeling fine although I think he is a bit put out at the idea of having to work so hard after a month in a warm climate. He left Sue in Florida, but she came back a few days later. She says she felt so good that she wanted to come home and show off. She really seems made over.

Yesterday we had a reorder from McClurg for 1000 *Babbitt*. All the signs indicate that it is holding over beautifully. The total of sales up to December 31st is 140,997.

You'll be glad to know that our problem of new quarters is solved. I almost bought those two houses on East 49th Street, but the prospect of building this year looked worse the more I looked into it, and Monday we signed a lease for 20 years on a floor in a new building on Madison Avenue at 47th Street. We have the whole fifth floor, and we plan to sublet two or three pieces of it for briefer periods which will provide for growth. We will probably be moving about the first of July.

The next time I see you will probably be in England, for I fully expect to go over in the spring. We all send our love and good wishes. Give De Kruif my warm regards.

Yours,
Don

February 1

Dear Red:

If I don't get a letter to you off now, you may not hear from me before you get to England. I have been back a fortnight after a good holiday. The spring business in general opens up well and *Babbitt* had a good sale in January.

I think it is a good thing that you are going to London after the circuit of the West Indies. I take it that means the book is getting itself ready to write rather rapidly, and that after you have filled up on material you are going off to London to start writing it. You have all the time in the world to do that with and all the loving care you want. I think we will keep legs enough under *Babbitt* and get legs enough under the earlier books so that it probably would not be wise to publish the new book this year, even if you did get it ready in time to do so, though I don't think there is much chance of that.

I think, too, that this job will give you a satisfaction of another and better sort than the earlier books. I think you said once that your distinguishing personal characteristic is a hatred of bunk. I think that is true, though at the same time you understand it and don't hate the persons but only their bunk performances. The hero of this new book is perhaps the only hero you picked so far that feels as you do, and that ought to warm up the book a good deal.

I hope you are well and happy, are you?

Ever yours,
Alf

At Sea, between Puerto Colombia
and the island of Curaçao.
Tuesday, Feb. 13

Dear Alf, Don, Hal, Ellen, Gus, JES, and the rest:

Between going ashore at assorted places and working reasonably hard on *The Barbarian* (that, or just *Barbarian*, without the article, seems to stick by me as the title) and trying to write adequate letters to Gracie and my father and meeting all sorts of variegated people on the ship and ashore, I've been kept too busy to be much of a correspondent.

The whole trip has gone splendidly. First as to the book: I'm fairly sure that it will be the best I have done—more dramatic, bigger characters. And this is not merely desire and pipe-dream, for the book takes shape rapidly, despite all our sightseeing. There are hundreds of notes, schedules, maps; and the actual skeleton from which I write the book is well under way. It will take me till I reach England—about three weeks from now—to finish that skeleton; it may even take a couple of weeks longer; but then I can begin the actual writing of the ms. . . . This is well in time—I didn't start the actual writing of *Babbitt* till the middle of August, two years ago.

The trip has been jammed with sights and people amusing in themselves and as material useful for this or later books—officers on the two steamers, wandering Americans and English and Germans and Dutch and Spanish, all the curious races of the West Indies and Spanish America— English settled there for ten generations, Negroes with curious dialects, thousands of Hindus in Trinidad, Chinese there and in Panama, feeble little Colombians, sturdy Indians, all kinds. Our intimates have been curious contrasts—on the *Guiana*, a roughneck English engineer; in Barbados, a prosy but capable old English doctor; in Panama, Major General Sturgis and his wife; on the *Crynssen*, the cheerful first mate and a regular stage Englishman who regards drafts (window ones, not bank drafts!) with indignant astonishment. De Kruif and I today counted 155 separate persons whom we've met since January 4th and whom we seem to know intimately!

It gives me joy to inform you that De Kruif is perfection. He has not only an astonishing grasp of scientific detail; he has a philosophy behind it, and the imagination of the fiction writer. He sees, synthesizes, characters. You've sometimes said that my books are meaty; this will be much the meatiest of all—characters, places, contrasting purposes and views of life; and in all of this there's a question as to whether he won't have contributed more than I shall have. Yet he takes it for granted that he is not to sign the book with me. And he loves work—he's most exuberant when we're pounding on the book, and when we're not making plans, when I'm compiling notes into a coherent whole, De Kruif is preparing more data—clear, sound, and just the stuff for dramatic purposes.

On the boat from Curaçao I met a young American named Richard Whitcomb. He sells flour to merchants all thru this territory, but he's one of the numerous big, energetic young Americans who are not suited to this land of lazy men and low energy. He is more or less planning to return north and, sizing him up, I conceived the idea that he might be a good man for you—perhaps put him in your retail bookshop [1] for training, then send him out on the road. So I gave him a letter to you.

I hope you're advertising *Babbitt*. How is it going? I know nothing as to how it's gone since Christmas. Please try to have a letter waiting for me in England—or coming to me as soon as possible after March 6,

[1] The Harcourt, Brace Bookshop was to open in March at 4 West 43rd Street, New York.

when I arrive; and let me know how much *Babbitt* has sold, how it's going now, and all the personal news. Send me any especially interesting new press comments on it—tho I've seen, in Panama, the mention of it in the Mennen's Shaving Cream ad, and Hugh Walpole's summary of the novels of 1922—juh see that in the Digest for Jan 13 or so?

I hope Alf has had a splendid trip to Florida, and that Sue is entirely well again, and that you-all are succeeding in finding the building you want. My most affectionate regards to all of you.

Ever,
SL

Lots of luck! Look for a good time with B A R B A R I A N. Send a copy of the new biography of S.L. to me if it's done. . . . If any of you are going to be in England, make it after I get there—or cable um to wait there for me, if possible.

> On board the S.S. *Crynssen*
> Just passed the Azores—March 1st—
> five days from Plymouth—fine weather except last night and today and these only moderately rough.

Dear Alf and Don:

I was delighted to get letters from both of you when we stopped in at Barbados. Glad to hear that you have been able to decide about the new quarters, that *Babbitt* goes on selling; grateful that you have helped Grace make investments for us; and most particularly and extremely glad that Sue is well again and that there is a chance Don will be in England this spring. He'll find me there, very much on the job, and I'll tell him all about *Barbarian* plans. All I'll say now, in addition to previous remarks, is that it continues unfalteringly to go on, that I like it ever better, and that from Barbados here, with no ports to stop at—and with the passengers agreeable and very English and totally uninteresting and bridge-playing, I've done a very devil of a lot of what seems like first-rate work. No, the book won't be done before some time next year—in time for publication in fall of 1924.

De Kruif will be with me in London—thank God! His gift of disappearing for the whole long day (even on this little ship) when I want to work alone, is as remarkable as his ability to be right here when I need him. In London he'll be working on articles, but right on tap when I need to confer with him about not merely scientific points but the whole texture of the book for, even where I and not he have created a character, his understanding is perfect and always inspiring. You watch (entirely aside from this book) that man. I have the same respect for him that I had for a couple of brats named Alf Harcourt and Don Brace, back in—Gawd, it makes me feel old!—1915 or so.

Write me with speed—expect to be at 10 Bury St., but shan't know till I land—and accept my liveliest greetings. Let me know when Don comes and whether he'd like me to get him hotel accommodations—if there happens to be room at 10 Bury, it'll beat the Cecil all hollow. I'll meet him and try in my gentle way to keep him from drinking licker.

Ever,
SL

March 9
Dear Red:

All this traveling and infrequent letters between us are quite in contrast with the cheek-by-jowl work we did last May. We have just had and passed around your good letter of February 13 written at sea. You can imagine how eagerly we have all read it and how glad we are that the trip, and the plan, and especially the De Kruif part of it are working out so well. Aside from what I know it means to you personally to have such companionship and collaboration, it means a great deal to the book and to your work on it.

By the time this reaches you, you will probably have seen Cape and know that the transfer of *Main Street* from Hodder-Williams to him is arranged and of his plans for publishing the old books in England. We have enjoyed Cape's visit here. He is a nice chap and gives that sense of real integrity which makes business so comfortable.

The bookstore is just opening. Of course it is a little place, really a shop. It may grow, but now there is not any room in it except for the two girls who run it, the books and, we hope, for customers.

Babbitt has sold about a thousand a week instead of the thousand or 1500 a day that *Main Street* had in its second season. We have spent since the first of January about $1500 in advertising, but the sales, as you see, are not at an extraordinary rate. Don't be discouraged by this. So far as I can see, it is the only big book of last fall, except Dorothy Canfield's *Rough-Hewn*,[1] that has held over at all. We have sent out only just recently, so as not to conflict with the early flood of this year's books, the three earlier novels together with the reprint of the Sherman article and the biography.

[1] HB&Co., October 1922.

Personally we are all in good trim. We plan to move in June to the new office building opposite the Ritz. It is as good a location as we could find; and we managed to get low rental and long term.

Don is rather aiming to get away to England just after the middle of April. Write as you have time. Of course we are eager for news of you.

Ever yours,
Alf

March 22

Dear Sinclair:

We were delighted to get your letter from on board the steamer. Now I think of you as happily located in London—at 10 Bury Street I hope—all settled down and at work. It's fine that *The Barbarian* goes so well. I feel that if you are satisfied with the way it's going it has passed its most exacting critic.

I cabled you Saturday, and Monday morning we deposited $14,000 to your account. Just after cabling you I went over to the Chatham, found Grace, had a delightful lunch with her at the Crillon, and put her safely on board the 2:20 for Hartford. Alf goes to Bermuda the day after tomorrow with his family to be gone eight days.

I wish I could tell you on what date I shall sail, but I don't know. I still expect to come this spring. Mr. and Mrs. M. F. Quinn[1] left here in February for the Mediterranean trip and their schedule brings them to London April 23rd to 27th. Their address is care of The American Express Company. If you feel inclined to look them up, I am sure they will be delighted, and it might be fun for you too.

Everything goes on in about the usual way with us. We have all been reading Edith Kelley's manuscript. In many respects it is a remarkably fine job with rather too perfect a representation of the life of her people to make it a novel. I suspect that we shall have to publish it, but I am not sure of our decision yet.

I shall certainly not go to the Cecil again. Alf recommends the Metropole. 10 Bury Street would be nice.

Affectionate good wishes to you and De Kruif,

Don

[1] Michael F. Quinn, founder of Quinn and Boden Company, printers for Harcourt, Brace.

[1923]

10 Bury St., St. James's,
London, March 24

Dear Alf:

Your letter of Feb 7 went to Barbados and following me here and your letter of March 9 have both arrived, and now I feel that our lines are straight again. I'm all settled and on the job; De Kruif's wife has arrived, and they've taken a little flat in Chelsea for six months, so that we can work together when necessary yet be altogether independent of each other in between. I've seen Cape and some of the changes he has made in *Mr. Wrenn*—they seem well-advised—few phrases here and there Anglicized.

I've seen, of course, a lot of people since I arrived, but the only new ones of importance have been Bertrand Russell—as charming as he is wise, Lloyd Osbourne, who seems to be a great *Babbitt* booster, Sir Philip Gibbs—another corker, and a bunch of physiologists and bacteriologists, met thru De Kruif. I'm in the old place on Bury Street, where Don might stay when he comes—if he'd like to, he ought to let me know date ahead, so I can engage a place. Sue will tell you how nice these little flats are. When Gracie comes over, we'll probably go to the country, after a bat in London. . . . I have a feeling we'll stay in Europe till, say, late fall of '24—at most, a year after that, then return to US, to Washington or N.Y.—NOT, b' God, to a Hartford!

All well.

Ever,
SL

April 4

Dear Red:

I am back from a week's trip to Bermuda coinciding with Hastings's Easter vacation. We had a good time. Now I am settling down to hold the fort as long as may be necessary, which probably is at least through Don's trip to England which is getting pushed off toward late May and through our moving and getting settled in the new quarters in the summer.

It is good to find your note of March 14 with the Bury Street address. You have been happy and comfortable in that house and have done much good work there. We have had to turn down Claude Washburn's new novel. Hal and Don and I each read it and none of us could see it. It was all too mild and, despite a few interesting characters, it was just too much tea on the terrace and also luncheons, dinners, and breakfasts and the talk at them in and around Florence. We must not clutter ourselves up with books that seem to us second-rate.

Spingarn is just back from the South looking better than I have seen him in a long time and seeming to feel better.

Ever yours,
Alf

London, April 10

Dear Alf and Don:

All goes well, mit book and feelings. I've seen a fair number of people—tho not too many. Weekend this past w.e. at H. G. Wells's—met the Countess of Warwick, and Ramsay Macdonald. The weekend before—Easter—motored with Frazier Hunt, an American representing the Hearst magazines here, and Boardman Robinson (now living here) and his wife to Devon, stopping at Bath and Wells. Norman Hapgood [1] has been here—he did not speak of serializing *Barbarian;* I guess that he and Ray Long now realize that with the price I would want and the non-breaking-for-serial type of books I write, they're lucky not to get it, and if that is so it will save future fussing.

By the way: about the title. Is just *Barbarian*, sans article, too much like *Babbitt?* I don't think so. And there has, dammit, been a book called *The Barb* published recently, which might interfere with using *The Barbarian*. One or the other seems to me we'd better use—they fit the book. Which do you prefer?

I still think Don would like it here at 10 Bury St very much. Staying here just now is George Kaufman of Kaufman and Connelly, authors of *Dulcy*, the dramatization of *Merton of the Movies*, etc. Lunch this noon with Ferris Greenslet [2] and John Buchan. They seem to be ardent admirers of *Babbitt*. Dinner with Cape this evening.

I hope your moving will go well—I hope you've taken Edith Kelley's novel—I hope you are keeping sober.

Ever,
SL

April 23

Dear Red:

At last we are getting a little action on the earlier novels. I enclose the pieces from yesterday's Times and Saturday's Post.

[1] Norman Hapgood at this time was with *Hearst's International Magazine.*
[2] A director of Houghton Mifflin Company.

Had luncheon with Grace Friday. I'd say she is five years younger than last May and quite apt to run away with you when she gets to England.

About the title, it is tangled. *Barbarian* has an adjectival sense that *Babbitt* hasn't. I suppose the American high schools have made phrases like "barbarian invasion" jump into mind at the use of the word. It raises the question, "Barbarian what?" *The Barbarian* is rather too much like *The Virginian*. Can't you rather hear Ward Macauley [1] ask, "Is Lewis trying a Tarzan novel?" Aren't both satirical titles? Is not that aspect of your work apt to be over-emphasized by critics anyway? Better let the title simmer a while longer, though I know it does mean a lot to you to write to a title. I don't say at all that I don't like either of them. But let's cogitate about this carefully.

Thank you for your cable suggesting that you do the cutting on the Edith Kelley novel.[2] We had just sent the manuscript back with our suggestions of cuts. Hal Smith did a careful and excellent job on it. We sent her a few hundred dollars to give her leisure to pull it together. There's great stuff in it. I think it will come out as a good book. If it doesn't, it will be a long time before we fuss with another job of editing, if the editing looks like a serious undertaking.

Ever yours,
Alf

London, April 25
Dear Alf and Don:

There really isn't a devil of a lot of news except that *Barbarian* marches on, I'm well, I've seen a lot of people, and I'm awaiting Gracie's coming—she sails in ten days now.

The new people—Lord Beaverbrook, weekend at Lady Astor's (incidentally she is an extremely interesting person, and Lord Astor is really a charming fellow, somewhat overclouded by her fame) where I met Philip Kerr who was L George's secretary during the war—he's just been in America. Met a number of scientists and been in several laboratories watching actual work, which will make much more real the stuff in *Barbarian*. Lunch with Sir Walter Fletcher, head of the Medical Research Fund of the Brit govt. A day with Philip Gibbs in the country. AND so on. I've seen Cape several times, and like him better and better. By the way, he's interested in the new book on sea-power and blockade of my friend Prof. Maurice Parmelee, of whom I've written you now

[1] Prominent Detroit bookseller.
[2] *Weeds*, HB&Co., 1923.

and then; if it comes to you, sent by Curtis Brown's [1] man, give it unusual attention—might be one of the books which, sole authorities, go on selling for twenty years.

I cabled you, after receiving a letter from Edith Kelley, that if you liked I'd be glad to look over her book in *re* cuts. I do hope this pans out well. I judge she has a real future—and present! Don't plan to cut *too* much—remember that well-known vollum *Main Street* which, from certain points of view, might have stood a hell of a lot more cutting, yet which did go, as I remember the figures, extremely well for the work of a young author.

Quinn is here, and Cape and Howard [2] and I have given him a lunch and shown him a printing establishment & I'll see them again.

Will you, on receipt of this, please deposit another thousand dollars to my credit? I might be able to get thru till Gracie arrived mit money, but better not take a chance on running short. . . .

My very best, and looking forward eagerly to Don's coming. Only I wish the whole damn firm were coming!

Ever,
SL

London, May 3

Dear Alf:

Gracie will arrive here the 14th, and from about the 17th to, say, the 25th we'll probably be down in the country, so if by any chance it happened that Don arrived here at that time I wouldn't be here to greet him. But from about the 25th to mid-June or July 1st we'll be right here at Georgian House and the whole family can have some good times together.

The plan all finished, with magnificent scientific stuff from De Kruif as background—not necessarily all to be used but as reference when needed—the book itself is booming ahead and seems to go very well indeed. . . . I *think* BARBARIAN, sans the article, is the title, but as you say, we must mull over it—we have almost a year before the title must be finally fixed, so that you can announce it. Here's the list of other titles that seem possible: BARBARIAN—COURAGE—HORIZON—WHITE TILE—CIVILIZED—THE MERRY DEATH—THE SAVAGE—MARTIN ARROWSMITH—TEST TUBE.

Love and kisses,
SL

Any real sale on *Wrenn—Hawk—Job?*

[1] London literary agent.
[2] G. Wren Howard, associate of Jonathan Cape.

[1923]

May 7th
Dear Lewis:
I had a little visit with Grace over the telephone Saturday morning just before she went to the steamer. She was delighted to be sailing. Later in the morning your letter came.

It was nice of you to make something of the Quinns while they were in London. He's a fine old boy and on several occasions has stood his plant on its head for our mutual benefit.

Another occasion of the same sort may present itself to you within the next month or so. Miss Grace Thompson of L. S. Ayers, Book Department, Indianapolis, is on your side of the water and will be in London about the end of May. I gave her a card to you and if it comes handy she is worth some attention. She's an awfully nice girl of the Marcella Burns [1] type but younger, and is doing the same sort of thing for Indianapolis and thereabouts as Marcella has done for Chicago. This is her first trip abroad. She used to be salesgirl under Melcher when he was in Indianapolis and for the last three or four years has been building a first-rate department in the town's best store. She has used a good many more than her quota of your books and is a warm friend of ours.

Things are going well with us. Papini's *Life of Christ* [2] is the best-selling non-fiction book in the country; in fact, Baker & Taylor say it sold more last month than all but one novel.

Sincerely,
Alf

May 11
Dear Sinclair:
As you will have suspected, I am having a lot of difficulty in getting away to London. Now the date has been postponed until about the first of June. I am inclined to think I will come then unless I decide in the next few days that it is too indecent to be away during moving and in the midst of getting the fall list ready. That is as definite as I can be about it this morning. I suppose when I do get to London you will be in the country or somewhere, but if you are not farther away than Egypt I will see you anyhow. This will find you a reunited family; I hope Grace has had a good voyage and that she finds herself even happier than she expected to be on reaching London.

Ever yours,
Don

[1] Marcella Burns Hahner, head of the book department of Marshall Field and Company, Chicago.
[2] *Life of Christ* by Giovanni Papini, HB&Co., March 1923.

London, May 26
Dear Alf and Don:
Is there any more sale on *Babbitt?* and are *Wrenn* etc. starting to sell? Cape is making a fine splurge here with *Wrenn,* with subway posters and plenty of ads in the papers.

Don's last notification is that he may be sailing by June 1st. I think we shall be right here at 10 Bury St. till July 1st, then somewhere in the country in England, and we shall be awfully eager to see him. I wish you were both coming. . . . I shall watch for Louis Untermeyer and Grace Thompson.

Gracie seems to like the plot of *Barbarian* enormously, and the beginning of the actual ms so far as she has read it. She thinks it will have a chance to be much the biggest book I have ever done. . . . Alf's last letter suggests that *Martin Arrowsmith* seems to him just now the best title. Well, it's certainly a possible one. You might add this to the list I gave: STRANGE ISLANDS. BUT no doubt it sounds too much like a South Sea island romance. It's probably a choice between *Martin Arrowsmith* and *Barbarian*—without the article.

Gracie and I have just come back from a bully week's walking tour in lovely Devon, and are off today for a weekend at H. G. Wells's, and next Monday I shall get back on the job, to some extent—tho probably I shan't be completely back on it till we get off to the country. But I'm well ahead of my time-table if *Babbitt* may be taken as a standard.

All goes well. Wells Lewis is sent off to a jolly boys' school till we get off to the country; Gracie is enjoying London; and me I feel wigorous.

Ever,
sl

June 5
Dear Red:
Don will have given you what news there is. Carl Sandburg came in yesterday afternoon and said that he'd seen the picture of *Main Street* in Chicago.[1] I'm happy to report that he liked it. He said a curious thing seemed to have happened—that while the scenario did violence to the story and to the ideas you wanted to put over in it, the actors had taken the thing back into their own hands, so that the spirit after all was near enough that of the book. The only thing he really objected to was their making a caricature of Miles Bjornstam and a comic out of the maid Bea. He thinks it may go big.

Yours,
Alf

[1] Carl Sandburg was writing motion picture reviews for the *Chicago Daily News.*

[1923]

Le Val-Changis,
Avon, Seine-et-Marne, France
July 7

Dear Alf:

I've scarcely even sent you a note, the past six weeks, both because I've been with Don, and I knew he would give you the news, and because Grace and I have been busy, first making up by a lot of London parties for her dull winter in Hartford and second house-hunting in France. By the same token I haven't done a lick of work. But now here we are most agreeably settled in a charming house with a shady garden on the edge of Fontainebleau; I'm settled down again for from three to five months, and damn glad to be. We got in day before yesterday and already I'm started at work.

It was pleasant to play about London—all sorts of people from Lord Beaverbrook to Stacy Aumonier, H. G. Wells to Donald Ogden Stewart, but that sort of thing entails staying up too late, rushing too much, and too many cocktails, and much tho I like all those decorations, I've been overjoyed here, with a simple supper, cooked as only a French cook can do it, on the terrace, looking down the lawn to thick woods, then getting to bed early.

Don will probably reach NY before this letter. Tell him I was awfully sorry not to see him again—his note came this morning. I hope the rest of you will agree with Don that Paul de K's story of microbes [1] will make a good book. Personally I'm enthusiastic, and if you'd like I'll back the financial obligation of the advance.

Let me know how *Babbitt* and *Wrenn-Hawk-Job* are going. What's being done about serial on *Babbitt?* What's the office news? Meantime you may picture me here, in a quiet room off a garden, working like hell on *Martin A.*

Our best,
SL

July 19th

Dear Red:

It's good to have your letter of July 7th. There has been no particular reason why we should correspond as regularly this year as we have in past years, and I have pumped Don for all the news of you folks and the book which he could give. Nevertheless it is good to have a direct letter.

Don had a good time in London; really, I think one of the best

[1] *Microbe Hunters*, published by Harcourt, Brace in 1926.

times he has ever had. Good for him and good for the business, too. Spingarn is a good deal better and beginning to take hold again. Hal settled down to be a real comfort and shows signs of being a bit of a genius as an editor. The new quarters are fine—much better light and space and arrangements for everyone except, perhaps, me. I grew to be extremely fond of that front room at 1 W. 47th Street. Business is good —our sales for the first 6 months were $100,000 ahead of the same period last year, thanks considerably, though not entirely, to the success of Papini's *Life of Christ*. It looks as if that will hold over to a big autumn sale. I am sending you a fall list and you'll see that it is a nice lot of books.

The second serial rights of *Babbitt* are released the first of August through the International Feature Service.

I like the outline of De Kruif's *Story of Microbes* and I am glad to report that Don grew to like De Kruif very much personally after what he saw of him in London. I do not think that you should guarantee the advance to De Kruif on this book. It is generous for you to think of it.

Sales of *Babbitt* last spring were just under 10,000 copies. The earlier novels have not seemed to find any new life here. In fact, it would be my guess that we have spent at least a dollar in advertising for each copy we've sold. The Harper editions kicked around the bookstores just enough to foul the market and to make the trade unwilling to stock them.

Don liked what he saw of the new novel and he was also much impressed by the idea for one which grew out of the talk after Tinker[1] spent an evening with you.

Ever yours,
Alf

July 31

Dear Sinclair:

After you left I finished up my last week in London in a mad rush with hardly any sleep, but I had a fine voyage home, and I have now had a little over two weeks at the office interrupted only by a trip up to Vermont near the Canadian border to see the children. It took a good deal of adjusting to get used to the new quarters after having sailed away from 47th Street. There must have been a kind of youth and informality about the other place; here the concern looks as though it might have been going on forever. The offices are fine with plenty of light, air, and convenience, and everybody is happy and busy. Hartman[2] came down last

---

[1] Chauncey B. Tinker, professor of English literature at Yale.
[2] The artist C. Bertram Hartman whom Harcourt, Brace commissioned to do the batik mentioned.

week with a batik for the reception room which is both lovely and amusing. JES seems much improved in health, and more happy and vigorous than I have seen him in a long time. Hal is taking a vacation this week. Sue is again not at all well and Alf is feeling a good deal of anxiety. Except for that, everything is flourishing.

I had a splendid time in London; it gets better the more I think about it. The fact that you and Grace were there is largely responsible for it. I hope you like the house and that by this time you are comfortable, happy, and busy. I wish I could have come over to see you, but I have a queer kind of conscience which makes me suspect my reasons for wanting to do things when they are too attractive. The talks we had about the new novel were rather scrappy, but I am very keen about the whole thing. It seems to me that your characters and situations are going to bite a little deeper even than they did in *Babbitt*, and it is sure to be a great book. I'll bet you're enjoying getting at it again.

Much love to you both,

Don

Avon, France
July 31

Dear Alf:

It was good to have your long letter. Keep the news coming—I'm out of touch with everybody here. We've been here a month, lacking three days, and it's been superb—quiet, beautiful, working like hell all day and practically every day—going off on an exploration tour to the lil villages about, every eight or ten days—and the book has gone tremendously.

I have two or three more titles to consider besides MARTIN ARROWSMITH—which is certainly very possible, and has, so far as I can see, only one objection—its resemblance to *Martin Chuzzlewit* and *Martin Eden*. These new ones are: *The Stumbler—Martin Arrowsmith, M.D.—Dr. Arrowsmith—The Shadow of Max Gottlieb—The Destroyer*. I like the first of these quite a lot—it's short, I *think* unusual, and fits the idea of the book, as you will see when you read it.

One thing I wish you'd have done before I forget it. Have Hal or somebody look up in the American *Who's Who*, the English ditto, the American Medical Register or whatever they call it, & the British Medical Register & Amer. Blue Book, to see if there are any, or how many, people having the following names: Martin Arrowsmith, Max Gottlieb, Gustaf Sondelius, Leora Tozer, Terry Wickett, T.J.H.Silva, Bruno Zechlin, Angus Duer, Clifford Clawson, Almus Pickergill, Rippleton Holabird,

(Mrs.) Joyce Lanyon. They are the chief characters—among some millions of minor characters. We wouldn't *necessarily* change the names if there were identities with real people—want to know who those people were, first. It sounds like a hell of a job, particularly if whoever does it has to report on several identities, but I'm remembering the lot of trouble we might easily have had a year ago with Geo F Babbitt of Boston. Fortunately out of all of these, most of them are on the good side—more or less a compliment to resemble 'em—except for Duer, Pickergill, and Holabird, who are goats.

Thanks for the deposit of the three thousand. It's not too cheap to live here, food surprisingly high, but still it is cheaper than London by a good deal, especially as we rarely go to restaurants.

Let me know how the *Babbitt* serial rights go.

Besides the Tinker novel of which Don spoke, I have eleven others which I could write, so I probably shan't dry up for some time yet—a few days ago I listed 'em, just to see how many of them were keeping fresh in my mind. *Neighbor*[1] is still in the list, but rather far down in it.

Now on the job, then a little tennis, a little bicycling, a little more job, dinner outdoors with long French loaf and Camembert and bottle of excellent vin ordinaire at one franc 95—about twelve cents—a little reading, and to bed early!

Ever,
SL

What's become of the Bill Benet—Elinor Wylie romance?

The death of Mrs. Harcourt in August interrupted the correspondence for more than a month.

September 18

Dear Red:

There isn't much news, but I do want to tell you that Grosset and Dunlap have just printed another 50,000 *Main Street* which makes 135,000 in their edition this year.

Hastings and I are back at Mount Vernon, and I wish you'd come and live with us whenever you feel like it. Everybody's well here, and business is good. I think Ellen has sent you a copy of Edith Kelley's *Weeds*. It is a rather powerful and promising job.

Ever yours,
Alf

[1] Lewis was contemplating a book on the American labor movement for which he had invented the title *Neighbor*. It was to be founded on the life of Eugene Debs, Socialist and labor leader. Lewis struggled with this conception for a novel for many years, but was unable to bring it to fruition.

[1923]

Avon, France
September 21

Dear Alf:

I'm delighted that you're back at work and that you had the wise long tour with Hastings. We leave here two weeks from now for a month's rambling in Italy (a rest I can do with, after three months of the most complete concentrated kind of work), then up to London, probably, to be settled and much at work for all winter—with a house, but with me off out of sight in a little office somewhere all day. We plan to see Venice, Verona, Lake Como, a few other places, and to take it very easy. Wells will be left with people near either Paris or London.

AND before I leave here I hope to have the entire first draft of *Martin* done!—certainly practically done. It will be about the same length as the first draft of *Main Street* and, like it, will be considerably cut. Seems to me it's been getting better and better—last part much better than the part Don saw. Paul de Kruif comes over from London next week to spend a week here going over it minutely—then later we must also have him read the proofs.

I expect the rewriting—or rewritings—to take me about five months so, with a month off for Italy, it ought to be done and in your hands by the first of May of next year. I'll come over with it. AND it may be before May 1st. I returned with *Babbitt* (but with a week of work still to do on it) on May 20th, last year. I'm for publication NOT TOO EARLY in the fall—so many publishers, this year, seem to have hit on the same trick of getting out their fall leaders early, even in August, and I'll bet a Scott hat they'll do so even more next year.

Does *Martin Arrowsmith* still seem the title? What about THE STUMBLER—ARROWSMITH—DR. ARROWSMITH. A complete list of possible titles as I now have them: MARTIN ARROWSMITH—THE STUMBLER—THE BARBARIAN—BARBARIAN—ARROWSMITH—DR. ARROWSMITH—MARTIN—M.D. —CIVILIZED—TEST-TUBE—THE SAVAGE—THE SHADOW OF MAX GOTTLIEB. Go over it, with Gus, Hal, Don, Ellen.

Grace went to London to have her tonsils out. She's been back here a week now and feels fine—as we all do. I'm tired, but it's been so lovely and quiet in this secluded place that I'm not too tired, though I've been spending most all my time facing this damn lil Corona.

Let me hear.

Love,
Red

Has Spingarn looked into the matter of Marcel Proust? One or two volumes of him in translation have been published in England—have any in America? He seems to be all the rage here. Edith Wharton, whom I've seen several times, is extremely enthusiastic about him.

P.S. II-67-B: Gracie and Paul still seem to like just *Martin Arrowsmith* best among all the titles. . . . Does the resemblance to *Martin Chuzzlewit* and *Martin Eden* bother you? . . . I think I've asked you this sixteen or twenty times but if I have, then, drat your soul, you've never answered it.

Avon, France
September 28

Dear Alf:

A joy to have your letter of ten days ago. This will presumably be the last letter I'll write you from here—we're off for Italy in six days. I shall have the first draft of *Martin* done before I go—only about two more days' work. Paul has been down here and read all but that two days of it. He seems somewhat more than enthusiastic. He thinks, first, that the scientific stuff is absolutely accurate and absolutely dramatized—fictionized—and second that it is much the best book I've ever done. But of course with his nearness to the book he is the worst as well as the best possible critic. Certainly he seems to feel that I have carried out all the high things we dreamed while we were planning it (& damn high they was!).

I've read Edith Kelley's *Weeds*. It is big, powerful, real stuff, with a professional touch in the style, a calmness, a sureness, which I had not expected from a first novel. I *think* you have something big in her & in this book.

In writing to her I warned her of one danger: Because she has, in various apparently different but inherently alike phases, led much the same life as her own heroine Judy—finding whether as Upton Sinclair's secretary, as wife of Allan Updegraff and teacher in NY East Side High Schools, as keeper of a farm-highbrow-boarding house in New Jersey, as Kentucky farmer or California farmer in all of them the same mill of discouragement, the same one-damn-thing-after-another—therefore there might well be that greatest danger of the author with one promising first book—the danger of simply doing again the same book with only apparent changes, the change of futile Kentucky lanes to inherently identical futile Harlem streets.

I *think* we have something here, arriving just at the time when the US, weaned from pink romance, is ready for her. Don't let her fail for lack of encouragement—particularly in the hard dollars which will make it possible for her to work.

I know—I KNOW, damn you—I've also sent Claude Washburn, Bechhofer, the Nonpartisan League historian, and Allan Updegraff to you, and they've all been washouts. But still—have I ever more than *sent* them to you for *your* own final decision—have I ever done much whooping for them when they have sent in bad work? The two whom I trust after seeing not their probabilities but their actual accomplishments are Edith Summers Kelley and Paul de Kruif.

BY the way: Edith ought to sign herself just Edith Summers. It would be no rudeness to her husband—Gracie when she occasionally writes signs herself Grace Hegger.

And BY the way: I see that Houghton Mifflin have just published a book called *Civilization and the Microbe*, by one Kendall, prof of bacteriology in Northwestern University. This may or may not at all interfere with the plans of Paul. I've told him to get a copy of the book the moment he gets home (he sails for US on October 25) and make sure—possibly modify his own plans if necessary. But he has been getting so much fresh material, hitherto unpublished, about Pasteur, Leeuwenhoek, and other European romantic heroes of bacteriology, and his mind works so differently from anybody else's that I don't believe they will be much alike, and it's good that his book will come a year and a half after this other. But let's take precautions to keep the courses different, now while it's early; so talk over Kendall's book with Paul. . . . If you could have seen how he went at *Martin* here—working night and day yet reading with such minute precision! My admiration for him is greater now than ever.

So! That's all, I think, before I start. . . . Don't you want to come over to London some time this winter?

Ever,
Red

Avon, France
Sunday, September 30
Dear Alf:

I finished the first draft of *Martin* today. It comes out 748 pages plus a certain number of insert pages—about 245,000 words long. How much it will cut I don't know—there's so much more *story* to it than there was to *Main Street* with all the strung-together incidents in *M.St.* that it may not cut so much as that first draft did. . . . But cheer up. Remember that most of the books that keep going, like *Old Wives' Tale*, are indecently long.

Again, like Patti,[1] we bid farewell.

Ever,
Red

[1] Reference to the continued "farewell" appearances of Adelina Patti, famous soprano.

I have read the new novels by Edith Wharton and Charles Norris, and *Weeds* is so much better than either of 'em that there's no comparison. The same is probly true of Van Vechten's *Bow-Boy*, except that the two are so different that it's unfair to compare em. As for Bill Woodward's *Bunk*, it's no good whatever, and as they want me to write about it, I shall (confidentially) fail to receive either the book or Harper's letter.

October 1

Dear Red:

I am delighted to have yours of September 21st. I hope you and Grace have a wonderful month in Italy. You can imagine how much interest all the news has for us. As to time for publication of the new book, we want to have it ready early enough to be able to publish it either late or early according to the situation we find next summer. It's true that everybody has been early this year. They will probably be late next year. Then the thing to do is to outguess the crowd, or better, size up book trade conditions. It was wise to publish the bulk of our list early this year. Booksellers had a good spring and were in the buying mood during the summer, but the last month has been rather flat with them and they have shut up pretty tight on orders for late books.

There seems to be no hesitation around here that *Martin Arrowsmith* is the best title. I am having a little leaning toward *Dr. Arrowsmith*, though I doubt if that's better in the long run. For the short view, it saves saying a thousand or more times that the hero is a doctor. The world pretty much knows now that your father was a small-town doctor, and it would readily connote to a good many thousands of people a more than glowing story with a hero of whom you approve as one of the bases of civilization.

We've been over the Marcel Proust matter several times—too early, in fact, because when we first went after it, the Frenchman wanted a thoroughly impossible sum and we had to let go. Later, Chatto and Windus got out the translation in England and sold some sheets to Holt of one or two volumes, which rather spoils the market for us.

Business is good. It looks as though we should have the biggest year so far.

Ever yours,
Alf

[1923]

October 10
Dear Red:

Yesterday afternoon Sewell Haggard telephoned that the Butterick people were extremely anxious for a feature serial for the Designer in order to put that magazine on the map next year. He said that he heard your novel was approaching completion and he wanted it. I said, "Do you want $50,000 worth?" He gasped a little at that and said he'd call me back. He did call later and said we could consider that we had an offer from them of $50,000 for the first serial rights. I told him that the book would turn out to be as long as *Main Street* and he said, "Well, that would mean we would run big chunks of it in each issue and get it out of the way so that you could publish in the spring of 1925."

So this morning I cabled you. I do not feel that I ought to decide this matter without having your views. I will say that if I did decide it now, I would accept. Of course we made a lot of plans on having your new book next year and hired another salesman to start in the spring, but we can use him anyway and we have a strong list generally. I know you and Grace are on a holiday in Italy and there may be some delay in the cablegram reaching you. If I am forced to a decision before I can hear from you, I will accept this offer.

Ever yours,
Alf

October 27
Dear Red:

Two weeks have gone by without a reply to my cable in regard to the sale of the first serial rights of *Martin Arrowsmith*. I understand that this has been due to your holiday and that you have probably not received my cable. Meantime, the Designer people, primarily Sewell Haggard, are pressing me for a decision. I am having lunch with them Monday, and if dates, terms and everything are all favorable to you and the fortunes of the book as far as I can judge, I shall accept their offer. I hate to do this without having your views, but in the first place it seems to me the wise thing to do for your interest, and in the second place it may relieve you of some embarrassment with your other friends in the magazine world. To have had the matter taken out of your hands and settled without your knowledge enables you to make me the goat.

The effect on our business in not publishing *Martin Arrowsmith* next year will be significant but not serious. If we did publish it next year, we were all set to pass a million dollars' business, but without this $200,000 and more of sales, I still think that next year will show an increase over any previous year. It all comes down to the fact that I cannot see any compelling reason why you should not have this $50,000 from serialization in a magazine that will not get in the way of book sales in any significant fashion.

Ever yours,
Alf

October 30

Dear Red:

The Designer people would not wait beyond yesterday for a decision, and for all the reasons which will readily occur to you, I have accepted their proposal. I hope by all that's holy that you approve. Unless you're entirely satisfied to have me settle things like this for you, don't again go out of the reach of cablegrams for so long. At any rate, this is the highest bona fide price for magazine serialization that I've ever heard of.

Yours,
Alf

Hotel Curzon
London
November sixth

(Address 58 Elm Park Gardens, S.W.10)

Dear Alf:

I'm cabling you today "Deposit two thousand Guaranty." As I omitted the PLEASE in a frugal and mean way, I herewith add it, also thanks. . . .

The address above is a rather charming furnished house we've taken for the winter—just on the borders of Kensington and Chelsea—taken it till next June though probably I myself will be coming home considerably before that, leaving Gracie and the kid there while I thresh round with you and Paul, and run out to Minnesota and so on. I'll be back on the job in couple days now. . . . Most agreeable time Italy—Venice, Vicenza, Padova, Verona, Milan, Mennagio (on Lake Como), Siena, and Florence. Got a beautiful rest and feel like work.

Now about the serial. I hate serialization but it seems foolish to lose fifty thousand. I promised Ray Long of the Hearst organization also Karl Harriman of Red Book a chance to bid against any others, and would they hurt book sale any more than Designer with the huge circulation

[1923]

drive they will be making? Give Ray and Karl the chance to bid—if it is still possible. In London, Don and I assured Frazier Hunt, the foreign representative of the Hearst magazines, that we would absolutely not serialize, so gave him no chance to talk business and Frazier is an intimate friend of mine. It seems impossible to decide what IS best to do in a case like this—and I appreciate the worry you must have had.

I'm thoroughly grateful to you for your thought and work on this, and I understand how much against *your* interests, as publisher, it was. One thing I wish to emphasize. I suppose Haggard will have to cut, but I will not change the thing into a sunny sweet tale nor will I permit him to. DOES HE UNDERSTAND THAT? Please let me know, for otherwise he can't have it at any price. (Not that there's much really *offensive* in novel, anyway. He needn't worry.)

Isn't there some chance that you will come over here this winter? Your room will be ready for you at the house, and we could have some marvelous times together.

Ever,
SL

November 8

Dear Red:

I received your cablegram about the serialization. I have cleared the record for you with Ray Long and his crowd. I will write an explanation to Karl Harriman the first chance I get. It begins to look as if it were fortunate that this matter developed as it did. After I had named a price to Sewell Haggard and he had accepted, I could hardly have used that price to start an auction, and the way it all happened lets you out. At any rate, we have made a good sale at a high price in a place apt to affect book sales little, if any, and with the dates so arranged as to release book publication at a useful time.

One of the pleasant episodes of a crowded week has been a visit from Paul de Kruif. He came in Monday, was much interested in the serialization news and approved of it heartily so far as his interest was concerned. He and his nice little wife were out to Don's to dinner last night. They are having lunch with me tomorrow. I have enjoyed seeing them.

Yours,
Alf

58 Elm Park Gardens
Chelsea, London, S.W.10
November 12

Dear Alf:

I wonder if in my letter about the serial rights of *Martin Arrowsmith* (yes, I think that title is probably better than *Dr. Arrowsmith*) I expressed my really very great appreciation of your efforts for me and your possible sacrifice. I do feel it! Have you seen Paul de Kruif? What does he think of the matter of serialization? Does he understand that the book is not to be injured for serialization? As I asked before, does Haggard understand there will be no sunny conventionalities tucked in?

I met Frederick O'Brien (*White Shadows in South Seas*). Writing a novel. Awfully good fellow. Is sore at Century Company. He's just sailed for NY. Told him I'd write you.

Though we don't move into our house till day after tomorrow, I'm already settled and at work—I have a room for writing, of all delightful places, in the Temple! . . . Are you coming over this winter? Come on!

Ever,
SL

November 21

Dear Red:

Of course we've seen De Kruif. He is delighted with the serial sale. Twenty-five thousand words of the manuscript are to be delivered in February. I haven't done anything about Karl Harriman, and I'm a little embarrassed about doing so. I never have met him, he has never asked me about the serial rights, and it would be a little gratuitous, it seems to me, for me to explain to him that I've sold them. You better write him direct.

I will talk with Hal and Don about Frederick O'Brien. He's probably worth our getting after, but we have about all the fiction we need for next year unless it is something or somebody whom it would be absolutely foolish to ignore. We could take O'Brien for the fall, but I am more and more convinced that we are right in holding our list to about one hundred books a year and doing our darndest with those we do take. The way authors are flocking around us, it takes a lot of independence to stick to this. It also means that we'll make some mistakes, but we mustn't worry about those. We have already counted over twenty novels that we've turned down on other publishers' fall lists. None of the twenty have made fools of us yet, but every once in a while we'll turn down something that will make a big success. Hal Smith said the other day that it is getting harder for us to take a book of creative literature than for the camel to go through the eye of the needle. Well, that's true and I guess it's right. It is right if we are going to continue to give special attention to each book we take and not let them merely go through the mill.

It would be lovely to go over this winter. Hastings and I are happy and comfortable at home. We are having probably the last few years of a rich and satisfying personal association. He is getting along well in school and I doubt if I'll go away for long until next summer. Also we're busy here. I'm devoting a good deal of time to the textbook department.

Yours,
Alf

London, December 3

Dear Alf:

Is the title understood then as *Dr. Arrowsmith?* Is that final? The thing against it is that Arrowsmith is much more Martin than Dr.—*it's his personal and scientific career that counts much more than his medical career*—Paul de Kruif can explain this to you. Will you please, P.D.Q., talk this over with Paul, then with Sewell. But Dr. is shorter, and quite all right. Please do give this thought before it's too late.

Have you sold any *Weeds* at all? You haven't told me a thing about how it's gone. Have you hopes for her next? My belief in her is very great.

I can see how you feel about not coming over here this winter. My own plans seem to be somewhat as follows just now: I hope to have *Arrowsmith* finished by the end of April or earlier, and to come over to the States with an expectation to stay for a long time. As soon as I've gone out West to see my father, and generally floated around a little, I'll settle down to the next book. This one may be much shorter and more adventurous, and you could probably publish it in the spring of 1926, a year after *Arrowsmith*, with the next, again a long one, coming a year and a half after that. I'll talk it over with you when I come home.

The revising of *Arrowsmith* goes famously. I'm raising hell with the first part, which starts rather too slowly. We're all well, though this blasted London fog does give us colds now and then. Does *Babbitt* keep on selling at all?

Frazier Hunt, now sailed for America, may come in to talk over his contemplated novel with you. He's a fine fellow and, if he settles down to it, may produce a good book.

Ever,
Red

December 12
Dear Red:
I do not understand that the title, *Dr. Arrowsmith*, is final. Haggard likes it, Paul likes it, and I like it, but neither Haggard nor I know anything about the book in detail, and Paul is inexperienced in this realm and inclined merely to acquiesce in what he considers our experienced judgment. The argument for "Dr." is about as follows:

It saves prefacing every statement in advertising and by salesmen with the explanation that the book is about a doctor. The first question anyone asks is "What is Lewis's new book about?" To have the title answer that is useful, distinctly so. You have become such a figure and information about you is so widespread that literally thousands of people know your father was a small-town doctor. Hundreds of thousands, perhaps a million or so, think that the most likeable character you have created so far is Doc Kennicott, so that besides defining the sort of person the hero of the new book may be, the word "Dr." in the title creates a hazy but nevertheless valuable predisposition in its favor to the effect that the hero is a character with whom you are in sympathy. Of course these arguments don't amount to much if they do violence to the book. If, when people have finished the novel, they feel that the "Dr." part of the title is wrong, then the title is wrong. As to this, under the present circumstances, you are the only one who can decide. If I had read the book or a good part of it, I'd think my judgment was worth something. Since you put this down as a possible title, I just assumed that it did not do violence to the book itself.

The best thing in your letters in months is the statement that you expect to come over here to stay for a long time. Bully!

We have not been able to get more than a thousand or fifteen hundred people to read *Weeds*. Critics who really dip into it like it and praise it highly but it just will not penetrate.

Babbitt has slowed up pretty much. I think I wrote of the contract for 200,000 cheap ed. next fall.

I haven't seen Frazier Hunt. Paul saw him last week.

Yours,
Alf

London, December 27
Dear Alf:
A quiet, very happy Xmas, with dinner with Curtis Brown. . . . Recent acquisition, Arnold Bennett—I like him. . . . Work going splendidly—I'll send Haggard about 43,000 words about January 10.

Title

I think your arguments for *Dr. Arrowsmith* as title are sound, and it does not do any violence to the book. The only thing then is: shall it be DR. ARROWSMITH or DR. MARTIN ARROWSMITH. The advantage of the latter is its impressing the full name of the hero on readers, that he may the better live. I'll write Haggard this same thing, and he and you can decide between you, by phone.

Book manuscript

If I were you (and in this case the you refers to everybody connected with Harcourt-Brace) I don't believe I'd even read the installments that go over to Haggard BECAUSE I am more or less cutting from the book-manuscript for serial use—cutting out bits of philosophy which will (I think) be of considerable value in the book and little or none in the magazine. Wait till about the end of April, and you'll have the whole book ms. When I come home we can at leisure go over the book ms and—this will be splendid—I can lay it away for several months and go over the whole thing again just before you start setting, a year or so from now.

Coming home

Both because I'm very comfortably settled here, and living rather quietly, and because when I do get home after a year and more of absence there will be so many people and things that I'll want to see that it'd be hard for a time to settle down to work, I don't want to leave till I have the book revised and done. Then I'll leap on a steamer (leaving Gracie and the kid here, till Wells's school year is done, or even for all summer) and skip back, see you, go over the book if you want to, go out West and see my dad, and generally cruise around, possibly spending next summer in the Canadian wilds to get some outdoor life after this sedentary year of writing and doing but little else.

Incidentally, Paul will get very little on the serial. He owes $10,000 on advance, and he owes me $1100 (approximately). Between having to accompany me to the West Indies, then here, outfit Rhea, and bring her over, he couldn't do it on a thousand a month, so I let him have some more, and told him not to repay it till money came in from the book—he wanted to repay it some time ago when, being settled in London and able to economize, he got ahead of the game again. It might as well wait till I get home, then we can settle it all up.

Oh. You had to cable me several times in *re* serial. Be sure that all these cables are charged to my account—better have someone look it up, because they quite possibly were not so charged.

I feel very well and as soon as I've had a good lay-off next summer, preferably in the wilds—Canadian woods or Rockies or some place—to get this book out of my system, I'll be ready to go at the next book. I'll talk it over with you when I come home. It'll be, I think, either a lovely detective story I've enjoyed planning, or the big religious novel I've planned so long—paying my compliments to the Methodist cardinals, the Lords Day Alliance, the S.P.V., and all the rest—not slightly and meekly as in *M St* and *Babbitt* but at full length, and very, very lovingly. I think it'll be just the right time for this novel, and I think I can do it con amore. . . . And this one couldn't *possibly* be serialized! . . . Perhaps I'll do both—the detective thing will be short (100,000 or a little less). That we might serialize, and publish just a year after *Arrowsmith*. We'll see. In any case, I suspect I'll still do a few more novels!

This is about the longest letter I've written to you for a year, so it starts the giddy new year with a bang.

Ever,
SL

My very good friend General C. B. Thomson will probably be coming over to America to lecture this spring—possibly immediately—and I want you two to meet. You'll like him immensely. He's a sure-nuff British brigadier who, after 26 years in the army (he's still under 50) winding up with 18 months on the Supreme Council, resigned and went into the Labour Party (note that *our*), because it was the only one that seemed to him to have a program. But he seems as completely Tory and army as anyone could want. He knows everybody from Ramsay Macdonald to the Queen of Roumania, and he was the most charming of all the guests we had in France last summer.

The third possibility for the next novel is a university-president story —do him as lovingly as I did Babbitt. Paul and I have talked of doing this together. It would be great fun for us two to get off into the Canadian wilds or the Rockies next summer, and plan it. Sooner or later, we probably will do it. The only objections to making it the next one are that people would buzz if we had two books together in succession and that I long to deal with the religiousers soon.

[1924]
London, January 5

Dear Alf, Don, and Gus:

Not to be interrupted too much in the production of a masterpiece of literature, I'm answering Alf's note and Gus's letter and Don's all in this one, with much New Year's greetings to all of you.

[1924]

I'm awfully glad of the Stuart Sherman review of *Weeds*. I sent off last week a letter to the N.Y.Sun about *Weeds* and Elinor Wylie's splendid *Jennifer Lorn*—God I wish we could have kept her, now! [1]—deliberately designed to start some discussion, decidedly con as well as pro, and perhaps help the two books a little.

I VERY much approve Don's suggestion of Monty Belgion as an addition to the shop. I know that he would like to go to America; I know that though he writes more or less he looks forward to a career in something like publishing rather than writing; I know that he would, everything going well, be perfectly satisfied to stay in the States for good. He is not only industrious and capable but an extremely good fellow; one who would fit beautifully with the somewhat unusual spirit of the house. . . . I find him one of the few Englishmen to whom I can talk with perfect ease. . . . He has, or would acquire, the peculiar American virtues without losing the English ones. Yes, do go ahead on that.

Arnold Bennett wants me to "do" the great and heroic days of the early railroad building—say the Great Northern or the Union Pacific. That came out the other night. We had him for dinner with Sir George McClaren Brown, head of the Canadian Pacific in England, and when SGMB and I were being profuse about those great days, Bennett, says he, "You ought to do that; it's never really been touched; you've scolded enough so you can be romantic for once with a clear conscience." Worth thinking of. I once did talk of a Jim Hill novel. It wouldn't come, then, but perhaps it might.

New Year felicitations.
May you enjoy Lady's Day,
Twelfth Night, and Boxing Day.
SL

January 11
Dear Red:

If you are in such danger of getting the British point of view about business as your suggestion that we charge cable tolls to you on the serial sale, it's time you came home and stayed a while. Except for this indication, I'm pleased you thought of it. We never did and won't again.

What you say about the next novels is interesting, of course, and we have all read it here. But the best fun will be to talk all this over when you come back.

Yours,
Alf

[1] Harcourt, Brace published Elinor Wylie's volume of poems *Nets to Catch the Wind* in 1921, but rights were later transferred to Knopf.

January 25

Dear Sinclair:

After being kept at home for a few days with a hard cold, it was good to find on my desk your letter of January 5th. All this was last week, but the approaching wedding [1] brought some local excitement which put the thought of writing to you out of my mind. This was last Saturday, as you already know. Alfred returned to the office Wednesday morning after an unextended trip.

When I wrote you about Montgomery Belgion, I didn't know that Miss Eayrs would be leaving so soon, and I merely had her leaving in mind as something that would happen perhaps next summer. Certain adjustments have to be made immediately, and I can't tell how or when we could use Belgion until the future is a little clearer. I am glad you thought of him as I did.

Thank you for selling *Weeds* to Cape. I had almost given up hoping to find an English publisher with the nerve to do it. It will be fun to see General Thomson whenever he arrives. I remember him from the Sunday luncheon at the Webbs'. It's good to realize that we are going to see you before many months.

Ever yours,
Don

London, Feb. 9

Dear Alf:

Thirty-nine, day before yesterday. I'm becoming an antique! I vastly appreciated the cablegram signed Alfdongusellenjeshal, and the signature struck me as so Oriental, so Kubla-Khanish, that I evolved the enclosed noble poem.

> Alfdongus Ellenjeshal
> King of the Eastern Riding,
> Tall as a temple of Bal,
> Swift as an evil tiding,
> His dolorous people guiding
> Rode with his white queen Zal,
> A golden tempestuous gal,
> Into the vale of Xiding,
> His runners beside him gliding,
> Shouting "Pashaw and Pal!
> Emperor Ellenjeshal!"

[1] The marriage of Ellen Eayrs and Alfred Harcourt.

You will have noted before this that our friend General C. B. Thomson won't be coming over to lecture for six months or a year or six years or something like that, because he has been made Minister for Air, and been given a peerage. The British certainly know how to lay on the nomenclature: "Secretary of State for Air, Brig. General the Right Honorable Lord Thomson, P.C., D.S.O."! Now that's what I call a name! C.B. is quite unspoiled by his honors (honours) and takes them and himself and sometimes even the Labor (Labour) party with a chuckle.

The book rolls on evenly. In about four days I'll be sending off another 25,000 words to Haggard. Regarding the first 40,000 he has cabled me, "Story splendid."

There's something (where have you heard these words before?) I wish you would do for me. I may take up the preachers in the next book, and I want to make some plans. Can you get and send me the chief periodicals of the Methodist and Baptist churches—not so much the ones that would be read by the laity but by the preachers, if there are such periodicals. And there is a magazine devoted to the business of evangelists. I'd like to see a copy of that. I doubt if you could get these at Brentano's; I think they'd have to come from the Baptist and Methodist publication offices. (For God's sake don't let 'em know who it is as wants 'em!) Could you have someone get these for me?

All well and cheerful. Been seeing millions of people. Spike Hunt sends his love to Don (he's just back from America). Infinite personal greetings, Alf.

Ever,
SL

February 9

Dear Red:

You can imagine how pleased Ellen and I have been over your warm and friendly letter which came to Mount Vernon the other day.

Ralph Block of Famous Players has approached me definitely about the sale of the motion picture rights of the next book. Warner Brothers are undergoing a sort of reorganization. I told Block that I felt we ought to give Warner Brothers a chance to go on with your books if they wanted them; that I thought we would not decide until you came home, or until I had the entire manuscript. By that time, I think Warner Brothers' situation will be clearer and we will know what to do.

Ever yours,
Alf

February 29

Dear Red:

Our birthday figures do begin to sound like middle age, but let's keep the middle age part of it just a far-off sound. I will be glad to see that you get the religious periodicals.

About Belgion. As whatever he should do here would be particularly under my wing and as I have never seen him, I do not think it wise to get after him. I have a little notion from what I have heard of him and seen of his activities that he may be primarily an author and literary feller rather than a business man, and the birthday figures of Don and me and Hal, Spingarn, and Gus are now significant enough so that we ought to take very few chances of spending three or four years training a man who is not fitted to push at least one of us off the chairs we now occupy. We are still young enough, though, so that we can take youngsters out of college or little more than out of college and let them really learn the business under our wings. Young Hilary Belloc [1] is here now, another boy is coming in September out of Yale, and then a Rhodes scholar. We got a likely youth from Harvard last fall and another from the University of Wisconsin, and the folks who have been here with us are coming on beautifully. It would sort of take the heart out of these boys to have someone come in from the outside and pinch off the good jobs they now see they have a chance of working up to. I rather cotton to the idea of having a number of these youths around and letting it be a free for all.

Everything is serene here and business is humming.

Yours,
Alf

London, March 4

Dear Alf and Don:

I'm skipping off to Spain with Gracie for a couple of weeks—probably be gone three weeks in all including the travel down. I have finally completed 96,000 words of the story, of which 30,000 are now at the stenographer's being copied and to be sent off to Haggard the moment I return. . . . Haggard writes me that he thinks if the whole novel is up to the first 40,000 words, it will be the best thing I have ever done.

About the title for the book. We can settle that when I come home. If *Dr. Martin Arrowsmith is* too long, then I think the only desirable contraction will be *Martin Arrowsmith*. He so definitely is Martin, more than Dr. Arrowsmith; yet just to call the book *Martin* would be senti-

---

[1] Son of Hilaire Belloc, the English writer. Young Belloc was on the staff of Harcourt, Brace for a brief period.

mental—lady-novelistish—and so would *Dr. Martin*. As for the *Doc*, which suggestion Alf hastily scrawled after a bibulous lunch—I spit!—it would be like calling *Jude the Obscure, The Country Kid*.

I hope you'll both have some free time and be able to read the book P.D.Q. as soon as I come home (which, with this Spanish interlude, will probably be mid-May) because I shall probably not stay long in NY City. I expect to be able to go with a Canadian Government Indian Treaty trip way up into Northern Saskatchewan—canoeing, camping—for a couple of months, starting about mid-June, and before that I'll have to skip out to Minnesota and have at least a week with my father.

Movies

I imagine it would be better to have Famous Players than Warner do the *Arrowsmith* film, if there is to be one—Warners are pretty damn amateurish at everything but finance. . . . I think I'd wait till after Haggard has done a lot of publicity and advertising on the serial before closing any bargain, and I'd see to it that both Block and Warners do see that advertising. It ought to whet their hungers considerably. I'd ask $50,000 *or more*.

Despite the tiredness from long-continued concentration, and despite the London fogs, I feel very well (as do we all) and I'll return to work with bells on. I'll have the whole thing done by about mid-May all right. I think you're going to be enthusiastic. Ah, but when I get to *Neighbor!* That's going to be THE book. And in less than five years I shall get to it.

Fred Howe is here—we lunched with him yesterday, and this afternoon I take him to the House of Lords on tickets Thomson (he's now a peer) gave me.

And tomorrow—SPAIN!

Ever,
SL

London, March 26

Dear Alf:

This in answer to your letter which was awaiting me when I got back from Spain. It was a good trip and, as we were shameless about not doing our duty as sight-seers, a good loaf. Toledo is a particularly interesting and unspoiled town and both there and in Seville there's plenty of Moorish architecture left.

I think we'd better wait till I come home and talk about the annual drawing of money for investment. However, it may be that I shall have only a few days in NY—I'm due in Prince Albert, Saskatchewan, on about June 8—and I may ask you and Don to do the actual investing.

Have I told you much of anything about the summer trip? I join a Canadian Govt trip—a "Treaty Party"—which goes annually to the Indians to pay them off, adjudge legal cases, etc.—and for two or two and a half months I shall be in complete wilderness in No. Sask., outdoors 24 hours a day, which will be just the thing to set me up after a year and a half or more of much too sedentary life. I'm glad to say that my doctor brother will be with me. I'll be back in what we call Civilization by the end of August and perhaps between then and December I'll go over the whole *Martin* ms again, and carry out any changes on which we-all may agree. Fortunately we have oceans of time, so everything would go all right even if I could have only one day in NY on landing—which depends on when I finish the *Martin* work.

About Belgion: Use your judgment. I quite see your point about youngsters, and admire you for it—your way is exactly the opposite of Doran and old Freddy Stokes,[1] neither of whom had any real notion of training youngsters.

Ever,
SL

April 7

Dear Red:

Hendrik Willem (Van Loon) sends me the enclosed prospectus of the Dutch edition of *Babbitt*. You can try your Dutch on it.

The Designer publicity is good. Seeing the title in print tends to convince me that *Dr. Martin Arrowsmith* is too much of a mouthful for a title, and if I had to say this minute it would be simply *Martin Arrowsmith*. But all this can wait until you come, of course.

Yours,
Alf

April 9

Dear Red:

Glad to have yours of March 26th. Your letter is the first definite word of the Canadian Government trip. It sounds fine. I only hope that the mosquitoes don't eat you up, and aside from this detail it does seem to me the ideal thing for you to do next. It will get you toned up physically

---

[1] Lewis was employed as a manuscript reader at Frederick A. Stokes Company, 1910-1912.

and do all sorts of good things to you. Of course we are a little disappointed not to look forward to a longer visit with you after you land, but it will be perfectly simple to do our work together in the autumn.

It certainly will be good to see you again.

Yours,
Alf

London, Saturday April 12

Dear Alf:

I shall sail on the *Scythia* on May 10, arriving late May 18 or early 19. My plans are to stay in NY to about May 27th, then a couple of days in Chicago, on to Sauk Centre, about six days there, then trip with the Canadian government party, and be back late in August.

I expect to arrive home with the book quite all done. You might meet the *Scythia*, if it doesn't arrive at too ungodly an hour, and plan for a dinner. And will you please engage a room for me at the Chatham? And we might all get right after the book. There won't be the final lookover which I had to give when I came home with *Babbitt*.

I'll see Paul in Chicago on my way home, unless he happens to be in the East. It'll be damn good to see you all, and I think you'll like the book. I feel as well satisfied with it as I ever do with anything.

Next fall, *probably*, we'll find a house in Washington for the winter, and stay put nearly a whole year . . . unless we go to California . . . or, *you* know, maybe just a flyer down to South America.

Six million salutations.

Red

As I'll be out of sight all summer and as she wouldn't have any too much fun without me at an American resort, Gracie is going to France for the summer, then will join me about September first.

Could you call up Henry Mencken at the Amer Mercury, tell him when I'm coming, and ask him to arrange a party for some date between May 19 and 26th at his—and your—convenience?

April 28

Dear Red:

Of course we are delighted to hear that you are coming and to know of your plans with some definiteness. I'll telephone Mencken, reserve a room for you at the Chatham, and we'll have a fine time while you're here. Ellen and I want you to stay out at the house as much as you can. Plan to be there several days, and I'll just stay away from the office and go over the book.

I'll meet you at the steamer and then take the book and read it in twenty-four or thirty-six hours. I suggest that you play around for a day or two while I am reading it and getting my head around it and then spend two or three days with us mapping out useful things to do to and for it.

I'll be so glad to see you.

Yours,
Alf

London, April 30th

Dear Alfred Harcourt:

For the sake of small Wells I am returning to the States this summer. I shall arrive on the *Veendam* in New York June 13th. I shall first go to my mother in Forest Hills where I shall sit down in the midst of my luggage to decide what is the best thing to do with my summer.

This last week I have been reading *Martin Arrowsmith*, most of it for the first time. There is a depth, an intelligence, a bigness, and a beauty about this book that seems almost epic to me. It has come to me that it is absurd to read a Sinclair Lewis novel as if it were a Peter B. Kyne. It should be read with leisure and with thought as we do the good books which have lasted more than their generation. Do you think this rather monumental of me? But you know, like Mrs. Merton of the Movies, I am his "severest critic" as well as "his dearest friend."

Grace Lewis

SIX
Travel on Two Continents

On May *19th Lewis arrived in New York with the manuscript of* Arrowsmith *and took up with the office details of its publication.*

[1924]
New York, May Twenty-three

Dear Alf:

Do you remember that bird—I think he lives in Brooklyn—whose chief delight in life is taking a book that is already published and marking on it the most marvelous corrections that have ever been made? He did it with *Babbitt* and *Main Street* and found a number of errors that all of us had missed.

Although he is an amateur he might be able to do it, for filthy lucre, with *Martin*. As we have so much time before the publication of *Martin* we might get him to read the galley proof, make a list of proof suggestions and make use of as much of them as we may wish. As I remember it, his one fault is that occasionally when a thing is said sardonically he takes it literally and makes a proof correction which is absurd. But he is one of those geniuses who may be valuable to us.

Your loving little boy—go to hell!

Sinclair Lewis

After a few days Lewis headed for Sauk Centre, from where he and his brother were to start for Canada.

Sauk Centre, June 4

Dear Alf:

Your good letter this morning. I already begin to feel rested & start off cheerfully for Canada tomorrow evening. My father is well but not awfully strong. . . . Send me a note now & then this summer so they'll be here when I get back. My best to all of you.

Ever
SL

This was the last note Lewis wrote the office before starting for Canada. In it he mentions a letter from Harcourt, no doubt written longhand, for there is no copy.

June 23

Dear Sinclair:
    I have just had an enjoyable half-hour reading the interviews from Winnipeg. They are marvelously good, and the reporter who describes his visit with you in the hotel room comes pretty near to genius. I know you won't get this letter until after your trip is over, but the interviews and the pictures indicate you are going to be fit to enjoy it.
    For the sake of the record, I'll tell you that I met Grace at the steamer on Saturday, the 14th, and saw her safely started in the direction of the Forest Hills Inn. She and Wells are looking splendid and appear to be completely fit. Grace is going to spend the night with us in Pelham tomorrow night.
    Martin is completely set up and we have proofs, which the movie people are reading. I have also sent a set to Paul.
    New York is full of the Democratic Convention this week, and after lunch Alf and I watched the parade on Fifth Avenue, made up chiefly of politicians in silk hats and policemen. Imagine the Police Glee Club, during a halt in the parade, singing "Sweet Kentucky Babe" and a lot of similar songs on Fifth Avenue. It wasn't very different from the 4th of July, 1897, in my small birthplace in New York state.
    It will be nice to see you—soon, I hope, after you see this.

Ever yours,
Don

There was no word from Lewis while he was en route until his letter of June 30th.

Ile a la Crosse
Sask—June 30

Dear Alf—Don—Hal:
    This is my last chance to send you a note before vanishing quite beyond post-boxes until I emerge at The Pas, Manitoba, some time between Aug. 15 & Sept. 5. . . . This settlement (Hudson's Bay store,

Revillon post, log cabins of Indian fishermen) tho it is 150 miles (by canoe) from railhead has a postal delivery every single month!

The trip is going beautifully. I've already quite lost my jumpiness, my daily morning feeling-like-hell; haven't had a drink for eleven days & haven't missed it in the least. I don't *have* to do any work at all—the Indians do that—but I paddle enough to get a lot of exercise. The ground no longer feels hard to sleep on, & I wake at 4, ready for bacon & coffee, with great cheerfulness. I shoot *at* ducks; catch pike; & listen to the agent's stories—he is a delightful fellow, knows the wilds, & has a sense of humor. All goes beautifully—& I hope it does with you.

Ever—
SL

July 3

Dear Grace:

Yesterday I was really moved by the picture of *Babbitt*. I stayed and talked with the Warner people; they do not seem to think the picture will make money. They say it did well when it opened in Los Angeles but it has not done well in Boston. I told them I thought they could count on almost any other part of the country but Boston to respond to the picture.

Ever yours,
Alfred

On July 8th Mrs. Lewis went with Wells Lewis to Nantucket Island, Massachusetts, and there was a constant exchange of correspondence between her and the office while Lewis was in Canada.

July 26

Dear Red:

I was really surprised by your telegram yesterday saying you were again in touch with civilization. I meant to have two or three letters waiting for you at Sauk Centre, but the days have slipped by. Of course those of us who have been holding the fort have been especially busy and it has been a stinking hot summer. Most of the staff have been away on vacation and there is still a number to go. Hal left for a cruise last night. I think he plans to stop in and see Grace at Siasconset, where according to her letters she seems to be enjoying herself.

There is nothing to report on the motion picture rights of *Martin*. I have sent galleys to all of the leading producers and Ralph Block is the most interested of the lot. Warner Brothers say they lost some money on *Main Street* and expect to lose some more on *Babbitt,* and of course this has spread. The lack of success of these pictures makes the other producers a little wary. It may be that the sale will not be made until the book itself is under way and we have an assured box office title for it.

We have done nothing but send out some galleys to the motion picture people and in every case I have insisted that these be returned to us after they have read them. It seems important to me not to allow the book to be pawed over so far in advance of publication; in fact I have steered the office away from it and have kept the reviewers from reading it. I don't want anybody to read it and get het up about it and then have a chance to cool off. Not that they would really cool off. I find that I like the book more and more myself as I think it over, but you know how it would be with the reviewer if he reads it now, and then next February started to write an article about it.

Ellen and I and Hastings expect to leave about the tenth of August for ten days or so. I think that is all the news. I'll write again if anything occurs. I'll bet you had a wonderful time. I would like one like it myself.

Ever yours,
Alf

The Tavern-on-the-Moors
Siasconset
Nantucket Island, Mass.
July 29th.

Dear Don:

I am having a better and better time. Fola LaFollette and George Middleton are here. And yesterday I ran into my adored Marc Connelly and Tony Sarg and Bob Benchley. Great fun.

Did you see the telegram from Hal which was forwarded to me from your office last week? It reads thus: "Weather fine and party is ahead of schedule and I have cut off last loop of trip so am back at railhead feeling superb real rejuvenation. Going Sauk Centre so hustle mail there and wire present address and a funny and take day off to write me enormous letter. Shall know plans better when see mail but unless you like to come to St. Paul for bat shall probably go East in about three weeks."

Enough is enough apparently. The wilderness is all right in its place but not too much of the same place. I do hope the creature will come up here and love it as I do.

Grace

Lewis stayed in Sauk Centre until August 5th and then drifted East by way of St. Paul, Chicago, and Detroit. He arrived in New York the end

[1924]

of August, and joined Mrs. Lewis at Siasconset. While he was there he read galley proofs of Arrowsmith. *There were several letters written back and forth, principally about the proofs.*

September 5
Dear Red:

A minor piece of business: The head of the English Department in one of the large St. Louis high schools is making for us a collection of short stories to be read by high school pupils. He is extraordinarily keen about your short stories and urged us to make a collection of them some day. I report this as backing up the suggestion I made to you when you were in the office. Incidentally, he would like to include one of your stories in his collection—"Old Man Axelbrod." Have we your permission to reprint it? I think a little of this sort of reprinting for high school pupils is a good thing to steer them toward an author's complete work. I often wonder how many new readers of fiction come into the market each year—a darn sight more than die off, I think.

I do hope you found Grace and the boy all right and that you're enjoying the crowd at Siasconset.

Ever yours,
Alf

Have you tackled proofs yet? Mencken asked for an advance set again the other day. I stalled him off.

Siasconset, September 6
Dear Alf:

Yes, use the "Old Man Axelbrod" story if you want to in the short story collection. About a collection of my stories: As I'm going abroad for God knows how long, I ought to look them over before I go—or else take 'em with me, for examination and possibly revision. Now if I remember aright, I gave all the copies I had of my stories to Ellen, just after *Main Street*, and they're probably stored somewhere in the office.

No, I haven't done a lick of work on the proofs. I've never been more agreeably and profitably lazy than here, in this island of sea breezes and moors. But I probably shall do quite a little work these next two weeks.

Don't stall Mencken off on the proofs so long that there'll be any danger of his getting sore. I think he'd respect release date if it was emphasized to him.

See you soon. Love to Ellen, Don, Hal, Gus.

Ever,
SL

September 19

Dear Sinclair:

Paul has been in this afternoon, explained that he will have to go away without seeing you, and brought up the point of the acknowledgment to be made for his share in *Martin*. He suggests, either in small type on the title page or in small type on a following page, simply this: "In collaboration with Paul H. De Kruif." Or if this doesn't seem all right to you, he wishes nothing to be said at all. You can tell us what you want to do about this when you come in.

I hadn't looked at the book since I read the manuscript, and I find myself neglecting other things to read the batches of proofs as they come in from you. It's even better than I thought it was.

See you next week.

Yours,
Don

Mrs. Lewis went to the Forest Hills Inn, Long Island, on September 19th, a few days before Lewis left Siasconset. In New York Lewis discussed with the office the form of credit to be given to De Kruif in Arrowsmith. *The Lewises sailed for England on the* France *early in October. Lewis read page proofs of* Arrowsmith *on board.*

Bord S. S. "FRANCE"
Monday noon, October 13

Dear Don:

We are less than twenty-four hours from Plymouth. About this time tomorrow we ought to be ashore—IN ENGLAND! It's been a fine easy trip; no very exciting people aboard but no one disagreeable. It's a fine ship in every way, especially as regards food and service, and I recommend it. The only rough day has been today—she's pitching, rather, as I write—the typewriter shows an unmanly tendency to approach me then back off from me.

Don't forget that all thru the page proofs the running heads have to be changed to just *Arrowsmith*.

Feel fine, rested after the excitements of NY, for tho I've worked pretty hard on these damn proofs aboard, I've also had the finest lot of assorted sleep.

Ever,
SL

Lemme know what Paul says *re* credit page.

[1924]

October 30
Dear Red:
Your cable authorizing the change of the word "suggestions" to the word "help" in the acknowledgment to Paul [1] has just come in. You already know that everything else has arrived, and as far as I can see, there will be nothing else for you to look at until you get the finished copies of the book.

All Paul said about the acknowledgment was that he'd be content with a compromise in regard to that one word. I thought you wouldn't mind this; hence the cable.

I hope you'll soon be settled down for a good winter. Everything is flourishing here.

Ever yours,
Don

The Lewises stayed in London until November 11th, and then went over to Paris.

c/o Guaranty Trust Co.
3 Rue des Italiens, Paris
November 12

Dear Don and Alf:
We've done nothing but loaf and get over the final rush in NY all this month. Tomorrow morning, early, we're off for Switzerland, where we'll put the kid in school for several months. Then we'll return to Paris and there, and All Points South, view the wonders of the nation for several months till I feel like getting on the job again. I think the only sensational thing this past month has been having Bernard Shaw in for tea. He was charming, and very young, and his wife, of whom one has heard very little, seemed to be a very real person.

Ever,
SL

[1] The following statement of Lewis's obligation to De Kruif was printed in *Arrowsmith:*
   To Dr. Paul H. De Kruif I am indebted not only for most of the bacteriological and medical material in this tale but equally for his help in the planning of the fable itself—for his realization of the characters as living people, for his philosophy as a scientist. With this acknowledgment I want to record our months of companionship while working on the book, in the United States, in the West Indies, in Panama, in London and Fontainebleau. I wish I could reproduce our talks along the way, and the laboratory afternoons, the restaurants at night, and the deck at dawn as we steamed into tropic ports.

November 21

Dear Red:

No news yet about the motion picture sale of *Arrowsmith*. I think it will drift now until after the book is out. We have settled on March 5th as the date of publication.

Paul and Rhea have been at our house for a day. They are apt to settle down somewhere around here for a few months. I am just reading the first two chapters of *Microbe Hunters*, and they are fine.

As a piece of news: You remember Hal's friend Arthur Hildebrand started last August with two others to sail from Norway to Labrador over the Viking route. They have not been heard from since, and it looks as if they were lost. It's a shame!

We have had a busy autumn. Nothing has had an extraordinary sale, but the whole line has been moving, so that the year has been a good one. We have already done just over 20,000 of *A Passage to India*, which is so many more than the sale Forster has had before in America that he ought to be pleased.

We are all heading up now to work on *Arrowsmith*, and it's going to be great fun.

Ever yours,
Alf

November 25

Dear Red:

I just have your note announcing your arrival in Paris. I envy your having Bernard Shaw for tea. I always see him now in a raincoat, talking and wringing his hands, as he did that day at Ramsgate. I hope by the time you get this you will be all settled and comfortable wherever it is in France.

We have nearly finished printing the limited edition of *Arrowsmith*, and in a few days we shall begin printing the first regular edition of 50,000 copies. We may have to print more before publication, but this will at least give us something to start on.

Paul is back here for the winter probably and has just found a flat in Mount Vernon. We're all well and busy, the same as usual.

Ever yours,
Don

In the three weeks they were in Switzerland, there was no communication from Lewis.

[1924]

>L'Elysee-Bellevue Hotel, Paris
>December 11

Dear Alf and Don:

Hunting for a school for Wells in Switzerland—we found a good one, too, at Glion, just above Lac Geneve; an eight-day walking trip among the mountains in the most glorious Indian Summer weather, with no baggage except a small rücksack; a week here looking for a suitable hotel. And now we're settled down in this comfortable place out on the Champs Elysee, and I've started my French lessons and reading Voltaire. We both feel superb and being dug in here we see almost nothing of the Wild Boys who do their drinking at the Dome or the New York Bar. 'Ve seen Fred Howe several times.

About Jefferson: I've read the Muzzey and Morse biographies, and while I find Jefferson interesting, I'm not really stirred to specialize on him—certainly not yet.[1] But I am planning *The Yearner*, and second novel, much bigger, containing the novel about the Methodist preacher which I've planned so long, but also other and more dramatic elements.

We'll be here about two months, then off Eastward—to Czechoslovakia, Greece, Turkey, or Lord knows where. If either of you are (is?) planning to come over here, please make it enough before February 15th so that I shan't be gone. Or make it May-June when I'll probably be back.

In advertising I think I should emphasize the "first novel in the two and a half years since *Babbitt*." People may forget it's been that long.

I'm most terribly sorry to hear about Arthur Hildebrand. Perhaps there may still be a hundredth chance of his being at some Esquimo village.

Tell Hal that if he can by some miracle be stirred to write to me, I'll send him a handsome answer. Tell him that I may beg him to go off to China and Siam a year from now. As for Paul, remind that low form of micro-biologic life that he owes me about two letters now, damn him.

>Ever,
>*Red*

>Paris, December 27

Dear Alf:

A quiet but agreeable Xmas. We spent the afternoon wandering among the old tumble-down streets on the Butte de Montmartre. Arthur Maurice is in town, and we dine with him this evening. So is Tommy

---

[1] For many years Harcourt kept suggesting Jefferson to various authors as the outstanding comparative vacancy in American biography.

Wells—saw him on the street the other day and asked him to phone me when he had time for lunch or something.

I don't myself know the exact dates of the first editions of my books—that is, I hate to depend on my memory. I believe they're to be found in *Who's Who*. I think—in answer to your questions—that I'd include *The Innocents*, but omit the Stokes boys' book [1]—if later it gets included, all right, but let's not facilitate the process, and meantime most copies of it, lying dusty in boys' libraries, will have vanished from the collectors' ardent view.

Cape writes me that he is coming over. When he gets there, discuss with him whether it would be better to send English or American editions to people in England. AND, besides the individual doctors, the editors of medical journals, the A.M.A. officials, and the college bacteriologists, HAVE PAUL make out list of other scientists to whom it should go in advance. Talk over with him whether, perhaps in some guilty hope of starting controversies, it ought not to go to people—e.g. Flexner—who may not like it quite as much as those who will.

Then what about the big foreign scientists besides the British? Talk that over with Paul. I suggest specially D'Herelle (who is mentioned so much), Roux, D'Arrhenius (oft mentioned), Bordet, Gratiot. If Paul can get the American, British and Continental scientists to write either for the press or at least to him—— Talk over for his letters a delicate phrase which may suggest that to them.

Finally, what about sending this to the big critics everywhere? What about Spingarn or you sending it to Brandes, Croce, et al? What about sending it to James Joyce in Paris, Gilbert Seldes and Wilson Follett and other highbrows in America? And just for the fun of it, to Freud, Jung and Adler and see if they'll roast it among their disciples? And get off copies for translation-agents as early as possible—may get good European reaction, esp. in Germany.

Grace suggests, apropos of my hint tother day of Britishers who might review book for America—West, Wells—that they ought NOT to have May Sinclair do it; as she did *Babbitt*, it will begin to look like logrolling. Have some one get after Edith Wharton early—perhaps cable her with prepaid reply—it would not be easy to get her, but valuable if possible.

Ever,
Red

[1] *Hike and the Aeroplane*, Frederick A. Stokes Company, 1912. Lewis wrote this under the pseudonym of Tom Graham.

[1925]
January 7

Dear Red:

I am glad you are comfortably fixed in Paris, that you're feeling well, and that *The Yearner* is continuing to take shape. The new season has started off with a bang; we seem to have been more than unusually rushed getting samples ready for the spring books and getting the travelers ready to start.

Ernest (Brace) and his wife left for Paris on New Year's Eve on the *Ohio*, planning, I think, to stay there at least for part of the winter. I expect to come over in the spring. Our plans are to leave here the end of March, probably go straight to Italy, and then come to Paris, spending probably three weeks altogether on the Continent, which would bring me to London about one month after leaving New York. Or I could just as well reverse the route, going to London first and around the other way. Unless we fail to make suitable provisions for the rest of the family, Ida [1] will come with me. I certainly want to see you.

Louis Untermeyer, Paul, Chris Morley, Hal, Alf, and I have just been having lunch, interrupting the ribaldries long enough to talk about *Arrowsmith* and you. I can't see anything in sight this spring to compete with *A.* in any real way—nothing within miles of it in scope, or depth, or any kind of importance. I've been rereading here and there from the printed sheets—it gets me more each time I go back to it.

Ever yours,
Don

Early in December the fly-leaves for the limited edition of Arrowsmith *had been sent to Paris for Lewis's signature.*

Paris, January 10

Dear Alf:

I cabled you day before yesterday that I have not yet received the fly-leaves for the special edition. They've probably been caught in the Xmas mail.

I've had photographs taken by Man Ray, an American who follows after Stieglitz, Steichen, etc. I'm awaiting proofs and will send you the best.

After I had suggested various bacteriologists to receive advance copies of *Martin*, it occurred to me that there MIGHT be a danger that too many editors of reviews might have the bright idea of having the

[1] Brace's wife.

book reviewed by a scientist. One or two such reviews would be fine; too many would be fatal—it would suggest to the public that the book was not a piece of literature but a scientific manual. So don't suggest profs as reviewers to too many. I hope Carl Van Doren will do the book for somebody, and that Stuart Sherman himself will be moved to do it for the Evening Post. And Menck of course.

I'm still loafing but beginning mildly to think about novels. But it'll be some time before I go to work. I'm thinking about a month or more in Germany. Meantime I learn some French . . . a little!

I have a letter from one Leon Kochnitzky, who was secretary to D'Annunzio during the great Fiume days, whom I met in Rome, and who has been in Russia recently, that one Domher wants to write to you about Russian rights. I'm answering—"sure, let him write—if he has a publisher interested." . . . ARE there any publishers in Russia except the State? I don't know. But Louise Bryant tells me there are a lot of Russians interested in my books, and I should suppose that at best we'd get darn little out of Russia in money, so it doesn't much matter who publishes there. . . . Happy New Year.

Ever,
Red

January 15

Dear Red:

Yours of December 27th came in the first of the week. The day was a hectic one, as Don had to have an emergency operation for acute appendicitis. It was a close squeak for him, but last night his temperature, pulse, and breathing were about normal, and I really believe he is out of the woods.

The only thing that isn't going right is the flyleaves for the special edition. We are having them traced. If they do show up, may we have a cable so that we will surely wait to bind them in the books?

We are waiting for the special photographs. Ellen and Hal are attending to the advance copy stuff. Paul has read your letter and is making notes, and he and Ellen are going to devote Friday to getting that part of the job in shape. In one thing I am sure you have gone a little too far—in suggesting free copies. For instance, "professors of bacteriology in ALL American medical schools, and in all the larger colleges and universities." We mustn't cheapen the book by being too free with it.

While we are working up the critical reception of the book with a good deal of care, I am devoting most of my attention this time to getting the trade started. After all, they are the folks who hand out the copies on which we pay you royalty. Gehrs has worked out a really clever advance order scheme. We will have a dummy of the book, the inside of which is really an order blank, with a little poster projecting from it, on the front of the fiction counter in each of the stores for three weeks before publication. I explained the scheme to Marcella Hahner yesterday, and I told her I'd give $25 to the girl in her store who had the most orders booked by the morning of March 5th. When she saw how it works, she said she'd be disappointed if they did not have 1000 retail orders on the day of publication. That means 1000 people from her store alone will be reading the book immediately and talking about it. It is important for us to emphasize this aspect of *Arrowsmith* for a number of reasons. The main one is that *Babbitt* seemed to stop so suddenly that there were some copies of it around for a considerable time. Another reason is the serialization. These give the booksellers excuses to cut down their advance orders. We have to do something to get them thinking in terms of 250 and 500 for their first orders instead of 50 and 100.

We now have a full page on the book every week in The Publishers' Weekly, so that booksellers will know for dead certain that the day after Calvin Coolidge is inaugurated they will have nothing else to do but sell *Arrowsmith*.

No more now.

Yours,
Alf

Paris, January 25

Dear Don:

I'll wait here in Paris for the new set of fly-leaves. Otherwise I'd be off to the Riviera right away—not because I don't like Paris but because I want to see a lot of other places in the few months more of loafing which I can take. . . . As soon as I have them off to you, Grace and I will be leaving, with Germany *probable* after Riviera. . . . I don't believe we'll go out as far as Constantinople, though we had thought of it.

Where I'll be when you arrive in Paris I don't know, but I'll plan to meet you here or in London when I know your dates more definitely. I saw Ernest and Reeves (Brace) a couple of times here. They are now off to Vence, a little and, I am told, very agreeable town not far from Nice.

Ever,
Red

January 26
Dear Red:
I have your note of January 10th. Ellen and Paul have worked out the list of bacteriologists who are to receive *Arrowsmith*. I was at once aware of the danger of there being too many reviews by scientists, and I have already squashed a scheme or two in that direction, especially with Canby who has decided that he is very anxious to review it himself. The scientific reviews with one or two exceptions ought to be confined to the scientific journals. We will need two or three of just the right comments from those sources, but not more, and I want that crowd to realize that they have gotten into literature and that they should buy and read the book rather than expect to have copies given to them.

Cape's steamer is due today, and I suppose he will be in tomorrow or the day after. Don got home from the hospital yesterday.

Yours,
Alf

Paris, January 28
Dear Alf:
I was frightfully worried to hear of Don's illness. I hope that long before this he will have been out of danger. About the time you get this, or a little after, I'll be off to the Riviera.

The damned fly-leaves for special edition never showed up till yesterday afternoon, and I've sent them off to you today. The three original packages are now in one package—*together with* ten new photographs just taken here.

I'm a little sore about Paul's being unable to find time to write me one single line in about four months. You may show him just that, if you'd like. . . . If he *has* ever written, I haven't heard from him since the letter which came to me just as I left Nantucket. . . . Meantime I've written him at least three times—whether postcards or long letters.

Many ideas about *The Yearner*. Agreeable days with Bill Woodward, now in Paris, and beautifully grown since the days of the Publishers Newspaper Syndicate, and Mencken's great friend, Philip Goodman, the theatrical manager—a hell of a good fellow.

So! Now you can catch your breath.

Ever,
SL

Paris, Feb 1
Dear Alf:
I'm going to write a play! I shall enjoy it in contrast to novel writing, and it will only take me about three weeks. I shall be working more or less with Philip Goodman, who will then produce it some time this year. We're going off to Munich to do it in a few days now. Then, probably, Riviera. Meantime *Yearner* grows and rounds itself.

Ever,
SL

Paris, Feb. 1st
Dear Don:
I was shocked and distressed when I heard from Alf of your operation but, as I have had no further news, I let myself hope that you are convalescing beautifully. I saw with Gracie the extremely beneficial results of an appendicitis operation and I hope it will be the same with you.

How will this affect your plans about Europe? Just now I'm going up to Munich for about three weeks; then Gracie will either join me there or we'll go to the Riviera. In any case, I shan't go out to Constantinople, and I'll be in reach whenever you come.

Drop me two words whenever you are able. . . . Need I tell you how heartily and completely Grace and I send you our affection and good hopes? She has skipped off to Switzerland for a few days, to see Wells. This morning I talked to her over the long distance telephone—they got the call in about ten minutes and it seemed so strange to be talking from the flat plains of France to a place in the mountains, and high ones, of another country!

Ever,
Red

Paris, Feb. 6
Dear Alf:
Today I started off the second—emergency—set of fly-leaves for the special edition of *Arrowsmith*. Jeezus! Have you ever tried signing your name 500-odd times—keeping the sheets from getting blotted meantime, whereby the floor about your table is covered with a snow of fly-leaves—and then going to a French emballeur (Gracie being in Switzerland for a week to see Wells, who seems very happy there) and trying in damn bad French to explain that you want theseĥere carefully wrapped in

strawboard for shipment to Amerique? Then you ain't been nowhere and you ain't done nothin'.

About Maurois. And Disraeli. I have seen Grasset, his French publisher, twice; and thrice I have seen his very delightful secretary—qui s'appele Alice Turpin and who speaks an admirable English but who is completely French. And this noon, thanks to Dr. Dawson Johnson, director of the American Library here, I lunched with Maurois himself.

The situation is this. Maurois is now writing a series of five short things dealing with Goethe, Byron, and three others. And he has the documentation for two books on Disraeli and Wilson—yes, H.H. the Late Revered Woodrow. But not a word of either of these has he written.... He is a very charming fellow (incidentally speaking perfect English). He is, unfortunately for us, much interested in his business (he is by profession a silk manufacturer or something of the kind) and in his children—his wife died some short time ago and he is devoted to them. Also he is well pleased by Appleton in America, Lane in England.

I told him what a hell of a bunch of guys Messrs Cape and Arcour-Braas were. There is a vague long-range possibility that you might have with Grasset here in France something like the same relation you have with Cape in England. . . . He is young—about forty—energetic, free from silly tradition, and at the moment about the most successful publisher in the country.

I'm off in a week now for Munich.

Ever,
Red

February 13

Dear Red:

Don is back at the office and in better trim than for a long time. Ellen and I are starting South tomorrow afternoon for a holiday. We will be away ten days or so.

Consider yourself damned in Ellen's best New England accents for not having sent the photographs by first class mail and not having had them taken earlier. The review copies of *Arrowsmith* to the monthlies and weeklies of large circulation have all had to go with the best of the old photographs we could find. Of course the new pictures will be darned useful in special places, and we will make all the special use of them we can.

About Paul: I am almost certain I have heard him talk of having written to you, but I'll show him what you say. There is one thing you can be dead sure of—he has been most expertly and completely helpful in the advance publicity work on *Arrowsmith*. He spent days with Ellen on it, and between them they have done a careful and scrumptious job. We are already beginning to get a few letters saying that the scientific crowd are pleased to have this special and unusual attention.

The news about your writing a play is splendid. You will enjoy the work, and it is about time you pulled one. How long ago the first night of *Hobohemia* seems!

Advance orders for *Arrowsmith* look to be thirty-five or forty thousand, but the big accounts are just beginning to come in. Mencken has read it and is as enthusiastic as we could wish. You know he is now syndicating a weekly article to 45 newspapers. His article on March 7th will be a review of *Arrowsmith*, and then he will do it over again in the April Mercury. As you know, Hal is endlessly enthusiastic, and the stuff he and Gus have worked on for the trade has been splendid. The book grows on us all all the time.

Yours,
Alf

February 13

Dear Red:

I am back at the office after my operation, apparently in good condition. As far as I know, my plans for Europe will go through about as I told you. I expect to sail for Naples on March 26th. Meanwhile I have a lot to do, and Alfred is going to Florida tomorrow to get a holiday before mine begins.

Spike Hunt came up to lunch day before yesterday, bringing recent and good reports of you. Jonathan is here now, too.

Barring strikes, accidents, and other acts of God, I think you can count on my being in Paris for a few days toward the end of April and in London during the first two or three weeks in May.

Ever affectionately yours,
Don

Hotel Elysee-Bellevue, PARIS.
February 28

Dear Alfred and Don:

After two weeks in Munich Phil Goodman was called back to Paris to see some one—and also Munich is a town which, however sharming, becomes a little bit dull after a few days—and so we have returned to Paris to complete the work on the play. As soon as it is finished, which will be in from two to four weeks more, Gracie and I will start off for a long hike through Germany and Austria.

We enjoyed Munich immensely, particularly as it centered about the Kurt Wolff Verlag. No one could have been more charming than Wolff and his wife. They had us at a couple of parties, as it was in the midst of the Carnival, and in general did everything possible to make our stay agreeable. Wolff strikes me as being one of the most intelligent and promising publishers I have ever met, and I shall be glad if it is possible to make an agreement with him for *Arrowsmith*.

Gracie had sent to Munich—and therefore I missed—the new pamphlet about me [1] which, she informs me, is amazingly charming and valuable. I am glad to hear that the book starts in with a promising advance sale and that Mencken is as enthusiastic as we had wished.

Having told you something like 16,347,222 times how much I appreciate your work on all my books, need I again repeat it on *Arrowsmith?* I would say—if it were not for the fact that Phil Goodman is sitting across the room listening in a great bronze buddha bored Hebraic way to this letter when he wants to work on the play, and were it not for the fact that the letter is being dictated to Ellen Barrows—that as soon as I get this God damned play done and as soon as I have had a joyful hike in Germany, I shall go to work on *The Yearner*, which will naturally be the greatest novel which has ever been written in the northern countries of southern Iowa.

Ever,
Red

Paris, Mar. 4

Dear Don & Alf:

The play is no good. It tends to be cheap & sensational; so I have chucked it, absolute, & with pleasure I return to thoughts of *Yearner*—tho it will probably be a couple of months before I start writing it . . . in England, in the Tyrol, in Sweden, in Connecticut, or one (at least) of those places.

So at last Grace & I start off on a real hike. As it's rather early, we plan (tho you know how often we change our plans) to go from here to Marseilles, Cannes, the Italian Riviera, then direct from Genoa to Munich, on to Vienna & Budapest, to Berlin & possibly Stockholm, Rotterdam & Brussels. . . . I'll probably, therefore, see Don in London after May 1st rather than here. But I want him to keep me posted as to his

---

[1] Biographical pamphlet *Sinclair Lewis* by Oliver Harrison (pseudonym for Harrison Smith), issued by Harcourt, Brace.

movements. From time to time I'll wire from Xdzboda or some other agreeable place.

I have Hal Smith's new pamphlet. It's a corker.

Ever,
Red

March 6

Dear Red:

Arrowsmith is published, and all the signs point to success. I was intending to enclose with this letter a number of the early reviews, but Hal tells me he is writing you and enclosing them. Stuart Sherman's review is splendid, and Canby's is good too. Hal has had a wonderful time with the advertising and has managed things with much skill and of course with no end of interest and enthusiasm. The advance sales are, we figure, 43,000. We shall have to start another printing the first of the week. It is pretty clear from the early comments that there is going to be controversy of one sort or another about the book; everything looks favorable.

I am due in Naples on April sixth. You might write me in care of The American Express Company in Naples where you expect to be in Paris the last few days in April and in London after that.

Ever yours,
Don

March 6

Dear Red:

The eventful day has passed. Last month there was a total eclipse of the sun. This week New York had its first earthquake since the days of President Grant and the police reserves had to be called out to quiet the swarms from Harlem. Yesterday *Arrowsmith* was published. Today I am writing you a letter. The connection between these events does not need any astrologer.

In short, *Arrowsmith* is going over with a bang. There are reviews everywhere—publicity everywhere—ads everywhere. Vanity Fair devotes a page to the photo with the twisted column and the enigmatic Lewis at its base; Arts & Decoration (God save the mark!) another; the rotogravure sections of newspapers will have you; and the women's magazines cry for them. Even the biographical squib by that imposingly unknown critic Oliver Harrison is selling and will probably have to go into another edition. For ten days people have been going into the bookstores and trying to buy Gus's dummy copies—which, with their virginal and blank leaves are still a better buy than many of the new novels, having the merit of complete honesty and the dramatic quality of suspense.

Up to date Canby likes *Arrowsmith* immensely; Stuart Sherman thrusts back at that red-whiskered Boyd, and proclaims that it's your best novel. His is a completely satisfying estimate of the book, at least to me. Fishbein and Keith Preston in Chicago have come up to scratch. It is all very exciting, and you ought to be here to flavor it. Laurence Stallings, now out in Los Angeles working for the movies, is the only discordant note so far, coming out with an abortive, brief and unfair review which appeared two days before the book was out. Carl Van Doren tells me he likes it immensely, and I am waiting breathlessly to hear from that dean of American critics who is now (heaven help us!) editor for Doran's, John Farrar.

This will have to serve as a brief résumé of the latest dispatches from the front. To be concise, you have captured the American front line trenches of the enemy. In another week Gus will have the entire public on the run—into the bookstores.

Personally I am well, cheerful, and wish to God spring was here. The same to you! A letter from Gracie says that you are in Germany with one Philip Goodman, and I can only wish that his name was Harrison Smith. But still, perhaps he knows something of that accursed language, which I could never manage to twist my tongue around. However, Europe is not for me for two or three years as yet, and why I should think it should be then, I don't know. Are you really going to the Orient? Knowing something of China and Japan, I recommend it with all my heart. No one has really seen the world until he has been there. You are beginning to do the job so completely that you ought to absorb the saffron and the brown people and perhaps the black, although if you are like me you will be more interested in the weird varieties of whites you meet out there than in the natives.

Some good books out in the last few weeks, though nothing can in the least degree rival *Arrowsmith*—Item: *The Constant Nymph* by one Miss Kennedy, and *God's Stepchildren* by Sarah C. Millin.

If there is anything I can do for you, any messages I can bear, or rears that I can kick, let me know. You will hear from me again. My love to Grace, and if you will get yourself a bottle of good wine and pretend that I have paid for it I will be satisfied.

Alf is down in Florida but comes back Monday. Don sails soon. Paul is the same as ever, and he and Rhea are going to move into Don's house and look after the youngsters while the Braces are away. We have Spike Hunt's novel, and I am going to try to read it tonight.

That's about all the news I can think of. Cape has been here and goes back tomorrow. He is a good scout.

Yours,
Hal

March 11

Dear Red:

With Don planning to sail for an eight or ten weeks' holiday at the end of the month, I suddenly realized that my last chance for a holiday in some time was rapidly passing. And, during the last week before the publication of *Arrowsmith* and the few days after it actually appeared, there was nothing I could do for it—all the wires were laid and the book itself was at work—so Ellen and I slipped away to Florida and had a splendid time.

I spent last evening reading through all the reviews so far. They're fine as a whole. A number of the reviewers are a little at sea as to just how to take it. They're going to be ashamed some day of their "ifs" and "buts." I am glad to see that most of them recognize Leora for part of what she is—just about the best woman character in American fiction that I know of. I have no doubt that we shall surely sell 100,000, and I have hopes that it is going much beyond that.

I have also read your letter about Maurois, Disraeli, etc. What a fine and careful job of going to the bottom of a tangled situation!

While I was in Florida, I read Spike Hunt's novel and sent it back to Don for him and Hal to look at. I said I thought we ought to try it—it's honest and it's real. I haven't heard what they think of it. If they share my hopes, we'll try it; if they share my doubts, we may not.[1]

You must have enjoyed Munich and the play. I hope you and Grace have a wonderful time in Germany and Austria. Then it's time to start writing another novel.

Yours,
Alf

Hotel Bellevue
Cannes
March 21

Dear Hal:

Yesterday, forwarded from Paris, came your letter & the first batch of reviews & the big ad. God bless you! The ads are corking—the use of the arrow as symbol for the book is superb. I should think they would

---

[1] Frazier Hunt: *Sycamore Bend*, HB&Co., 1925.

hit everybody square in the eye. I'm so glad, of course, of Sherman's review.

We're off on a two months hike—here (Cannes is lovely, by the way), Italian Riviera, Munich, Vienna, Berlin—then, God knows. But *probably* we'll be back in America in May, & I'll settle down to writing the new novel, which I have been pondering endlessly. . . . The play which I started with Phil Goodman proved N.G., & we chucked it; anyway we had two agreeable weeks in Munich.

You *must* plan to go out to Siam (via China perhaps, or India if by way of Europe) in fall of next year.

Ever,
Red

Hotel de L'Hermitage
Monte Carlo
March 26

Dear Alf:

I have your warming letter of March 11. Grace & I are *really* enjoying our progress along the Riviera—Cannes charming, Monte Carlo really sensationally beautiful with its gardens between sea & abrupt mountains. And we've peered at Hyères (Mrs. Wharton likes *Arrowsmith* best of all), Marseilles, Carcassonne, Nîmes, Avignon. . . . From here we go to the Italian Riviera—esp. San Remo & Porto Fino—then north to Munich, Berlin, Vienna. . . . In eight weeks or so I'll be settling down to the new novel, tho' whether abroad or in U.S. we haven't yet decided. . . . G. has had a touch of 'flu but she is all right now, & we feel fine. . . . The new novel will be, I hope, not over 100,000 words, & be ready for publication in fall of 1926—I *hope*—and (I HOPE) be quite of the quality of the last three. . . . I think it should certainly *not* be serialized, & I am enclosing a letter on that subject to the Designer.

Our most affectionate greetings,

Red

Any thoughts on pulling wires for *Martin* for Nobel prize?

[*Enclosure*]

March 26

Loren Palmer, Esq.
Butterick Magazines

Dear Mr. Palmer:

Greetings! I am writing from Monte Carlo—the lights have just gone on in Monaco across the little harbor, the yachts are twinkling, and it is the perfect stage-set. What is perhaps more important is that I am trying to get used to a Corona again after long use of a Royal, and my typing hasn't perhaps the perfection it displayed when I used to be valet-secretary to the King of Iceland.

Your letter of March 10 has just come in. I am delighted that *Arrowsmith* should have been enough of a success as a serial so that you should want to hear about my next novel. But in the first place that novel isn't as yet even started—I've been taking my first long loaf in years—and in the second place I doubt if it will be available for any serial use whatever, both because as it now outlines itself in my head, it has no suitability for serial use, and because I don't want to get into the habit of having things serialized. With *Arrowsmith* it was all right, because the novel was complete, at least in its first draft, before I had the slightest notion that it ever would be serialized, so I did not work toward that purpose ever. But if I knew, or even rather thought, that the new book was to be serialized, it would badly cramp my style—rob me of the freedom without which very few decent novels are written.

One might say, "But why not just work ahead, forgetting all about serial purposes, in complete freedom, then consider serialization afterward?" Because one doesn't work that way; even a subconscious notion of serialization would cause one to insert this and omit that—especially when one has had as dreadfully much practical experience in magazine hacking as in the past I have had.

I'm awfully grateful to you for your interest, please understand that definitely, but unless I should happen to go broke some day, or happen by an improbable chance to turn out something really splendidly suitable to serialization—some romantic interlude between longer books—I don't believe I'll ever have another book serialized.

Sincerely yours,
Sinclair Lewis

April 4
Dear Red:

I was awfully glad to hear that you are thinking of coming over to this side before long. Seven months in Europe and five months here is not a bad program.

Everyone is discussing *Arrowsmith*, at least when I am around, from all possible angles. One night I dined with a well-known children's specialist who seemed to have been neglecting what little sleep his practice afforded him in order to finish the book. He said that the medical profession ought to offer you a vote of thanks for exposing all the cant, hypocrisy and bunk that go with that job. The "tonsil snatcher" had gotten under his skin, just the same, and he assured me that for a long time he had been intending to give up that lucrative branch of his work.

The attitude of the English critic seems to me to be much less complicated and more straightforward than the American, and I think the reason behind it is that the American critic is not quite able to get over a feeling of resentment which he is not willing openly to profess. You have attacked American materialism (let us say) and you sell enormously. Here are two crimes which irritate these gentlemen. The English critic is delighted to have you strike at American crudities, since he belongs to the country of Wells, Bennett, and Galsworthy, and he has sense enough to know that a great writer may also be extremely popular. This may seem nonsense to you, and anyhow it doesn't really matter. Over here some of the adherents of the Boyd clique have come around to your side. The Bookman published its first fair estimate of you as a writer in Grant Overton's article, which I am sending you, and Burton Rascoe has flung his floral tribute at your feet. The attitudes of Broun, Stallings and F.P.A., representing the World, of course, have been curious. The book has never been competently reviewed there, and after Stallings' first review (which seems to me to be entirely unworthy of him) the paper has said nothing beyond a few digs. Personally, I think Stallings is a little shaky about it. He came in to tell me that you were a great man, that he took his hat off to you, and that you were the greatest journalist writing fiction since Dickens (whatever that means). We are maintaining an attitude of polite reserve accentuated by daily advertising in the World, and it will be amusing to watch the final result. It's a rather interesting illustration of American criticism, to my mind. Stallings, busy in California with a movie, reads the book and writes his review at a time when he is too busy and too angry to write about anything, and certainly in no mood to consider so important a book as a new novel by you. His pride would not allow him to recant, and since he is attached to the World the rest of the paper backs him up. Oh well, what's the use! As Alice said, they are only a pack of cards. The writers whom I meet and the people who merely live and read books now and then have no reserves about it. They like it enormously.

Claire [1] sails on the *Orduna* on April 25th with the whole outfit, and in addition her mother and aunt and a friend. I shall be on the job all summer with the exception of a holiday cruise, and if you come back I want to have you spend some nights with me on board.

We're having an interesting, exciting time just now around the office, and it looks like a prosperous year. Extraordinary how fascinating this

[1] Smith's wife.

work is. You will be delighted to know that we have sold Sandburg's life of Lincoln [1] to the Pictorial for a sum which gives him over $21,000. It means putting the book off till next spring, but that can't be helped. Sandburg is one of the most lovable men in the world and has always been poor; I don't believe that he has ever been more than three or four thousand ahead of the game at any time. You can imagine what it will mean to him. This book of his is magnificent, and I doubt if it would ever have been written without Harcourt. And incidentally, there is no other publisher in America who would have had the intelligence to see the latent possibilities in Carl.

Eh bien, spring is here and I am beginning to be restless. No word from Hildebrand. It looks as if he were gone for good.

Good luck, old son, and don't forget to come back this spring. My love to Grace, if she wants it.

Yours,
Hal

Hotel Continental, München
Apr. 8

Dear Alf:

Fine trip: Riviera lovely; fine walks in hills near Genoa with Claude Washburn; Monte Carlo & Alassio especially beautiful. In 5-6 days we're off to Vienna, Budapest, Berlin. I *think* we'll probably come home late in May, & settle down while I get busy with *The Yearner*—for which I have numerous notes, & which is now well-formed in my mind.

I don't know where I'll see Don—probly not till May, in London. I've written to him in Naples.

I've seen a lot of reviews—thanks to H.B.&Co. And how go the sales? . . . All well & happy & interested.

Ever,
Red

April 10

Dear Red:

Yours of March 26th with letter to Loren Palmer is just in. You're right about this serialization business. Serialization cut down our advance orders at least 25,000, I should guess, and it dulled the edge of the event which the publication of a new book by you should be. Advance sales of *Arrowsmith* were just over 40,000. Incidentally, our record of gifts

---

[1] Carl Sandburg: ABRAHAM LINCOLN: *The Prairie Years*, 2 vols., HB&Co., 1926.

totals 1500. We sent it widely for review and to the book trade, and your suggestions and Paul's ran into a large total. Most of this is worth while, but 1500 is a hell of a lot of books, and, in general, I think a man thinks more of a book he buys than he does of a book that's given to him. The upshot of all this is that I think you're dead right in your state of mind about your next book. We'll make the whole bunch hungry for it rather than take the edge off their appetite in any way.

Heywood Broun has decided he likes the book, according to his column this morning. He is rather niggling about it, but I enclose it. We found from the Publishers' Weekly that the book was the best-selling novel in March, according to their reports.

Don gets to Rome tomorrow. He'll be home the end of May. Ellen and I are rather planning to get abroad with Hastings for a few weeks in July. Of course, wherever you are happiest is the place to write the next novel, but I rather hope it is America.

I have looked into the Nobel prize procedure. Their prize is awarded by a close corporation of professors consisting of 18 members. The procedure seems to be foggy. I have made a delicate suggestion to Stuart Sherman that he take some steps to that end from America. I have written to Cape to see what he can get done in England, and I have asked him to have your Swedish publishers see if they can start something in the Scandinavian countries, and I am sure Kurt Wolff would help.

Write when you feel like it, and of course let me have early word of your plans if you decide to come home.

Ever yours,
Alf

Hotel Sacher, Wien
Apr. 18

Dear Alf:

Superb time in Vienna—a Viennese baron whom I knew in Munich came on here with us; he is youngish, very intelligent, amusing, & a damn good banker; he's introduced us to a lot of people whom we like—& most of whom speak admirable English. . . . Vienna does not *seem* poor; there are few outer signs of poverty, but they all say they're rather discouraged. They look so to America.

To Berlin day after tomorrow, with a day in Prague on the way. I'll see Don in London—*possibly* in Paris. We'll probably sail before the 20th of May. All well.

Ever,
SL

[1925]

April 24
Dear Red:
 Much interested in what you say about coming home in May to start the new novel. I am pretty sure it will be a good thing for you to write it here. I don't know how dependent you have come to be on people and change, but why not try it? There have been some nibbles on the motion picture rights but nothing significant yet. Don is evidently having a fine time in Italy. You may be seeing him in London.
 Has anyone told you that Gene Saxton has gone from Doran's to Harper's? He is to be a side partner for Briggs. He sailed last week—I suppose to do what he can to dislocate some of G.H.D.'s British authors. It will be interesting to watch the developments both at Doran's and Harper's.

Ever yours,
Alf

Lewis returned to New York on the Albert Ballin *at the end of May with Philip Goodman, Donald Brace, and their wives.*

May 29
Dear Red:
 I am much disappointed not to be able to be at the steamer to meet you. Six weeks ago I made an engagement to go with some friends up to the Arlington Valley over the Decoration Day holiday. You will remember I have headed in that direction at this time of year for a long time. I remember the trip you and Grace and Hastings and I had there just three years ago. I really can't get out of the trip now, especially as I have told Dorothy Canfield about it, and she has the manuscript of her new novel for me to read. I will be back Tuesday night. Of course I don't know what your plans are, but I do contemplate your being in this part of the country for at least long enough for us to have a real visit. There is your old room and a warm welcome for either or both of you at the house.
 I don't understand what has happened to the book market this spring. Hood told me their sales of fiction for the last three months had been between fifty and sixty per cent of normal. Perhaps the public is pausing for breath before they decide to go off on another reading bust—maybe in a new direction. We will know more about that in the autumn.
 I have had letters from Don in London saying you were in great shape. I am eager to lay eyes on you.

Yours,
Alf

The Lewises remained in New York until the middle of June when they rented a farmhouse for the summer at Katonah, New York. During this time Lewis's contact with Harcourt, Brace was through personal visits and the telephone.

Louden Farm,
Katonah, New York
Aug. 26

Dear Don:

As to book form of short stories, etc.: My story "The Willow Walk" appeared in E. J. O'Brien's annual *Best Short Stories of* —— for, I *think*, 1918. And my article on Minnesota appeared in *The United States* (I'm not quite sure of that title) published by Liveright (1924 or 1925).[1] And I have a piece in a co-operative book on the short story edited by Blanche Colton Williams,[2] published when & by whom God only knows. And haven't Harcourt, Brace & Co. published one of my short stories in a volume edited by somebody from the West?[3]

Cheerio,
SL

Lewis came down to New York and stayed at the Shelton Hotel all of October.

New York, October 3

Dear Alf:

I told you so! I knew that the Brooklyn wizard of proofreading might easily take a whack at *Arrowsmith*, and God Almighty look at the things he has found in a book said by all scientists to be totally free from error.

Of course it would be impossible to make many (it may be impossible to make any) of the corrections indicated by him. I have red-penciled a few which you might care to use if there is ever another big edition of *Arrowsmith*. I don't, for instance, see why in the phrase "smart aleck" I should capitalize the "Aleck." True it was once a definite reference to an unknown gent named Aleck, but now it has come to be a phrase with little consideration of the personal in it.

You may remember I said the one trouble with Feipel was that he had almost no sense of humor. This is clearly indicated on the last page

[1] *These United States* edited by Ernest Gruening, Boni & Liveright, 1924.
[2] *Book of Short Stories*, Appleton, 1918.
[3] "Young Man Axelbrod" in *Short Stories* edited by H. C. Schweikert, HB&Co., 1925.

of his letter where he questions "feetball coach"—in which Pickerbough was, of course, trying to be humorous. And when he says: "What are we to understand by 'told G.U. stories' (17), 'wimpish little men' (288), 'a scad of money' (331), and 'club-tie' (410)?"; of course it isn't my fault if he doesn't get the implications any more than it would be his fault if I didn't get the implications in a letter of his.

If you want to make the red-lined corrections, you have my beneficent permission. Don't forget him as a person some day to be used on a book of, for instance, the type of Mencken's *American Language* in which, as a scholarly work, every syllable is subject to the most carping criticism (though why a carp should criticize is a question to be decided not by me but by Mr. Feipel).

Yours sincerely,
Sinclair Lewis

In this period Lewis had been at work on a short novel in which he used the Canadian trip as background. It was written primarily as a serial.

The Shelton, New York, October 24

Dear Alf:

Collier's will publish the last installment of *Mantrap* in their number for June 4, and they agree that you may publish the book any time after June 1st. I should think it might be a good thing to have it not later than June 3 so that it will catch most of the outgoing trans-Atlantic business.

Yours sincerely,
Sinclair Lewis

At the end of October Lewis sailed for Bermuda and stayed at the Hotel Frascati. Mrs. Lewis rented George Arliss's New York flat for the winter, at 157 East 75th Street.

November 6

Dear Red:

If *Mantrap* is to appear in June, it should be in our spring announcement list and have the benefit of the entire range of spring traveling. So it is time to ask you for an almost final decision on book publication. You have had all sorts of advice from all sorts of people on the question, but you know the considerations perfectly well yourself and your name goes on the book. Now that you have been away from us all for a little while, it will, I think, have fallen into order in your mind so that you will have a sure hunch as to what is best to do. So will you take a walk, think it over, and let me know?

Everything serene here; we miss your visits. I hope Bermuda is fun. Shall be glad to have letters and know how you fare.

Yours,
Alf

Hotel Frascati, Bermuda
November 10

Dear Alf:

I am extremely happy to be in Bermuda. I like it just as much as you said I would. After a week of loafing—except for a book review for Canby—I am feeling superb and now into the play with all four feet. I should think I shall be here another three weeks.

I still don't see any reason why we shouldn't publish *Mantrap* as a book. Looking back at it I recall nothing shoddy in it, and as for the critics who insist that I have no right to do anything but social documents, they may all go to hell. I have pretty much worked on that theory with them anyway and I have seen no evil results. I am enclosing a sheet giving my idea of a description of the book, and from it you may get one or two suggestions for your descriptive material.

Regards to all the shop,

Ever,
Red

P.S. I am enclosing a letter from the man who is interested in an Italian translation of *Babbitt*. Will you please take care of this? Ordinarily, of course, we refuse to give any one person the exclusive rights to translations. But from what I know of Italian publishers, I rather think that this man is absolutely correct in saying they are tricky birds to deal with and that, if they got the right to the book, they would be very likely to hire the cheapest and least competent person possible to do the translation. In any case the amount of money involved will necessarily be very small and we can't lose more than a couple of billion Russian roubles, which is the precise price of a drink of Canadian Club in the happy isle of Bermuda.

I have a letter from Mrs. Brody, the translator of *Babbitt* and *Arrowsmith*, saying that Kurt Wolff has decided after all to bring out *Arrowsmith* complete, without any cuts, although they will have to make two volumes of it, amounting in all to about 800 pages. It seems to me that those people are really giving every conceivable effort to doing a splendid job, and I'm damned glad that we are hooked up with them. As soon as you set up *Mantrap* send proofs over to Wolff—they will probably faint with joy at having at least one short book to translate . . . providing they don't think the damned thing is too lowbrow for the German savants.

Equally ever,
SL

The correspondence with the office continued while Lewis was in Bermuda and dealt chiefly with matters pertaining to Mantrap—*proofs, jacket drawing, descriptive material, and a possible sale of film rights.*

Bermuda, November 26

Dear Alf:

I shall leave here on December 12th and be in New York on the 14th, going to the Shelton. According to the way the steamers run, I shall not be able to get any mail sent later than noon of December *4th*.

The play goes on well and I feel fine. It has been a good stunt coming here. There may be a letter or two coming from you on the next two steamers (before the 12 days during which there will be no steamers at all) but in any case I'll see you in about two weeks.

I do hope you have called up Gracie once or twice and perhaps had lunch or something with her. I am going to the Shelton when I go back, but I shall certainly have Christmas with her and I hope for any number of agreeable teas and that sort of thing without impairing either her independence or mine.

Ever,
Red

After returning from Bermuda on December 14th, Lewis remained in New York and spent Christmas and New Year's in the city. A couple of weeks later he went to Kansas City to get material from friendly ministers for Elmer Gantry.

ELMER GANTRY

SEVEN
Portrait of a Preacher

[1926]
Linwood Boulevard Methodist Church,
Kansas City, Missouri
Jan 23d

Dear Don:

Here's end of galleys (of *Mantrap*). I've never been so busy in my life as I have been here, rushing around being took to warious organizations, but I feel fine & it's been darn valuable, darn interesting. Stidger [1] is a corker (& his book sermons are excellent) & has helped me a lot on preacher novel. I leave here for Santa Fe on Thur. to begin loaf—I'll buy car there or El Paso, depending on weather. Regards.

Ever,
SL

La Fonda Hotel
Santa Fe, New Mexico
Feb. 3

Dear Alf:

By this time you will know from my telegram that I found it rather cold here and that I am going on to San Francisco and work back—buying a car there—so as to see this country again in warmer weather. But cold or not it has been interesting. I spent a night at an Indian pueblo with Mary Austin and some other people in order to be there to see an Indian buffalo dance the next morning. And a damned good spectacle it was.

I got more out of Kansas City for the preacher book than could be imagined; it was not only Bill Stidger—I wrote to Don how really excel-

---

[1] William L. Stidger, pastor of Linwood Boulevard Methodist Church.

lent his book sermons are, and I hope you send him out all the books he wants—but at least a dozen other preachers of all denominations who varied from mild sympathy to real friendliness. I am going back there to start planning the book, as I can ask any one of these dozen or more preachers for the information I want, stay there a couple of months, and after that . . . God knows! I feel fine and think the adventure is in every way a great success.

Ever,
SL

February 9

Dear Red:

I am risking this to the St. Francis in Frisco. Your letter of February third came in yesterday. I was away then; my mother has had a slight stroke and I had to go to see her. In fact, Don and I were having a little holiday down in South Carolina when I was called back on account of her illness. Don is sticking out the two weeks. I saw Collier's this morning with the initial installment of *Mantrap*. They seem to play it up nicely.

I am endlessly pleased at the tone of these good letters from you. They sound as if you were having fun and going strong and running your own show. I have had some nice letters from Stidger. You can't imagine how pleased he was to have you with him. When Don and I were in Washington, I saw the big weather map in the station there and noticed how cold it was at Santa Fe—something like 26 degrees the day before— and we said that you would not be hanging around such cold parts long. I think it is sensible for you to go back when it's warmer. Keep traveling and working, and you'll be happy. Good luck!

Ever yours,
Alf

Hotel St. Francis
San Francisco
Feb. 11

Dear Alf:

San Francisco at last, and in a few days will start driving Eastward. I have a couple of ideas which I wish you would think over. You may have noticed two articles by George Sterling in the Mercury recently, one on Joaquin Miller and one on Ambrose Bierce. I wonder if we could get George to do a whole book on the golden days of California literature, with such personalities as Bierce, Miller, Jack London, Gertrude Atherton, Stoddard, etc; the old days of Carmel and Monterey; the early days of the good San Francisco cafes, and the Bohemian Club, and so on. It's not so much that any of these people, except London, were very important, as that the old life was peculiarly brilliant, gay and romantic, against a romantic background. Much of this George has gotten into the Miller article in the February Mercury. I think he might be tempted to do the book if you were interested, and if you are you had better get after him before Knopf does.

The other idea is a kind of Funk and Wagnalls stunt in which there might be a few agreeable millions. Is there at the present moment any good up-to-date household medical book—"doctor book"? If there is not, I don't see why one could not be sold to almost every household in the country. My idea would be to have it edited by someone like Dr. Morris Fishbein, editor of the Journal of the American Medical Association. Certainly as editor of this great sheet, Morris could get hold of the best people in the country. My idea would be to have chapters done by people as well known as Will Mayo, Richard or Hugh Cabot, and Pusey (I think that is the name of the big dermatologist) and to make the book a complete popular encyclopedia of diets, sanitation, preventive medicine, symptoms of diseases, and the like, with particular attention to the care of children.

If you like either of these ideas, I give them to you as a birthday present . . . I suppose you must have birthdays, though I have never caught you in the act.

Yours sincerely,
SL

February 18

Dear Red:

It was good to have even a faint talk with you over the telephone yesterday. I gather that it is a book in which Pola Negri, the movies and Gouverneur Morris are all mixed up and that you want to talk in terms of $5000 advance. That's all right as long as the advance depends on a look or more information.

The George Sterling idea is fine. I remember his articles in The Mercury. When your letter came, I reread the one on Bierce, and I have written to him making a definite proposal to publish such a book with a $500 advance if he will write it.

The family doctor book by real authorities is worth thinking about, but I think it should be done by someone more inclined to sell books by subscription or by house-to-house canvassing. And I have heard of another similar enterprise nearly ready for publication which we ought to see before we get much excited. I shrink a little from the book which is, after all, a symposium. It is such a job to drive a team of so many horses, and if the editor and the authors are good, they all ought to be well paid until the publisher hasn't much left for his labor except his pains—and they're apt to be fairly painful.

We are in the midst of February's worst weather. The soft coal smoke has added a new word to New York's vocabulary, "smog"—smoke and fog. It's worse than London! Business is good. Monty [1] and Hal and everyone are well. Don is coming back next week from a three weeks' holiday by himself in North Carolina. He seems to have had a really good time. How's your secretary working out; where have you been; and what's all the news? Dictate a good long letter to me when you have the chance.

Yours,
Alf

Del Monte Lodge
Pebble Beach, California
Feb. 19

Dear Alf:

The situation about the Pola Negri book is this: I met her here with her friend Gouverneur Morris (and, incidentally, with Valentino, to whom she is reputed to be engaged, which seems slightly doubtful). Morris told me that she had written a book—that she really HAD and that it was not by some press-agent—and I got a shot at it. After an examination of it, I rather think it is possible that she did write it—certainly it has none of the earmarks of the press-agent or literary hack. What you would have in the book is a not disgraceful performance backed up by the strength of her name. I suppose that Pola is about as well known an international actress as there is, although perhaps her screen fame is not so great as three or four others. Whether it is waxing or waning is something I cannot determine. So on the whole while I was distinctly interested in the book, I certainly did not feel like making a definite offer for it—you may remember that I have an authorization to do that in case of emergency. I telephoned you principally to find out whether you would be willing to make a fair advance with, of course, good royalty, if the book

---

[1] Although the possibility was discussed several years before, Montgomery Belgion joined the staff of Harcourt, Brace in September 1925.

should prove of interest to you. Morris is going to send the book on Pola's behalf to Paul Reynolds.[1] I wish you would call up Reynolds and tell him of your interest.

Pola herself is really a very lively and agreeable person, and while she probably thinks a good deal about the well-known sex appeal, she is certainly not the lanquid vampire, but rather lively and good fun.

We are leaving here in three days for Los Angeles, and I hope to find mail there. Where I shall get mail after that, God only knows.

Ever,
SL

P.S. Why don't Hake and my nephew Freeman [2] go to Europe together next summer? If Hake and you are for it, I think Freeman and his father could be made to see the light.

Los Angeles Biltmore
February 24th

Dear Alf:

It was good to have your letter of the 18th when I arrived here yesterday. I think that in my letter from Pebble Beach I covered almost all the news. There is nothing to add to it except that since then we have had a fine three-day drive from Pebble Beach through glorious mountains and valleys, and that we are hovering here for just a couple of days to get mail and have some laundry done. Tomorrow or next day we are off to Phoenix and Tucson, via the Imperial Valley.

Grace is going to join me in Tucson on the 6th for two or three weeks' motoring, after which she will return to New York and the kid, and I shall settle down in Kansas City to start the plan on the book. It will be terribly nice to have the hike with her—to be with her and yet not tied up to the necessity of going to parties and all the rest of the parade which is so fatiguing in New York. She is, of course, the most delightful and amusing companion conceivable for a motor hike and loves the "wide open spaces" even more than I do.

I say start the plan of the book, but actually the plan is already formed in my head in a rather complete way. It is now largely a question of developing the details of which I have already thought. I have been going to a lot of churches since I first hit Kansas City, including a fair number out here on the Coast. . . .

Go in and kiss Don, Hal, Monty and Gus on the ear for me. I have

[1] New York literary agent.
[2] Freeman Lewis, son of Lewis's doctor brother. "Hake" is Hastings Harcourt.

no particular choice as to which ear you select. Tell each of them that I have enjoyed the good long letters they have planned to write to me and have never written, and I hope they have enjoyed my equally long replies.

Ever,
SL

February 25

Dear Red:

I just have yours about the Pola Negri book; we also have your telegram with the Tucson address; and Grace was in for a visit yesterday morning with her word of your plans. So I feel quite in touch with you again. I'll call up Reynolds at once, and we'll see what we shall see about Pola Negri.

By the law of contraries, I suppose you're having glorious weather and bright sunshine. Today we're deep in rain and slush, and all the lights in the office are turned on.

The idea of Hastings and Freeman going abroad together has some points to it, but Hastings is now pretty well committed to a summer of arduous and special tutoring on the chance of making college next autumn. And when he seems to want to work so hard, I don't feel like stopping him. Also he went abroad last summer. I'd be inclined to wait on this idea for a couple of years.

Ever yours,
Alf

Santa Rita Hotel
Tucson, Ariz.
March 3

Dear Alf:

Safely in Tucson, which is a hell of a nice town with some intelligent people. It has been a great motor trip down from Pebble Beach with plenty of desert and one delightful four hours across in old Mexico with some real beer. Gracie arrives here the end of this week and we will be motoring off for three weeks or so before she returns to New York. I think there is no news except that I feel bully and am thinking constantly of the book.

Ever,
SL

[1926]

March 8
Dear Red:
Glad to have your cheerful letter from Tucson. I wish I could be with you for a week without taking the God-awful trip from here. This town has been a mess of slush and fog and dirt for the last month.

I "see by the papers" that Pola is thinking of resting in the arms of Rudolph with some permanence. I suppose it is the rebound from the attentions you paid to her.

I'll scratch my head over the matter of the second serial rights of *Mantrap*. I don't think we ought to promise them to any one yet.

Ever yours,
Alf

Somewhere in the desert between Douglas, Arizona, and Lordsburg, New Mex. . . . March 16

Dear Alf:
Neither Gracie nor myself has ever had quite so joyous a hike as we are now enjoying. She arrived in Tucson on March 6, and after we had loafed about that agreeable university town (to which I had motored from San Francisco, and where I fired my secretary, a nice boy but too damned collegian to be efficient yet) for a few days, we hired a motor caravan for a couple of weeks, and with it we are now proceeding in a delightfully slow manner on a circular tour which will bring us to Phoenix in ten days more. Then we'll drop the caravan, and go on just with my car toward Santa Fe. Perhaps Gracie will go as far as Kansas City with me; depends on how long we take on the way, because for once we are keeping ourselves from going so darn fast that we don't see anything.

We motor by ourselves, in my own car, top down, all day; then at evening we have waiting for us, in the motor caravan, a perfect dinner prepared by a Jap who is a real chef; and sleep in the bunks on the side of the car, outdoors in the soft yet rousing desert air, and wake in the morning, miles from any house, to look across cactus and sagebrush to huge rock mountains bright in the morning sun. . . . On the way we have crossed the Mexican border at Nogales for a bottle of beer; and we stayed for two days on a real ranch; and for the first time in fifteen years I was on horseback and, though naturally I got pretty sore auf der bot, I enormously enjoyed it. Great hike! And G and I have never been so serene.

Have you ever been bitten by a rattlesnake? Neither have I. I have a Winchester carbine, and I'm such a dead shot at bottles and tin cans that when I come into a grocery store, all the groceries vault howling from the shelves and hide.

Ever,
SL

March 20

Dear Red:

I am very happy over your splendid letter from "Somewhere between Douglas, Arizona, and Lordsburg, New Mexico." It does sound fine for you both. Don't hurry away from it—the days of rest and outdoors, with enough to do to keep your fingers busy.

Everything serene here. Travelers' orders are coming in encouragingly for *Mantrap*. I think we'll have advance orders for between twenty and thirty thousand on publication and then be ready for a quick turnover. I suppose some folks would tell you that advance orders would run between forty and fifty thousand. They may, but I am sort of getting the habit of prophesying minimums.

The office is pretty much shot by the flu. Monty is out at our house recovering, and three or four people are out every day with it. Upstate is particularly bad. So you're both lucky to be in Arizona. I'm going down to Pinehurst with Hastings today for a week. He is home for his spring holiday.

Ever yours,
Alf

Hotel Adams
Phoenix, Arizona
March 22

Dear Alf:

We've finished the circular tour in the motor caravan through Southern Arizona, very happily, through the most glorious mountain and desert scenery you could possibly imagine; we drop the caravan here and tomorrow Grace and I start for Santa Fe on our own. Both of us feel suberb. (That last word seems to be a cross between suburb and superb—interpret it as you will.)

I have read *Microbe Hunters* at last, and I am quite daft about it. I have never read finer drama, finer sarcasm, clearer exposition, deeper perception of human purposes; and those things must be in the writing as well as in the thought.

I note that the Los Angeles Times is going to publish *Arrowsmith*, second serial, beginning next Sunday. I had forgotten, or I never knew, that the second serial rights had been sold. How many papers are publishing it, and at what terms?

I'll be in Kansas City in about two weeks, and very keen and ready to start on the preacher book.

Ever,
SL

La Fonda Hotel
Santa Fe, New Mexico
March 29

Dear Alf:

At last we have motored into Santa Fe, the end of our motoring. According to reports, there is now mud pretty near all the way to Kansas City, and good ripe juicy mud, through which there would be no fun motoring, so I am hiring a man to drive my car on to K.C. and after a couple of days here, Grace and I are going on there by train. She will stay four or five days, then back to New York. I shall get some kind of furnished apartment and stay in K.C. at least two months. In a week from now, I hope to be hard at work on the book, for which I am very keen and ready. Next summer I may spend in the Middlewest, but wherever I am, I'll be settled down and at work. I'll probably spend next winter abroad, but I hope to have the whole first draft of the book complete before I sail, and revise it over there.

Damn it, the title *Sounding Brass* is gone. This spring Duffield's will publish a book under that title by an English girl named Ethel Mannin, one that has already run into seven editions in England. I know this because they have written asking me to do a preface for the book (which same I ain't going to do). So we must have a new title. What do you think of this? The chief character is going to be named Elmer Bloor, and what do you think of Rev. Bloor? Actually, I suppose it would be more distinctive than *Sounding Brass*, with its metaphorical nature.

I'm enclosing letter from Russia. I think you might send these people a set of my books, Hal's biography of me, and one or two of the press photographs. Charge the set to me, if you'd like. And why don't you send them Carl's *Lincoln?* How is Paul's book going?

Ever,
SL

March 30

Dear Red:

I am just back from a few days' holiday with Hastings and have your note from Phoenix. What a splendid time you and Grace must have had! I'm really happy about it.

In regard to the second serial rights of *Arrowsmith:* We finally made an arrangement for release early this year with the Reader's Syndicate, an energetic off-shoot of the McClure crowd, run by R. M. Cleveland and C. B. Brown. They set off their broadside and exploitation the middle of January, and we haven't yet had a definite report of sales. You will have a report by next month.

I have been watching the Pulitzer prize business all winter, and I'd bet about eighty to twenty that *Arrowsmith* will get the prize this year. It ought to mean something to *Arrowsmith*—how much, I don't know. It certainly will be a great help in getting *Mantrap* started, as the prize is announced at the time of the Columbia Commencement, the first week in June,[1] just when *Mantrap* is to be published.

Let me know how you organize your life and work in Kansas City. It's fine to think of you started on another novel.

Ever yours,
Alf

Hotel Ambassador,
Kansas City, Mo.
April 4

Dear Hal:

Gracie and I are safe in Kansas City, after 3200 miles of motoring, on some 2000 of which she was present. She leaves tonight for NY and tomorrow I shall be settled down in the Ambassador and busy on a definite plan for the novel. I'm going to work for a while with a Unitarian and generally disillusioned preacher who was for ten years a Methodist preacher, whom I'll use as cyclopedia for data about church organization and the like. He will not, however, have anything like the share taken by Paul in *Arrowsmith*, and it is distinctly understood that he is temporary assistant—in no sense a collaborator. . . . I'll probably stay here a couple of months, then find some reasonably cool and quiet place for work all summer. I'll doubtless go to Germany for the winter some time in the autumn, but I hope to have the first draft of the book all done before I sail. . . . It looms up better and better; lots of new dope. Grace may go to Germany in June; in that case I'll join her, say late in October.

[1] The Pulitzer Prizes are actually announced early in May.

The trip has been a great success. I wish you could have been with me in Arizona—day after day of grim mountains, desert—but not dead desert, rather alive with constantly changing flora, cactus, poppies, palo verde trees, mesquite cedars. Men who combine Western virility with some tradition of courtesy probably from Virginia. Real cow ranches and some riding. Funny little pioneer towns, then Tucson with its university and yearning would-be writers and new houses in the Spanish style, rather striking. Gorgeous sunsets behind mesas. Waking in the morning to cool sweet air. Great!

Ever,
Red

Hotel Ambassador
Kansas City
April 4

Confidential:
Dear Alf:

I hope they do award me the Pulitzer prize on *Arrowsmith*—but you know, don't you, that ever since the *Main Street* burglary,[1] I have planned that if they ever did award it to me, I would refuse it, with a polite but firm letter which I shall let the press have, and which ought to make it impossible for any one ever to accept the novel prize (not the play or history prize) thereafter without acknowledging themselves as willing to sell out. There are three chief reasons—the *Main Street* and possibly the *Babbitt* matters, the fact that a number of publishers advertise Pulitzer Prize novels not, as the award states, as "best portraying the highest standard of American morals and manners" or whatever it is but as *the* in every-way "best novel of the year," and third the whole general matter of any body arrogating to itself the right to choose a best novel.

Just on the chance that they may give me the award, I wish you would secure for me, so that I may prepare a proper answer, Robert Morss Lovett's letter denouncing them—giving away their turning down the "committee of experts"—on the matter of *Main Street*. That letter you reprinted, as an ad for *Main Street*, and should have in your files. And can you get for me the exact wording of the terms of the award—that "stand-

[1] In 1921 the Pulitzer Prize Committee selected to recommend the award for the best novel of 1920 consisted of Hamlin Garland, Stuart Sherman, and Robert Morss Lovett. Their choice was *Main Street*, but the judges rejected their nomination and selected Edith Wharton's *The Age of Innocence*. A lively dispute in the press followed the announcement, and the Committee finally published their recommendations for the sake of the record.

ard of manners and morals" stuff? If you'll be so good as to send me these two before long, I'll be ready for them.

You ask how I'm going to organize my work here. Grace leaves for NY tonight, and tomorrow I move into the Hotel above; a most agreeable small furnished apartment with two bedrooms, one of which, mit beds removed, I turn into work-room, a living room, and kitchen-dining-room. I shall have a cook of my own, but also have hotel service to fall back on. A highy disillusioned and amiable Unitarian preacher here, who was a Methodist preacher, both in city and country (for a time an assistant to Chris Reisner, who is now building the skyscraper church in NY), will work with me in the matter of facts, of exact data. I already have the story so well organized in my mind that I hope to have the whole plan done in a month, and be into the actual writing. Next summer I'll spend in some such place as a cottage on some Minnesota lake. Probably I'll go abroad, joining Grace there, in the fall; but by then I hope to have the whole first draft complete.

Besides this Unitarian, I'll have at least thirty other preachers to whom to turn for information and—though Gawd how I dread it—I shall attend various churches with frequency. . . . Hence I'd better beat it now, and go to Easter service, this gray and snowy and generally joyous Easter morn!

Ever,
SL

April 5

Dear Red:

I am glad to have your letter and the telegram giving your permanent Kansas City address. I hope to see Grace soon after she returns to New York and hear about you and your trip in more detail.

We have sent a copy of *Microbe Hunters* to Fred Howe. Paul has just shown me your letter to him about the book. He is immensely gratified to have you write to him so warmly about it. The book is doing well —it has sold a little over 5000 already and is making its way to a good sale. And then, of course, it has all sorts of chances for special sales to reading circles and Chautauquas, and we are seeing what we can do to have it made required reading in introductory courses in bacteriology.

I am not absolutely happy about *Reverend Bloor* as a title. How would the two words *The Reverend* do? Throughout small-town America, that is the general term used in referring to the local minister and stands for ministers somewhat in the same way that *Main Street* stands for the small town.

It's fine to know you're really started to work again.

Ever yours,
Alf

April 7

Dear Red:

I have yours of April fourth about the Pulitzer Prize, etc. It led me to go digging back to the old box of clippings, and I certainly did get a kick out of the recreation of those most interesting days. I enclose a copy of the advertisement in which we reproduced Lovett's letter giving the exact phrase about "the wholesome atmosphere of American life, etc." Your decision in regard to the matter is wise and fine. I only hope it turns out so that the affair can be handled with just the right gesture. It would be a little awkward, for instance, if they should send you an advance announcement and ask if you would accept.

All that you say about the organization of your work on the new novel is mighty promising. Your letters have the old-time ring, and I am glad for you and for the book. I hope your Easter eggs and lilies and hallelujahs set well.

Ever yours,
Alf

In March Lewis refused an offer from Haldeman-Julius of a small outright fee for the publication of his short stories in the Little Blue Book series. This resulted in an exchange of correspondence with Haldeman-Julius that brought about the offer of a small royalty. But since the idea of the publication by Harcourt, Brace of a volume of his short stories had come up from time to time, Lewis decided against accepting.

Kansas City, April 8

Dear Alf:

If this damned preacher book takes me long enough we may possibly want to publish a volume of my short stories between it and *Mantrap* and so I think it would be much better, particularly as there is almost no money in it (And God knows no glory) to tell Haldeman-Julius that we are not yet ready to close with him, and if he comes back with a snotty letter tell him to go to hell.

I know what you mean about the soundness of *The Reverend* as a title but there are two things against it: It might seem rather flippant and prepare the reader for a cheaply humorous book; and in England and on the continent it would have none of the connotation it would carry in this country. Fortunately, there is no hurry about the decision on this. I wish you would have the two titles *The Reverend* and *Rev. Bloor* typed out (and you might add to it a third conceivable candidate *The Salesman of Salvation*) and show them to Gus Gehrs, the Baker & Taylor people, and some good high-brow like Stuart Sherman and see what they think. I think you will find that in the long run you will like *Rev. Bloor* better and better as it becomes more distinctive in your mind, just as we all liked *Babbitt* better and better as it became more familiar to us.

    I have heard from a source quite dissociated from you your hunch that I am to receive the Pulitzer Novel Prize and so I am waiting the more eagerly for the dope which I asked you to send me. I hope you will not think that my decision in this matter is altogether insane. Certainly it is not too hasty a one; I have been thinking it over any number of times during the last five or six years, though I never could believe that they really would give me the prize.

    Gawd, the new novel goes swell. I have a perfect corker to assist me on it—the Reverend Dr. Birkhead, of whom I wrote you. He is giving me exactly the dope I need. Twenty new scenes appear every hour and at the present moment I feel fairly sure it is going to be much the biggest and much the most dramatic thing I have done.

    May God help you in your prayerful efforts, brother, and any time you need the help of the clergy call on me and I will see to it that your petition ascends to the throne of God ahead of those of Alfred Knopf, Horace Liveright or Calvin Coolidge.

Ever,
SL

April 14

Dear Red:
    I'm tremendously glad to hear from you directly, though it's extraordinary how little I have been actually out of touch with where you are and what you've been doing. Even in a desert you have the faculty of bumping into a lot of people who apparently rush to the nearest wireless station, tell the world how you look, what you said, and how many glasses of beer you just had.

    I don't know what Kansas City is like as a dwelling place, but I daresay you can stand it if anybody can; and since you have been surrounded by the Middlewest and the Rev. Bill Stidger, I don't see why it isn't as good a place to turn out the novel as anywhere else.

I haven't seen Grace yet, but I met someone who saw somebody else who saw her on the Avenue, and she appears at third-hand to be in very good form. We're getting all primed for *Mantrap* around here.

Very hastily,
Hal

April 14

Dear Red:

We have cogitated over the title. *Rev. Bloor* doesn't quite suit us. It sounds a little too satirical. We want all the church people who take their preachers seriously to read the novel. Perhaps there is a clue to the title in what we have all fallen into the habit of calling the book—"the preacher novel." Why not call it *The Preacher?* I do not like *The Salesman of Salvation*, nor does anyone else here. Perhaps a name would be all right if it were not Bloor. The right title will come between now and next fall.

How do you intend to handle the question of serialization of this book? If you want me to handle it, I'll be glad to, though you can do it just as well yourself. However, I think it would be better not to get a board of editors buzzing around you until the book is done.

Ever yours,
Alf

Kansas City, April 21

Dear Alf:

About the serialization—I should seriously doubt if there will be any serialization at all. In any case, you are quite right in saying that if there is to be, it would be asinine to let the editors even talk about it before the book is finished.

About the title: just at present I am thinking rather affectionately of: THE REVEREND DOCTOR. But it is really much too early to worry about the title at all.

Everything about the book is going superbly and we are getting fine new dramatic scenes every day. All of this damned fool preaching in pulpits and so on which I have been doing has been largely to give me a real feeling of the church from the inside.[1]

---

[1] On one of these occasions while he was addressing a congregation, Lewis defied God to strike him dead and held a watch in his hand for ten minutes.

No, I am not satisfied either with *The Preacher* or *The Reverend*. I agree with you in cutting out *The Salesman of Salvation*.

Ever,
SL

April 23

Dear Red:

I am sorry to have to inform you that the frequent and delightful exchange of letters between us that has done so much to make a long winter endurable will have to be interrupted because I am sailing tonight on the *Majestic* to spend about three weeks at 10 Bury Street. I don't know whether you realize that you have been in England every time I have been there so far, and I expect I shall be thinking of you there perhaps even more often than I do here, which is oftener than you think from my letters. I see you're being mentioned frequently in the newspapers these days.

With all my blessings,

Yours,
Don

April 23

Dear Red:

I saw in the paper that the Pulitzer Prize organization met at Columbia University yesterday, and this morning I notice that the office is forwarding to you "a personal and confidential" communication from the secretary of the University.

I just have your letter of the 21st. What you say about your doubts of serializing the preacher novel warms my heart. If you can afford it when the time comes, it may be just the thing to forego. I like *The Reverend Doctor* as a title.

Your preaching business has stirred this part of the country. I enclose a couple of typical clippings and a letter. It is extraordinary the number of letters and telephone calls we have had about it. Luck and love!

Yours,
Alf

Kansas City, April 24

Dear Hal:

I have been delighted to receive your weekly letter—in the spirit—and almost overwhelmed with astonishment to receive one of them in black and white. I am getting into the preacher book with both feet and it looks excellent.

I am going to spend the summer somewhere in the Middle West working on the preacher book and then join Gracie in Germany in the fall. I expect to have a cottage, and a reasonably comfortable one, on some lake in Northern Minnesota or Wisconsin. Why don't you get away from your damned ocean for a while and come out and join me?

Ever,
Red

Kansas City, April 26

Personal and Confidential
Dear Alf:

Well, doggone it, it's happened—I've got the Pulitzer Prize, and I've been spending about as much time in refusing this thousand dollars as ordinarily I'd spend in earning it.

The following is the letter received yesterday afternoon:

April 23, 1926

My dear Mr. Lewis

I take very great pleasure in notifying you, in confidence, that the prize of $1000, established by the will of the late Joseph Pulitzer for the best American novel published during the year 1925 has been awarded to *Arrowsmith*, published by Harcourt, Brace and Co.

Public announcement of this prize will not be made until Monday, May 3rd, and in due course a check covering the amount of the prize will be sent to you.

Very truly yours
Frank D. Fackenthal

So. This gives us plenty of time. Go over with the greatest care the draft of my letter of refusal which I am enclosing. You have asked me to write them *lightly* but my God, you can't refuse a thing like this without giving reasons and without having in that refusal a document which stands on its own feet, completely self-explanatory. But I have tried to make it as unflamboyant—and as short—as I could while including everything necessary. I'm meekly (well—so so) willing to hear any criticisms. . . . I think you might have Don look it over and, still more, JES—both because of Jes's literary attainments and because of his hatred of the machine at which I want to hit. Do have him! Then I'll send it to them after May 5th. Perhaps you'd better wire me what changes Spingarn and Don and you think 'd better be made in the letter.

An asinine, fantastic, useless, expensive gesture, refusing this prize.

But . . . I can do no other. By the way, of course $250 of the prize would be coming to Paul, and if he wants, I'll pay him that rite now, or you are authorized to do so for me. I can't write to Paul himself; there has been no friendliness in his letters, no interest, and I'm through with the vain task of trying to pump it up. But he has every right to the quarter which I am thus arbitrarily refusing for him. Tell him so, when you see him.

You probably realize that most or all of this idiotic appearing in pulpits and general ecclesiastical hell-raising is to have the chance to be behind the scenes, completely in, with church matters, and it has worked like a charm. I have a Sunday School class of 15 preachers who meet for lunch every Wednesday noon and whom I razz amiably . . . and who like me. The definite plan is going down, fast, and all looks well. . . . Then lakeside quiet, and the book itself.

Let me know, P.D.Q., by wire or letter, what you think of my letter, and wht plans for issuing same to great heart of genl public.

Ever

SL

I *must* have in that Natl Inst Arts Letters stuff to make a complete case. They never let the news of my refusal out. I was too polite!

You remember, don't you, that "I can do no other" was Luther's justification.

April 29

Dear Red:

Joel and I have just had lunch over the Pulitzer Prize business, and we have gone over your statement with eagle eyes. Did you notice that the formal letter to you contained the phrase "for the best American novel" which is quite different from the actual wording of the prize conditions. Joel recalled a circumstance to my memory which I had forgotten. Since the *Main Street* affair, the committee recommended George Kelly's play *The Show-Off* for the Prize. Brander Matthews saw President Butler and had the Prize awarded to Hatcher Hughes's *Hell Bent for Heaven*—which is another instance of the dubious administration.

It would be even better if the press carried the announcement that you had won the Prize for a day or two, and then the announcement of your refusal. I think the Associated Press would prefer to carry it on the Kansas City date line, and I suggest that you hand your statement to their Kansas City correspondent. In the meantime, send me a copy in its final form, and I'll telegraph you when I have received it, so that at the same

[1926]

time you hand it to the Kansas City man I can take it to a friend of mine in the Associated Press upstairs.

Now as to the statement. It is not quite serious and dignified enough in tone. You're taking your proper position as the champion of the artist. You are not attacking the Y.M.C.A. or the taste of suburban dinner-tables —they may really be sympathetic to your point of view. What you're doing are three things: objecting to the standard set up in the Foundation; objecting to the misrepresentation of the standard; objecting to the dubious administration of the awards. And fourth, you're objecting to literary prizes and academies in general.

I think you might make a little more of the administration of the award. "Changing prize committee" is a loose phrase. The committee which recommends a book for the Prize is one thing: they are the people who recommended *Main Street*, for instance. The actual awarders of the Prize are the people to whom you refer by the words "imperial power." This should be cleaned up a little.

I would be definite and say that you declined election to the Institute of Arts and Letters some years ago, as this shows the consistent policy on your part.

The last sentence of the statement is a little gooey, and I don't know whether it is so damned "innocently" or not. I have pencilled in an idea for a concluding phrase, on which you might easily improve.

That's that. Congratulations and best wishes! I have had more fun over this since your letter arrived yesterday afternoon than anything else in a long while.

Ever yours,
Alf

Kansas City, Sunday, May 2

Dear Alf:

I have gone over all your comments with care and have, I think, accepted all your changes, besides making quite a few on my own behalf. The present form of the statement seems to be pretty compact.

I am enclosing two copies, one for yourself, one for the A.P. My many thanks for your labors on this. Joel has sent me a fine telegram which I much appreciate. Thank him for me if you see him.

The book tramps right on. I *couldn't* have a better man than Birkhead to give me dope. Personally most charming as well as most learned, young enough to be comradely, he has had ten years as a Methodist preacher, ten as a Unitarian, both observantly; and though he doesn't even smoke, he enjoys language of the type made holy by Paul and Spike and myself.

I'll be here two more weeks; then a week's interregnum while I motor to Minnesota and look over cottages; then settled down again for at least three months.

Ever,
SL

PS Have you taken up with Paul the question of the $250 which this causes me to owe him? Let me know details of what writers and publishers say privately about my Pulitzer Prize insanity. Lots of them will just call it publicity-hounding. The previous prize winners will probably all be sore—especially Booth Tarkington, who has twice accepted it (and for one bum novel, along with one good one).

This summer would be your inspired chance for Ellen, Hake & you to ship car by boat to Chicago or Duluth. Come see me for a few days, then motor to Yellowstone Park or farther, & let Hake & some friend drive back.

Letter to the Pulitzer Prize Committee which was enclosed in Lewis's letter of the second and which was later given to the Associated Press:

Sirs:

I wish to acknowledge your choice of my novel *Arrowsmith* for the Pulitzer Prize. That prize I must refuse, and my refusal would be meaningless unless I explained the reasons.

All prizes, like all titles, are dangerous. The seekers for prizes tend to labor not for inherent excellence but for alien rewards; they tend to write this, or timorously to avoid writing that, in order to tickle the prejudices of a haphazard committee. And the Pulitzer Prize for Novels is peculiarly objectionable because the terms of it have been constantly and grievously misrepresented.

Those terms are that the prize shall be given "for the American novel published during the year which shall best present the wholesome atmosphere of American life, and the highest standard of American manners and manhood." This phrase, if it means anything whatever, would appear to mean that the appraisal of the novels shall be made not according to their actual literary merit but in obedience to whatever code of Good Form may chance to be popular at the moment.

That there is such a limitation of the award is little understood. Because of the condensed manner in which the announcement is usually reported, and because certain publishers have trumpeted that any novel which has received the Pulitzer Prize has thus been established without

[1926]

qualification as *the best* novel, the public has come to believe that the prize is the highest honor which an American novelist can receive.

The Pulitzer Prize for Novels signifies, already, much more than a convenient thousand dollars to be accepted even by such writers as smile secretly at the actual wording of the terms. It is tending to become a sanctified tradition. There is a general belief that the administrators of the prize are a pontifical body with the discernment and the power to grant the prize as the ultimate proof of merit. It is believed that they are always guided by a committee of responsible critics, though in the case both of this and other Pulitzer Prizes, the administrators can, and sometimes do, quite arbitrarily reject the recommendations of their supposed advisers.

If already the Pulitzer Prize is so important, it is not absurd to suggest that in another generation it may, with the actual terms of the award ignored, become the one thing for which any ambitious novelist will strive; and the administrators of the prize may become a supreme court, a college of cardinals, so rooted and so sacred that to challenge them will be to commit blasphemy. Such is the French Academy, and we have had the spectacle of even an Anatole France intriguing for election.

Only by regularly refusing the Pulitzer Prize can novelists keep such a power from being permanently set up over them.

Between the Pulitzer Prizes, the American Academy of Arts and Letters and its training-school the National Institute of Arts and Letters, amateur boards of censorship, and the inquisition of earnest literary ladies, every compulsion is put upon writers to become safe, polite, obedient, and sterile. In protest, I declined election to the National Institute of Arts and Letters some years ago, and now I must decline the Pulitzer Prize.

I invite other writers to consider the fact that by accepting the prizes and approval of these vague institutions, we are admitting their authority, publicly confirming them as the final judges of literary excellence, and I inquire whether any prize is worth that subservience.

I am, sirs,

Yours sincerely,
Sinclair Lewis

May 4

Dear Red:

It is late because we have been standing on our heads to do a prompt and careful job on your statement. You have done a perfect job and I am proud of you.

The Associated Press here will distribute it tomorrow for release in the papers Thursday morning. They did not want it given to the A.P. in

Kansas City, as that might cause confusion. They have promised to send it complete to the New York, Boston and Chicago press. And they may send it complete to the entire country; they cannot promise that because of the British strike. We are sending out a thousand copies by mail, with the following statement:

> The Associated Press is distributing the enclosed letter for release Thursday A.M., May sixth. It is desirable that you have the complete text herewith.

In addition to the press, we are sending this to the Publishers' Weekly, the weeklies and monthlies, our list of booksellers and clerks, and to a careful list of about a hundred authors, such as Dreiser, Sandburg, Anderson, Cather, Mencken, etc. I went over the "best-selling" list for three years, and a list of best novels to catch all the most important names from Upton Sinclair to Hendrik Van Loon and from Ellen Glasgow to Edith Wharton. I am also sending the letter to the editors of such journals as the Christian Science Monitor. So I guess we have done a complete job. Tomorrow I shall send some to people in England who would be interested, including Don.

Macy's have just telephoned for a hundred *Arrowsmith*. I think the reaction will be splendid. Laurence Stallings came in yesterday morning and said, "Wouldn't it be splendid if Lewis would refuse the Pulitzer prize!" And I had all I could do to keep my mouth shut. That's all tonight. Fine business! Now sit tight and don't say a word.

Yours,
Alf

May 5

Dear Red:

Well, you certainly got a run for your money on the news of your refusal of the Pulitzer Prize. The Associated Press office is on the floor above us, and we have become acquainted with some of the people there. I discussed the policy of its release with them on a friendly basis. They promised complete distribution if they could handle it here. They carried the letter in full, as you will see by the enclosed sheets, which comprise a summary story released at 4:01 P.M., followed by the complete letter at 4:07, Pulitzer's comment at 7:35, and a day story for today sent at 1:45 A.M. I think I'd like to have you return these to me to stick in my first edition copy of *Arrowsmith*.

I have had the office send you clippings from the New York press. The World, Times, and Tribune made a first page story of it; in fact, your picture illustrating the story was the only one on the first page of the Tribune this morning.

The A.P. said the only thing that could interfere would be news of a revolution in England [1] or some such matter, which might swamp their facilities. To insure against this, I mailed a copy of your statement in full, special delivery, to the important papers in Boston, Philadelphia, Chicago, and New York.

I am glad you are going up to Minnesota for three months' work. I think it will be better for the book if the first draft gets done in this country.

It has been a beautiful job, Red. I'm proud to have had something to do with it.

Ever yours,
Alf

Kansas City, May 7

Dear Alf:

I have had so many corking letters from you in the last few days that to answer them in detail would take a month and so I shall reserve all of that energy for my loving little volume about the preachers and merely say that I am extremely grateful to you for the hundred things that you have done for me in this Pulitzer business and damn glad that you like the letter to the Pulitzer prize committee in its final form. I am sending some of the telegrams which I have received to Gracie and she will sooner or later show them to you. I cannot imagine a more thorough job than you are doing in sending out the complete copy of the letter to publications and authors. I am carefully avoiding making any comments on the comments which are wired from New York here and I more or less have the newspaper men working with me on this to keep fool wisecracks out of the press.

Ever,
SL

May 10

Dear Red:

I don't suppose there will be any more significant comment on the refusal until the weeklies and monthlies come along. I won't send on any more clippings unless something significant appears. In the first place, you've done a good job and might as well throw it over your shoulder;

[1] The general strike in England had aroused apprehensions.

in the second place, with Don in England and Gus at the St. Louis Convention, I'm very busy. Incidentally, business is good. It looks as if our sales would run over a million dollars this year.

Ever yours,
Alf

Kansas City, May 11

Dear Alf:

I am returning the Associated Press story herewith, and sending you a hell of a lot of stray letters which have come in from odds and ends of people. All these letters have been answered. When you are through with them, I wish you would send them up to Gracie and tell her to chuck them into the basket when she has looked them over. Tell her that if she sends them back to me I will make a special trip to New York to fight her.

I think you handled the whole business magnificently, and apparently there has been no confusion except in the delayed receipt of my letter by the Prize Committee. There came pretty near being a bad break here in the Star's getting the story too early, but a reporter risked his job by holding the story out on them for several hours so that they would not spring it too early. I must remember this incident whenever I get sore at the reporters for doing too much blabbing.

As I shall be leaving here next Monday, you will get this letter just about in time to make a change in my address. Until I wire you my summer address in northern Minnesota, please send my mail care of Dr. E. J. Lewis, Sauk Centre, Minn.

I am not going to send you these two letters [1] (of which copies are enclosed) but I think you will be glad to see the copies and know that my brothers in the church are sticking by their bishop when he is under fire by the sinful of the world.

Sincerely yours,
Sinclair Lewis

P.S. The enclosed picture may amuse you. I don't know whether or not I have told you anything about my Sunday School class. I have had from fifteen to twenty preachers coming to lunch with me every Wednesday, and I have had rather remarkable luck in asking them impertinent questions about why they are ministers. This is a photograph of one of the smaller meetings of the class taken out on the roof of the Ambassador, and in the picture No. 1 is Dr. Hanson, Methodist preacher and head of the Methodist Book Concern here in Kansas City. No. 2 is Bill Stidger of

---

[1] Congratulatory letters from Henry Mencken and George Jean Nathan.

[1926]

whom you have already heard a great deal. 3 and 4 are Shively and Rutherford, both Christian (Campbellite) preachers. No. 5 is Birkhead, the Unitarian, who is working with me on the book and who will spend all summer with me in the north, accompanied by his wife and boy (as Mrs. Birkhead is taking this dictation I cannot tell you what a low hound this preacher is, so I will have to confide that to you later). If you do take my dare and motor through Minnesota and westward this summer, as I hope to God you will, you will meet the Birkheads and find what a pious, pure, noble unblasphemous soul the Reverend father is. (Let me again remind you that as I am dictating this to Mrs. B. I don't mean any of these things, but will explain them in private later.)

No. 6 is Roberts, who is a completely modernist preacher of the John Haynes Holmes type. No. 7 is J. C. Maupin—you may remember reading in the paper about his successfully running for mayor as a modernist in Clarence, Mo. He is an ex-Baptist preacher who saved his soul by chucking the whole damn thing. 8 and 9 are a couple of laymen who were in as guests. 10 is Rabbi Mayer, the most important Jewish preacher in town. 11 is Burris Jenkins, who is, perhaps, the best known preacher in town, or indeed in all this section of the world. He is a Campbellite and it was in his pulpit that I spoke up to papa God. 13 is Clarence Reidenbach, a Congregationalist preacher, who is the president of the Ministerial Alliance here. 14 is the Rev. Earl Blackman, Burris Jenkins' assistant, former national chaplain of the American Legion, and one of the nicest fellows I ever met in my life. He is going to drive to northern Minnesota with me just for the trip.

No. 15 is Sam Harkness, Presbyterian preacher. He is coming to New York, by the way, in a few days, and I have given him a joint letter of introduction to you, Hal and Monty. He is a devil of a nice fellow personally—I think you will like him very much indeed, and he will be able to tell you at first hand all about the Sunday School class, about my contact with the preachers in Kansas City, and about my prospects for doing a really good book on the ministry. As to No. 12, that is the Right Reverend Bishop Doctor Lewis, the teacher of the class.

(*Some* P.S. says Mrs. Birkhead.)

May 17

Dear Red:

Thanks for your note and the further letters. The picture of your Sunday school class is fine.

It doesn't appear possible for us to get out to the coast this summer. Ellen and I may get to Chicago on a semi-business trip and might run out to see you from there. But even that is doubtful. Hastings is going to a summer school in Maine to polish off some college entrance points, and I am looking forward to hanging around here except for short holidays.

Ever yours,
Alf

There was only one more brief letter from Lewis from Kansas City written on the eve of his departure and concerned with minor matters. No further word was received from him until his letter of May 29th.

Star Route #2,
Pequot, Minn.
May 29

Dear Alf:

There's my address for the summer. It's not a luxurious cottage, but comfortable, and its charm is its location. It's amid a hundred acres of my own (temporarily) land, with a mile of shore front, fine sandy beach of Lake Pelican, so that I'll be absolutely secluded for work. Yet the roads are fine, and only five miles away is the best summer hotel in Minnesota, so that I can have a dance or a good dinner when I get sick of solitude. Mit fine swimming, fishing, tramping through largely unspoiled woods.

I'm writing from Sauk Centre, but I'll leave here about next Wednesday, and be on the job about Thursday, really hard at work, for the plan is all done and I'm ready to start the book itself.

Fine hike from Chicago here and north and back again, and I'm keen as mustard.

Ever,
SL

June 1

Dear Red:

It's good to have your address for the summer. We are publishing a novel entitled *Mantrap* the day after tomorrow. The advance orders will be between twenty-five and thirty thousand. The orders are best where the buyers have read the book. Even your old friendly enemy, Doc Wells [1] of the Powers Mercantile Company, Minneapolis, writes me an enthusiastic letter about it. You must know there is nothing that is more fun around this office than to publish a novel by S.L.

Ever yours,
Alf

[1] Leonard S. Wells, buyer for the book department, Powers Mercantile Company.

Pequot, Minn.
June 9

Dear Alf:

I have changed the name Elmer Bloor to MYRON MELLISH. Among the other objections to Bloor was one you more or less hinted at—it is so ugly, so scornful, that it prejudices the reader too early. I tried out *Elmer Mellish,* but the El-muh-mel assonance is bad. Myron has just the same color as Elmer, and I'm fairly well satisfied with the name now. I can see it in church notices, "The Rev. Dr. Myron Mellish will preach——"

Among other virtues of Mellish is: so far as I know, no one has that actual name—its made up from Melhuish. Now as Mellish is so much less objectionable, so much less indicative than Bloor, you may have less objection to the title *The Rev. Dr. Mellish.* But I'd be perfectly content with any of these three: THE REV. DR. MELLISH—REVEREND MELLISH—THE REVEREND DOCTOR. As I told you, my only point for holding out for the name in the title in this sulky way is that having the name of the man in the title makes people remember it so much better—it identifies the man and the book. For the present I'm going to call the book *The Reverend Doctor,* but will you please brood on all three from time to time.

All settled, and the book actually started. And tell Monty my invitation is opener than ever.

Ever,
SL

Doesn't this sound like *M. St.-Babbitt* days? The fussing that gets somewhere?

June 12

Dear Red:

The way *Mantrap* is getting along is fairly summed up in the two clippings enclosed. Broun, as you can see, likes it; the Brooklyn Eagle doesn't like it and reports it is the best selling novel in Brooklyn.

Myron Mellish is better than Elmer Bloor. Of the titles you give, both Monty and I like *The Reverend Doctor* best at first blush. But Monty is the only one I have had time to show the letter to yet. *Myron Mellish* might not be a bad title.

It's fine to think of you at work by a nice lake.

Ever yours,
Alf

>   Pequot, Minn.
>   June 12
>
> Dear Dr. Harcourt:
>
> No, Myron Mellish is not right. Besides, proves there was or is a well-known Episcopalian preacher, Howard Mellish. The name now is—and I hope will continue to be—ELMER GANTRY. Say it aloud. See if you don't like the sharp sound of the Gantry.
>
>   Ever,
>   SL

>   June 15
>
> Dear Red:
>
> Mellish was and Mellish is a rather "ishy" name. Gantry has a better bite.
>
>   Ever yours,
>   Alf

>   June 24
>
> Dear Red:
>
> The news about *Mantrap* is so-so—a steady sale but no walk-away. Publication date was the third of June, and we have actually shipped out a little over 30,000 copies. This is good but not wonderful.
>
> I hope the place and the book and everything go well with you.
>
>   Ever yours,
>   Alf

Only brief business notes were received from Lewis in this period when he was starting to write Elmer Gantry. *While he was in Pequot, Minnesota, Mrs. Lewis sailed on the* Mauretania *June 9th for Paris.*

>   Pequot, Minn.
>   July 22
>
> Dear Alf:
>
> Everything goes on well and steadily, and the Reverend Dr. Gantry progresses in holiness. Gracie seems to be having a quiet but very happy time in Austria after a good stay in Switzerland.
>
> I don't know what my plans will be after I leave here, but I am pretty sure that the novel will take me five or six more months, and I am

hesitating about going abroad before finishing it. I may possibly get a house in Washington for part or all of the winter.

Ever,
SL

Pequot, Minn.
August 1

Dear Don:

Thank you very much for letting me see the interesting English reviews of *Mantrap*, which I am returning. You have noticed the Atlantic Monthly review, haven't you? One of the best. Do you start advertising the book again soon? I've seen no advertising of it of late. I don't, of course, expect anything extravagant if the thing won't go over, but hasn't it a chance as a fall book?

I imagine the preacher book will have a chance to rival *Main St* and *Babbitt*. It's going on steadily, and looks good to me. I'd hoped to have it done by October first, but it'll be nearer January 1st; also I'd hoped to go abroad this fall but just now I don't want to leave the country till I have it all done and the galleys read. So when I leave here, some time in September, I'll probably go to Washington for part or all of the winter; and I'm waiting to hear from Gracie whether she'd rather stay abroad, and have me join her as soon as the work is done, or come back in September and join me in Washington.

Affectionate regards to all.

Ever,
Red

August 7

Dear Red:

I am just back at the office from a fortnight wandering around New England with Ellen in the car. We had a fine holiday. Don has shown me your letter of August first and the English reviews of *Mantrap*. They are first-rate, aren't they? Hal has just started on vacation, and I can't conveniently lay my hands on proofs of recent advertisements. I know he has been using an ad made up of these British reviews pretty generally.

What you say about the preacher book sounds fine. I too believe it will have a real chance of rivalling *Main Street* and *Babbitt*, and that it will take you to more nearly January first than October first to finish it is probably a sign in that direction. I should think Washington would be a good place to finish it. I hope you have been well and that the work hasn't taken too much out of you. Still, I guess that you live more on and for writing a good novel than anything else. It's not such a bad reason for existence or work, either. I am getting endlessly curious to see part of it and hear about the story. When you switch to Washington, I can probably have a chance either here or there.

Ever yours,
Alf

In the weeks following his letter of August first, there was no word from Lewis while he continued to work on Elmer Gantry. *The office wrote him news of the sale of* Mantrap.

August Twenty-sixth

Dear Red:

We are having mysterious letters and cables about a three-act play of yours called *City Hall*. Have you been concealing something in the folds of your robe? These rumors have all come from Germany and we have seen none of the original reports in German papers. Be sure to return these enclosures.

We had a cable "Hold mail" from Grace last week. Does this mean that she's coming back and that you have planned to settle down in Washington to finish the novel? How is it and how are you?

Yours,
Alf

Pequot, Minn.
August no it ain't—
September 3

Dear Alf:

The enclosures refer to the play which Phil Goodman and I tried to write in Munich and Paris, and which was a fluke—never got beyond the first act. No such play is in existence nor likely to be, and you might tell Wolff if he hears of anybody trying to publish a play purporting to be mine, to stop it by injunction and let us know.

Yes, Gracie is sailing on the *Arabic*, due in NY the 12th, 13th, or 14th, and I expect to meet her. I'll leave here tomorrow, spend a day in Minneapolis, a couple in Chicago, and be in NY some time the end of next week. See you then! I feel fine and ready for a good winter's work. The first draft of the ms is something more than half done and tastes good.

[1926]

Yes, we expect to have a place in Washington for the winter, with maybe a Bermuda or Cuba trip when the book and proofs are done.

Ever,
SL

Lewis arrived in New York September 10 and remained the rest of the month. In October he went to Washington where he and Mrs. Lewis had rented a house at 3028 Que Street, N.W.

October 7

Dear Red:

We are beginning to fuss with the jacket and to start a whisper about *Elmer Gantry*, so it's time to ask you for help in writing a description of the new novel. Will you try your hand at the two or three hundred words you would like to have the booksellers and the critics read about it?

I hope Washington is working out well and that you are feeling fine and working like hell.

Ever yours,
Alf

3028 Que Street, N.W.
Washington, D.C.
October 8

Dear Alf:

I'm enclosing, as you requested, my biennial burst of hurt modesty about an opus of the celebrated S.L. Yes, Washington is working out beautifully; the house is charming, and I'm hard at work, with an office up on the ninth floor of the Hotel Lafayette. Our best!

Ever,
SL

Brief letters continued to be exchanged—about new photographs of Lewis, a deposit to his account, etc.

October Twenty-first

Dear Red:

And how **is** Washington agreeing with you? I understand that you and Grace have gotten a house and that you are installed near the top of a hotel. I can imagine the devil peering in your window and rubbing his wings together in the most self-satisfactory way. You are, my dear fellow, with this book of yours, his most important advocate in America. I do not think that it is possible to exaggerate the love which his Sulphurous Majesty holds for you. If we can sell a few hundred thousand copies of *Elmer* (which is the most delightfully innocent name in the world) we can probably together increase his kingdom and later on the population of the nether world by vast numbers of the faithful.

All of the above, including my solicitude for your health, is a prelude to the jacket of your book. I saw this design, with two strong bars, black and red (which are, incidentally, the devil's colors) on a foreign poster. Stand off a quarter of a mile and look at it, and I think you'll see why it is good. It really makes a powerful jacket. Alf likes it and so do I. If you agree, we'll go ahead with it.

I was sorry not to be able to see you again before you left, but I couldn't help it. There seem to be so many people on my neck these days that it is difficult to be free for more than a few odd minutes. But anyhow, sometime this fall I want to get down to see you over some weekend, if you're agreeable. As I have explained to you before, your ways as the most important novelist in the U.S.A., etc., etc. are not my ways. But that isn't any reason why a friendship that has lasted ten years or more should peter out.

Yours,
Hal

Washington, Oct. 22
Dear Hal:

I think the *Elmer Gantry* jacket design's fine, corking. Yes, I'm more than comfortably settled here; and YES, we'd both be genuinely delighted if you could come down for some weekend—whenever you can—we have lots of room and plenty servants. I have a secluded and quiet room, with splendid light and air and lots of space, and I'm simply working like the devil. I'll have the book done (be sure to tell Alf this) by the first of January all right.

Ever,
Red

Washington, Oct. 28
Dear Alf:

Seems to me the jacket of *Elmer* ought to carry prominently—and the first ads ought to carry—something to this effect: "No word of this novel has ever been published before serially or otherwise." And, for the first ads, how about something on this order:

Somehow, the whole country has learned that Sinclair Lewis, after a year spent entirely with ministers of every sort, has been writing a novel about preachers. This is it!—*Elmer Gantry*.

Corking weather for work, just cool enough, and a perfect place for it—neither the country and lake, tempting one out to play, as in Minnesota, nor the noise and phone calls of NY.

Ever,
SL

And another ad:

Sinclair Lewis's long-promised novel about preachers—this is it—etc. (WITH the hope that not too many bar-flies remaining from the old days won't get an improper memory from the once magic words "this is it.")

October 29

Dear Red:

Your suggestions about advertising are dead right, especially as to the wisdom of emphasizing that the book has not been serialized and that this is the preacher novel which has been whispered about. I am told that Cadman [1] "whispered" about it over the radio last Sunday.

Ever yours,
Alf

Washington, November 1

Dear Alf:

I am enclosing a letter from Bob Sherwood [2] which made me madder than hell. I suppose that it is in many ways permissible to be a bookseller, to be 70 and to be a hearty good fellow, and I appreciate all these things about Mr. Sherwood. I also understand that this book is his one ewe lamb and that he is trying in this letter, with very poor success, to be humorous and that he probably does not know that he is being thoroughly insulting. But I'll be damned if his position as a bookseller can force me into giving a public endorsement of a book which seems to me thoroughly third rate. So far as I can remember, I have never met the man except once, at a booksellers' dinner and that for not more than 15 minutes. I am enclosing a suggested reply to him.

Mr. Sherwood called me up at the Shelton, said that he was sending up a copy of the book, and would I read it as soon as possible. I said that

---

[1] S. Parkes Cadman, president of the Federal Council of Churches of Christ in America.

[2] Owner of Sherwood's, bookstore in Beekman Street, New York.

I would. Then came this letter, which makes me just a little bit sorer than anything that has happened to me for at least two or three hours. There is only one line I like: that is the line in which he says that I am competent to tell people to go to hell!

The next bleating lamb is this bird from a town which I should think was probably Frauenfehl in Switzerland who wants some biographical material about me. Will you please be so good as to write him, explaining that I send him my almost overpowering love and shoot him the booklet by Hal?

God, it must be interesting to be a publisher and to be in touch with the sensitive and undemanding souls of these authors.

SL

November 5

Dear Red:

Alf has been in Chicago this week, and so your letter of November first with its enclosures has been in my care. I have mailed the letter to Sherwood today. Gus agreed with me at first in thinking it would be best to make no reply to the letter at all. But this morning Gus had a letter from Sherwood telling him a lot about the progress of his book and suggesting that maybe he'd see you in Washington. Of course you would be justified in ignoring his letter except it appears that might not be the end of it and you might as well tell him now as later.

Ever yours,
Don

November 8

Dear Red:

I spent last week in Chicago—most of the time at our sprightly new textbook office out there, which has been going for over a year but which neither Don nor I had seen. So I have just read your letter of November first. You're dead right to write to Bob Sherwood as you did. Of course you don't want to boost a bum book. We had the manuscript here, and he pestered us terribly to publish it for him and got Gus pretty much involved in it. But finally I read the manuscript and got up on my hind legs and said that the man couldn't write and that I'd be Goddamned if we would publish his book.

Ever yours,
Alf

[1926]

November 18
Dear Red:

I have refrained from telling any one that the duplicate manuscript of the part of *Elmer Gantry* which I read is in our safe, as I thought it better to have the complete book burst on every one here in its full glory. But I find that Hal has unearthed this manuscript, has read it and is completely carried away by it. I think he is planning to run down to see you some time within the next two weeks or so if that falls in with your plans.

Ever yours,
Alf

Washington, November 22
Dear Alf:

In the next few days I am possibly sending to you Horace Wylie, and I want you to do absolutely everything you can for him. He is one of the most pathetic cases I know of in the world. He was once upon a time a reasonably rich man, of an old and distinguished family, sitting about clubs in Washington and playing bridge. Then he fell for our friend, Elinor Wylie-Benet. They eloped, and in order to get a divorce from his wife he had to give up every single penny he had in the world to her. Well—of course, Elinor then divorced him and married Bill. Since then he has been trying to make a living by holding down a government job. This he has lost, and I am told that he is going up to New York to try to get a job as a holiday-time book clerk in one of the department stores.

This is not the familiar case of the ex-gentleman who is a drunk and a rotter; it is the case of a man who has rather too late in life tried to be efficient. (He's probably 47.) And he has really learned to be efficient; as a book clerk he would be the man for whom every bookseller must be looking. He knows books reverently; he speaks three or four languages; he would be equally courteous to the duchess and the ditch-digger; and the poor man at the present moment has no great financial ambitions.

You know every bookseller in New York and Chicago, and please have a very serious talk with Horace, if his pride permits him to come in and talk to you, and see that he gets a job with a possibility of permanency. It would seem to me that as that genius wife of his is in New York, it would be better if he went to Chicago. I think that Marcella would throw a cat-fit of joy to have him, and that Kroch would really appreciate him. Anyway, treat him as you would treat me, except for publishing his books (thank God he hasn't any, so you're safe!).

Bob Sherwood showed up here in Washington. I had him up for a drink and he was awfully nice. I think he understands now that I am not going to push his book. He would be a darling if he only did not think that he had a sense of humor.

Ever,
SL

Early in December Lewis came to the Grosvenor Hotel in New York.

The Grosvenor,
New York,
December 17

Dear Alf, Don and Hal:

This is just a memorandum in case I forget to speak to you about it later: I wish you would be particularly careful as to who goes over my manuscript before it goes to the printers. For example I do not capitalize he and who and so on referring to the Deity and the ordinary manuscript editor would carefully change this. I am going down to Washington a week from today and before I go I shall have the complete manuscript in to you ready to start setting. I hope you will be able to make the date of publication before April 1st; possibly even March 1st, because I am absolutely dead certain that there will be rivals coming along some time this spring, so great is the present interest in religion—as for one of many examples the "Religious Census" recently running in the New York World.

Ever,
SL

Lewis left the manuscript of Elmer Gantry *with Harcourt and returned to Washington Christmas Eve.*

December 27

Dear Red:

Gantry is splendid! Ellen and I had Monty out for Christmas, so he read it over the holiday as well as Don and I. We foregathered yesterday afternoon and gloated over it and finally thought to send you a telegram. Don thinks it's the best book of the lot. For me it is the best next to *Main Street,* and for Monty it is next to *Babbitt.* Though Monty and I both admit it has excellences not quite possessed by *Main Street* and *Babbitt,* I suppose those books were our respective first loves. You should have seen Monty laughing his head off and wiping his glasses a half dozen times in the course of reading it. What a sound job it all is!

I have a few general queries. I would be inclined to let the death of Sharon go without having Elmer finding her charred body holding a piece of the cross.

I think Elmer would have been more outraged on the occasion of his visit to Shallard by what the Ku Kluxers had done to Shallard, though he would have done nothing about it afterward or publicly.

I would tone down the vulgarities of Elmer on the steamship and in London and Paris. It is a little too blatant, and he must have picked up a veneer of manners from some of his parishioners by that time. It is just a little too thick. Cutting a little will do it.

We all agree you should consider the badger game episode more carefully and either change it or substitute something for it. A girl clever enough to get away with being his secretary and unscrupulous enough to badger him would not devote so much time to so unpromising a prospect financially. The labor, time, rent of apartment, etc. involved would come to more than Elmer's resources could stand. So clever a swindler would have gone after a man with a good deal more money and worked faster. While Elmer was about due to be badly caught in some of his philandering, he might also by this time be too clever and worldly wise to write letters and be caught so completely off his guard. There are a lot of difficulties in the situation as you have done it which the above observations will suggest to you. You either have to make the secretary a semi-innocent tool in the matter or provide more carefully for a number of contingencies. It occurs to us that you have Lulu ready at hand to provide the situation. She could do something foolish or hysterical. They might be caught in some piece of carelessness by the reporter who is on to him, and then have him make final use of Lulu and Floyd or Lulu alone in a made-up affidavit and statement which will clear his skirts.

I think the thing as it is would just get by, but it's too bad to have a soft spot at the end of the book, and if you mull over this between now and when you get the proofs, I am sure you can fix it to the Queen's taste.

Although you may suspect it, you don't know what a grand novel you have written.

Ever yours,
Alf

December 27

Dear Red:

Last night I finished reading *Elmer Gantry*, and this morning the manuscript is going to the printer. It seems to me amazingly good, even for you. I am glad I waited to read it when it was final and complete. I had no preconceptions about it except such as I got from talking with you and Alf and Melville. It seems so much better than I had expected from those conversations. It is sound and true and complete; it's funny just often enough; the characters are perfect. I was astonished to find how familiar the scenes and the lingo were to me from boyhood experience which I had forgotten. I should expect there are at least a million people who will get a similar or a greater pleasure from this rediscovery.

I marked a few things in the manuscript which seemed obvious mistakes in typewriting. I queried a few others which were not so obvious. It's amazing how complete you've got the various sides and shades of religious controversy through your characters and kept them all interesting. It's a great book, and I expect it will create some excitement among the shepherds and their flocks and even in the councils of the ungodly.

Ever yours,
Don

At the end of the month Lewis was back at the Grosvenor in New York.

The Grosvenor
New York
December 31

Dear Alf:

I have kept forgetting to tell you that Secretary of Labor Davis had a brainstorm when I was in Washington, to the effect that he might write an answer to *Elmer Gantry*—he had the vaguest of ideas as to what *Elmer*'s like, but I had told him that I was writing a book lambasting religion and he is, as you probably know, very well-known among the fundamentalist Christians. Why don't you write to him and see if he is authentically interested, and if he is send him an advance copy—but not too soon before the book comes out so that he will spill too many beans. I think that the spectacle of a Cabinet Member soaring into the book will be rather pretty publicity. Incidentally he will probably write a lousy book. Incidentally he is rather a nice fellow, for a Christian.

I'd be rather glad if you gave special attention to the volume of poems by Pierre Loving which you now have in the house. He is an extremely intelligent fellow and I think it is possible that something might come out of his work.

SL

[1927]
3028 Que Street, Northwest
Washington, January 4th.

Dear Alfred:

Please have the $2000 sent to me as quickly as possible, for it is the first of the month and I am strapped. Also I am closing this house up on January 15th. I am thro, quite thro, as far as Hal is concerned. This whole Washington venture was my last gesture, and it has failed. Physically as well as mentally I have reached the limit of my endurance. My last gift to him is complete silence until the book is out and the first heated discussion dies down. For him to divorce God and wife simultaneously would be bad publicity. I am really ill at the present moment, and I will go to some sort of a sanitarium to normalize myself.

Elmer Gantry is superb. I hate every one in it but "devastating" is the only word which will describe the cumulative force of the last third of the book. It must succeed tremendously on I don't care what score.

My good wishes to you all and wish me in return strength and *peace* in the coming year.

Grace

January 5

Dear Grace:

I have your letter of the fourth, and it's a good letter. Hal was all in last week, and we finally prevailed on him to go up to Bill Brown's Training Camp, Garrison-on-the-Hudson. I got him packed up and drove him up there New Year's Eve. I haven't heard from him since, but he has returned some thirty galleys of *Elmer Gantry*, which he took up there with him, carefully and sharply corrected. I do hope he gets into better shape there and builds up some reserves to go on with.

When you say *Gantry* is superb and "devastating," you've said it exactly. We are crowding the job of publication every way we can, but we can't publish before March—I should guess the 11th. The first edition will be 100,000, and to get those made and shipped around the country so that the book will be in stock in San Francisco on publication day is going to use every moment between now and the middle of March. I think the rest cure at Bill Brown's is insurance in that direction.

I do really hope you can achieve serenity in the course of time. Of course I hope Hal can also, but those hopes are much more faint.

Ever yours,
Alf

Lewis returned to New York about the eighth, and during this period of visits and telephone calls, there were only a few letters from the office about business details.

The Grosvenor, New York
January 25

Dear Alf:

I am laying up again in the Harbor Sanitarium for three days, but I really feel fine and on Friday I shall be buzzing about town, sailing at midnight on Wednesday next week. I have an awfully good fellow—Earl Blackman of Kansas City who motored with me from Kansas City to Northern Minnesota—to go along for the first four weeks, which is all he can get away. We plan to walk in southern England or in France if the weather is bad in England, which will both be lots of fun and get me into fine shape.

Ever,
SL

Lewis and Blackman sailed for England on February second, but there is no record of the ship they went over on.

EIGHT
Trouble in Kansas City and Boston

[1927]
February 9

Dear Red:

I hope you have had a good voyage and a good rest. We thought of you on your birthday this week. I have had a long letter from Stidger. He doesn't like the book, just as you told him he wouldn't, but hopes for its success. Kansas City seems het up by talk about it, and the sale there will start with a rush; in fact, it begins to look as if it will start with a rush everywhere.

I had a note from Mencken saying it is magnificent—even better than *Babbitt*, which you know has been his favorite till now. We are taking the line that the book is a great novel in the best tradition of English fiction, so that the inevitable scrap about it will head up between the two groups of readers and go over the publishers' and, perhaps to some extent, the author's head. You wrote it; we'll sell it; the public will scrap about it.

I do hope everything is going well with you and Blackman and that you're having a fine time.

Ever yours,
Alf

c/o Guaranty Trust Co.,
1 rue des Italiens, Paris.
Feb. 24

Dear Alf:

A hundred thanks for the letter with all the news about sales, Bill Stidger's letter, etc. (When Earl Blackman returns, he'll tell you not only about the trip and my worthy self but also about an amusing lunch they all had with Bill just before Earl left Kansas City.)

We had a beautiful crossing with only two rough days, and they not rough enough to bother us at all; ten beautiful days in England, both motoring and walking; now two days in Paris; and—since Earl has to hustle back—we're off this evening for a regular hustling American Tourist trip to the Italian lakes, Venice, Florence. Then I'll settle down here for God knows how long.

I really feel very well. I *am* still tired; it'll take a couple of months more for me to get that fundamental tiredness out of my system; and I'm living as quietly as possible. I had a beautiful rest on the steamer, and it was only in London, where I saw too many people, that I dashed about too much. And meantime the planning of *Evening* goes on tranquilly.

Ever,
SL

Let me know how Ellen is (and give her my dearest love), and what you see and hear of Gracie. I shan't write you very much—as part of my rest, I'm going to keep my correspondence down as much as I can.

March 4

Dear Red:

Jonathan sails tomorrow on the *Baltic*, and you may be seeing him and getting all the news that way. We are coming up to publication date with a rush. I have never seen anything to touch the advance interest in *Gantry*. We are refusing to let all sorts of people have copies in advance or preach on it in advance or write on it in advance. But I think every one who should have a copy has had one and feels correspondingly privileged.

We have given the Associated Press material of all sorts about you and about the book so that they can write their own story. The material covers the usual biographical stuff, the Kansas City Bible Class, and that the paper used on the first edition would make a path forty inches wide from here to Chicago, and so forth, and so on. Of course we are doing the same thing with the other news services and giving them a copy of the book so that they can work up their own sensational stuff in their own way. We have been careful to include in each statement that there are no portraits of actual people in the book.

We are printing up another carload of paper, which will make the actual printing before publication 138,000. The Book-of-the-Month Club will take between 35,000 and 40,000. I expect re-orders to come in promptly.

I received this morning an advance proof of Mencken's review for

[1927]

the April Mercury. It is three pages long and perfectly splendid. Jonathan expects the book to make an enormous sensation, now that he has read it all. Rebecca West is going to review it for the Tribune. I suppose she has to as visiting critic, but it's a little too bad they couldn't find some American to do it. The Evening Post is running two reviews next week, one by Bill Woodward and one by John Roach Straton.[1] A week from now we'll have a lot of stuff to send you.

I hope you're well and having some fun. What a job it was to write that book in the time in which you did it!

Ever yours,
Alf

Elmer Gantry *was published on March 10th.*

March 11

Cable to
Lewis
Garritus
Paris

Sales about hundred thousand. News stories everywhere. Kansas Star five columns. Reviews violent either way. Clergy hot. Reorders already. Letter and clippings mailed. Everything lovely.

Harbrace

March 14

Cable to
Lewis
Garritus
Paris

Reorders Monday eighteen thousand. Controversy hot. Dont talk. Love.

Harcourt

c/o Guaranty Trust Co.,
1, rue des Italiens, Paris—which will
remain my address till notice.
Wednesday, March 23

Dear Alf:

To thank you—and all the others—in detail for the splendid and complete job of publishing, and for all the letters, cables, clippings since

[1] Pastor Calvary Baptist Church, New York City.

would be quite impossible. I can only send you my loudest thanks. I don't believe I've missed anything here.

Tomorrow I'm off for Italy. I shall wander for several weeks, with Ramon Guthrie, who's doing a translation for you and who is the most charming of people. I plan on a cottage and the Simple Outdoor Life for next summer. AND probably beginning the new novel. If there is to be a divorce, I'm not going to do anything about it till next fall, to avoid scandal.

I've just come back from a very happy motoring trip in Touraine, the great chateau country, and I'm doing nothing but loaf and see a little of Ramon, his wife, Allan Updegraff, who has become extremely nice, Ludwig and Mrs. Lewisohn. I'm feeling well but still tired, which is one reason why I want to get out of Paris and into the country.

It's been a great battle, the *Elmer* row, and I imagine it will go on. Gor, what a gratifying review Mencken's is!

I'm delighted that Ellen is about again. Give my love to her and to the boys in the firm. I'm going to write very little—as you can imagine, I've had enough of writing for a while!—but I shall think of you a lot.

Best—BEST—!
Red

March 31

Dear Red:

The flag, as you know from our reports to you, flies high. I suppose that my share of *Elmer Gantry* has been more fun than anything that has happened since I entered this distinguished office. Now and then I hear of you, too. Ramon Guthrie writes that he attended a celebration in Paris to blow off steam after *Elmer* had sold its first hundred thousand. And the other day Earl Blackman came in and I had a long talk with him. I confess that I was a good deal distressed by him. He has the most ardent faith in the proselyting powers of the book, and actually wept from sheer emotionalism when he read Mencken's review. It seemed to me an extraordinary spectacle: a Presbyterian pouring out tears of joy at Mencken's most violent attack on what he was supposed to believe in. He also expected to lose his church when he got out to Kansas City, although I have a good many doubts about that. The same day I met his "boss" (whose name I have temporarily forgotten) and liked him very much. I am sure that he will do his best for Earl. After Kansas City settles down to whatever state of grace is customary in that fair city, I expect that everything will blow over. He is really an extraordinarily fine man (that is, Blackman is); I liked his earnestness and his simplicity. And he certainly is a wiser man than when he left these shores. If after all he has to turn into an expert plumber, there are worse professions than that—among which I would include preaching in a church that believes in the damnation of infants (or maybe that's the Baptist).

Everybody asks about you and I take great joy in telling them that you never were in better health. I think it was extraordinarily lucky that you had the sense to leave the country when you did. You would have been hounded from one end of the United States to the other by tabloids and by all the freaks in Christendom.

The publicity on *Elmer Gantry* is amazing, and it still keeps pouring in. We keep a daily bulletin of sales here, and it is very amusing to watch it catch on in one territory after the other. We are advertising it, of course, in every conceivable way from here to the Pacific Ocean. I am convinced that the vast majority of people are reading it because they at heart agree with your premise. Incidentally, the antics of the good brethren out in Kansas City have been marvelous to behold. I don't know how much of this rubbish you are absorbing yourself, but I am saving for your delectation the most extraordinary nonsense that was ever put on paper. Nevertheless, one finds defenders of *Elmer* and yourself in the most surprising places. Some little paper in the South or the West will burst into song in the most astonishing way. I presume that as a result of this book a large number of editorial writers and "would-be" critics have lost their jobs; but, as I have said before, there is nothing wrong with the plumbing industry.

I dined with Grace not long ago and took her around to Bill Bullitt's. She seemed fairly cheerful, although a bad cold had seized hold of the poor girl. Wells, as I understand, is in town with her now, and I am going to look her up again before long.

I can't think of any more news from home, but when we sell the two hundred thousandth copy of *Elmer*, which isn't so far off, I think we should send you a diamond-studded wrist watch, provided you promise not to hand it over to any fair Viennese. Good luck to you. Maybe I'll be over later myself, I don't know. Irita Van Doren sails April 9th for a round of literary activities in England and France. Perhaps you will run across her. She is a little terrified at the prospect of meeting so many distinguished strangers, and would probably leap right down your throat if she saw you.

Au revoir. Alf sends his love. He's been deep all day in negotiations for the motion picture rights.

Yours,
Hal

> Hotel d'Italie,
> Venice, April 2

Dear Alf:

More cables to thank you for. The book looks like a sure 200,000, perhaps more. I haven't seen the Bennett article yet.

I had to hurry so when I was here with Blackman that I've returned, with Ramon Guthrie, and it's a joy just to drift about in a leisurely way, not try to "see things" but just let them soak in. Spring is coming, with the Lombard plain, Milan to Verona, hot, green, shining with peach and almond blossoms, with the snowy Alps beyond.

I'm going to do a couple of very short (1200 words each) articles here for the Evening Standard, London, to keep my hand in and to broaden my English audience. I may work them up into a 3000 word article for America. I may ask you to handle it for me, if Collier's find it unsuitable. I plan to write a few short stories, this next few months, for knitting; and wondering just what *Elmer* had done to my sanctified reputation I cabled Grant Overton at Collier's yesterday, "Do you still want the short stories" and got back this morning "Eager to have first shot at any short stories you do." I may do two or three while wandering, and make expenses; then decidedly again not serialize next novel.

From here I'll drift some more in Italy, then to Germany, but Paris will remain my address.

Bill Stidger in his comments on my book must have been hit hard from the way he squeals! I shan't answer him; Birkhead will do that. Thank the Lord I can keep away from reporters here. The vast Venetian press (if there is any) is almost as much interested in my existence (if any) as in the fact that Sig. Teodoro Palmieri of Chiogga has a sow which has just given birth to piglets. Cheers!

> Ever,
> SL

> April 8

Dear Red:

On March 30th we cabled you that the sales were 150,000. The book is slowing up a little, but it is still selling at an extraordinary rate—1000 or 1500 a day. I enclose a memorandum of March advertising, which is the most advertising we ever did in one month for a book; in fact, I think it is the most ever done here. We have contracted for about $5000 or $6000 more. I am sending you separately proofs of some of the recent ads.

We are all so much pleased by your warm letter of March 23rd which came drifting in this week, especially in that you sounded as if you were better and happier than when we had last heard from you. I think the trip with Ramon Guthrie must have been fun. I hope it worked out well. The plan for a cottage in France in the summer is first-rate. Everything is serene here, but you've kept us as busy as a boy killing snakes.

Ever yours,
Alf

On April 12th Harcourt went to White Sulphur Springs for a holiday. Lewis wrote him a postcard from Ragusa, Dalmatia, Yugoslavia, on Easter Day (April 17th) reading, "It's even lovelier than the Italian coast; the men still wear thick jackets and zouave pants; & I feel fine. DOBAR DAN.—SL"

April 22

Dear Red:

I have just cabled you, in answer to yours from Yugoslavia, as follows: "Sale one hundred seventy-five thousand. Continuing nicely. Boston has suppressed." I envy you your present travels, and I hope you are enjoying them as much as I expect you are.

In regard to the suppression of the book in Boston: There had been rumors that it might be suppressed, and on the 12th District Attorney Foley notified the booksellers that any further sales would be followed by prosecution under the Massachusetts law. I enclose clippings which give the important details of what happened after that. You will see that it has turned into a general fuss about books in that city, and the booksellers, frightened by the possibility of arrest, have stopped selling a great many books which have not actually been banned. The Boston press has made a great deal of the matter, and so has the press throughout the country. Of course the intelligent opinion is everywhere that the suppression has made Boston ridiculous.

There seemed to be two courses of action—one, to issue a statement to the effect that this was Boston's business and that we would stop attempting to send our travelers and to sell books there and devote ourselves to selling them to the rest of the country; the other, of course, was to take some kind of legal action. We decided in favor of attempting something of the latter sort, but I have not at any time been in favor of going up there and getting arrested and having a sensational criminal trial with at least an even chance that an Irish jury in Boston might give a verdict of guilty. I understand the jails are not too good there and the law provides for a fine *and* imprisonment up to two years. On Thursday I went up to Boston with Melville and Gus. We interviewed various people, including booksellers, the editor of the Transcript, and the president of

Little, Brown and Company, and then consulted a representative of the Brandeis firm of lawyers and decided tentatively on the following course of action.

The idea is to refuse to accept from a given dealer in Boston the return of unsold copies of the book, we suing them for the payment of these copies. In defense, they claim that the book has been declared illegal and that this is a justification for non-payment. We expect that such a suit will compel a judge to pass an opinion as to whether the book does or does not violate the law. If we lose we can carry it to a higher court; if we win the booksellers can resume selling the book. We hope to be represented by very distinguished counsel and at least get whatever credit is involved in trying to maintain your rights and our rights and the general right of freedom of the press. There is some indication that the action of the District Attorney, a nice young Irishman who took office last January, is backed by the opinion of the Catholic Church, although, of course, the book itself is not considered an attack on that church. Their paper, however, The Pilot in Boston, has printed an editorial against the book, and his action in regard to this book and even in regard to books in general is popular with a considerable section of the voters. I hope you approve of what we do, though whatever we do will be done before we have a chance to hear from you. You're lucky to be away because you would have been besieged by reporters and hecklers of all sorts if you had been here. We will report as often as there is anything definite.

Alfred has been away last week and this week for a spring vacation but will be back at the office the first of next week.

Ever yours,
Don

P.S. I have just heard since dictating the above that Hays,[1] who went up to Boston and on behalf of Liveright made a sale of *The American Tragedy* to a policeman, was found guilty in court there this morning and fined $100. Enlightenment doesn't seem to be in the ascendancy in Boston at present.

Grand Hotel Imperial
Dubrovnik, Yugoslavia
10:30 PM. Apr. 25

Dear Hal:

Sliding into the shadow of the dark mountains the good (the extraordinarily unambitious) ship has just come to rest in Valona, Albania. I've just been prowling—below where on a hatch sleep Albanian tribesmen

[1] Arthur Garfield Hays, lawyer.

[1927]

whom we took on @ Durazzo this morning—one of them with dirk & old pistol, embroidered white wool trousers & shirt, black wool jacket sashed with red, pill-box cap with turbanesque veil on it & a face half Mongol, half old Greek. Entzückend! Tomorrow Corfu; Athens in a week. I feel superb—really—& I'm planning the new novel, tho I shan't get to real work for many weeks yet. I don't believe I'll be back in America till fall, if then.

 I was so glad to have your letter of March 31, which I got 2 days ago. I hope you really *have* had fun out of *Elmer*. Your work on it has been magnificent. The violent Kansas City blokes have been asinine. I'm grateful to them for proving the book.

 I wish to God I were going to see Irita, but I shan't—probably—be near Paris or London for months.

 Do write me again & give me all the gossip. I'm so far from it.

Blessings!
Red

May 6

Dear Red:

 We've all been too busy selling books around here to be much good as correspondents. Ellen and I have had a vacation in West Virginia and I think Don wrote to you at least once while I was away. I find two good letters from you and a postcard from Dalmatia. It all sounds splendid. I hope you can get back to France this summer and start the new novel, though there's no harm in a few short stories for Collier's to keep your hand in and the bank balance fat.

 There has been an endless lot of backing and filling and discussion about dramatic and motion picture rights (of *Gantry*). Stallings went to the coast and got absorbed in making two new motion pictures. Arthur Hopkins blew hot and cold and finally they both let go. The motion picture people have been afraid they couldn't get it past Will Hays and it became clear that the best thing to do was to sell the motion picture rights from the play if we could get the play arranged for and produced. I have today signed a contract in your behalf with Robert Milton as the producer (his last success was *The Bride of the Lamb*) and Bayard Veiller as dramatist (his most conspicuous success was *Within the Law*). One reason Ann Watkins[1] and I picked Milton is his great enthusiasm for the book. I think both he and Veiller would go to the stake for it. Milton seems to

[1] New York literary agent.

have ample backing and he has a good theatre in a good location free for it in New York. You have better than the minimum terms in the Authors' league agreement in practically every contingency. Melville has looked over and in fact drew most of the final contract incorporating the ideas Ann and I had so I think it's all in order.

Ever yours,
Alfred

There was a cable from Lewis from Athens May 9th, and nothing further until his cable of May 30th from Paris. Meantime Harcourt cabled twice to Athens and wrote Lewis a letter re sales.

Cable from Paris May 30

Harbrace
New York
Why dont Grosset start intensive campaign Trail Hawk which is really story Lindbergh.[1] Can hook up with fact we born forty miles apart.
Lewis

June 1
Dear Red:

I have your Paris cables. Grosset and Dunlap say they will get right after your suggestion about *The Trail of the Hawk*.

Sales (of *Gantry*) last week bring the total to over 200,000. We decided on at least another modest burst of advertising on our own hook before we received your cable. Now we will go ahead with the full program. You must know, Red, that this continued cooperation on your part in the arithmetic of publishing is really appreciated by us. I know it's good business and really believe it increases your total income, but you're a rare bird of an author to recognize it and to work with us the way you do.

All sorts of complications have come up in regard to the Boston suit and we have finally decided to drop it. I went up to Boston on the 18th of May and spoke at a mass meeting under the auspices of the Women's City Club. There were over 1000 people at the meeting. I also saw a good many people there in regard to the situation. There seems to be a definite and strong movement on foot to have the present law changed. As it stands now, the fate of a book can be settled on the basis of any words, or paragraphs, or even phrases which might "tend to corrupt the morals

---

[1] On May 21st Charles A. Lindbergh landed in Paris after his trans-Atlantic flight in the *Spirit of St. Louis*.

[1927]

of the young." The Women's City Club, the state librarians, and a number of first-rate organizations are getting behind the movement to have the law changed. I think in the present situation a real fight on the part of a New York publisher would be apt to embarrass them, especially as our Boston attorneys (Brandeis's old firm) are extremely doubtful if we could win the case under the present statute.

It will be nice to think of you settled for the summer. I hope you will feel like starting the new novel and that you are well and happy.

Ever yours,
Alf

Several business letters were written from the office to Lewis in the following weeks, and there is evidence that a letter was received from him dated June 16th, which was apparently of some length, but which unfortunately has been lost.

June 27

Dear Red:

Thanks for all you say about Ramon Guthrie. This business is really getting to be more and more like a club in the way new authors come in almost only on the recommendation of old authors. I had a pleasant talk with Guthrie at the time we arranged with him to do the translation of Bernard Faÿ's historical book.[1] I hope you can make it clear to him that we do want him to show us his work just as soon as he is completely free to do so.

Elmer is slowing up a little. The renewed advertising is helping it some in day-to-day sales. Publicity of all sorts keeps up. How your books do get into the lingo of the country!

Your summer plans sound fine. Write whenever you feel like it.

Ever yours,
Alf

Cable from Paris, June 29

Harbrace
NY

Leaving for another walking trip. Please inform Grace. Harry Savage of Stokes has idea republish Hike and Aeroplane. Tell him this impossible for credit both themselves and me.

Lewis

[1] *The Revolutionary Spirit in France and America*, HB&Co., 1927.

Munich, July 4

Dear Alf:

I've had about enough Europe-trotting now, & in three or four weeks I'll be heading for America—arriving in four or five. I'll bring with me the ms of Ramon Guthrie's novel. It's contemporary, alive, eager—a *corker*, I think, with sales possibilities. If you're away on vacation when I arrive, I hope you'll be reachable, so I can dash up & see you. Don't let anyone outside the office know I'm coming—caution Don, Hal, Gus, Monty et al. about this. I want to avoid undesirable interviews. I'll keep my name off the steamer list.

I go from here to Dresden & Berlin, return to Paris, & sail on I don't yet know which boat. In America I'll probably go for a while to Fred Howe's place @ Nantucket & work there. Perhaps you & I can have a few days' motoring. It'll be good to see you!

SL

Munich, July 6

Dear Alf:

It occurs to me, just as I am leaving tonight for Berlin, that if Ramon Guthrie takes a little less or more time in finishing his ms and that if I am amused in Berlin and stay longer than I expect, it may be better for him to send his ms directly to you. I wish that you would give it the most immediate and careful personal attention; and that if you are to be away, you'd leave word with Don or Hal to get right after it. This is because I think most highly of the novel (my own opinion is shown by the fact that I have gone over it twice, and with great pleasure), and of Guthrie as a Harcourt author. If you want the novel as much as I hope you will, I want you to make an offer immediately, by cable, to Guthrie. He would want an advance—simply to keep going till the next novel is done—but he would be satisfied with a thousand dollars.

Though this is not an aviation or war story, but fundamentally the story of a man's love for a woman conflicting with his friendship for another man, yet the man *is* an aviator (handled quite differently from any aviator of whom I've ever read), and it would be a good thing, if possible, to seize the present aviation interest.

So will you please give it more careful attention than anything I've ever sent your way; and cable Guthrie an acceptance or rejection; and above all, do take my word that not just as regards this one novel but as regards all his potential future, Guthrie is the sort of person you are seeking as a permanent Harcourt author.

God it's hot. Maybe it is in New York, too. But *me*—I have beside me long, golden, cool glass of Munich beer!

Ever,
SL

July 17

Dear Red:

I just have your note of the Fourth of July saying that you will be back in America the end of August. It will be good to see you and to find out just how you are. I think you will enjoy Fred Howe's place and be able to get to work there. I am rather aiming to be away the end of August, but I doubt if I will be very far away and maybe you could come and join Ellen and me where we are. We'll be very careful not to let out that you are returning home.

Ever yours,
Alf

DODSWORTH

NINE

Marriage and Divorce

[1927]
Cable from Berlin Jul 24

Harbrace
New York
Staying Europe several months more. Please inform Grace.
Lewis

White Grass Ranch
Jackson's Hole, Wyoming
July 25th

Dear Alfred:

Your telegram of the 23rd has just been brought in by a cowboy, so gloriously inaccessible is this place, tho a great deal of the glory is being dimmed for me. I had planned my summer pretty much up to October 1st when last week I got a letter from Hal in Munich dated July 2nd saying he would be back in New York in six weeks and would I go to Nantucket with him for the rest of the summer. My God! seems to be the only adequate comment on this. And now today your wire comes saying he is remaining in Europe for several more months. What with the altitude of 6000 feet and my low blood pressure, and the fact that I don't sleep at nights, I think I had better return East sooner than I had planned or I'll be inviting you to a rather tasty funeral.—Even so I think you and Hastings would adore this country, but it's no place to be *un*—certainly unhappy in. Keep me posted by wire of any new developments. God bless you and God help me!
Grace

Also my watch is stopped, my typewriter is busted, and I catch field mice every night in my room.

Berlin, July 26

Dear Alf:

As I cabled you a couple of days ago, I'm not, after all, coming home this summer. I like Berlin, & I'm getting the stuff here for *Blind Giant*. In August, I'm going to have some more walking—starting in England but possibly going to Scandinavia, then settle down here, possibly for months. So I'll see Don here, I hope. I hope to see Cane.

I had a lovely week doing the abortive revolution in Vienna [1]—& flew for the first time—comfortable, & slightly monotonous—with nice little paper bags to be sick into—which I wasn't.

Seems to me there ought to be a big new ad campaign on *Elmer* in late September, (I'd come in on it, of course), with entirely new forms of ads. Reprint the freak items—Billy Sunday's attacks; the story of the man in Kansas City who was arrested for stealing an *Elmer*, etc. But emphasize this: You have heard about *E.G.*, you have talked about it, *but have you* READ *it?* You may hate it or love it, but there must be a lot to this book which has caused more talk than any book since *Main Street*. Hundreds of preachers & editorial writers have said "The book can be ignored"—& then they've 'ignored' it for a whole column or a whole sermon. What is there in the book to stir them to such passionate interest? Read it & see.

How about it?

Red

Hotel Atlantic
Der Kaiserhof
Berlin, Aug. 3

Dear Alf:

Will you please send *Our Mr. Wrenn, The Trail of the Hawk, The Job, Free Air* and *Main Street* to Mrs. Dorothy Thompson, 8 Händelstr., Tiergarten, Berlin. These are to be charged to me.

I am off in a week for a month's hiking around England. The Berliners have been particularly nice to me and I have had a lot of literary editors come and call on me. Especially nice has been Lion Feuchtwanger, the author of *Jew Süss*, who wants to dedicate a new book to me. Rowohlt (publisher) is a truly charming fellow and I am sure that he is going to do much more with my books than Wolff did.

Ever,
Red

---

[1] Lewis met Dorothy Thompson one evening in Berlin, and when as the correspondent of the *New York Evening Post* she flew to Vienna the next day, Lewis obeyed a sudden impulse to take the same plane.

[1927]

There were no letters from Lewis while he was in England. He arrived back in Germany early in September when there was an exchange of cables, and then no further communication until his letter of September 30th.

Herkules-Haus, Berlin
Sept. 30

Dear Alf:

What's the news? Does *Gantry* keep going? When will the dramatization be produced? When's Don coming? I've been settled down very peacefully in Berlin ever since my five cheerful weeks in England & the Rhineland, & just to get my hand in before starting the new novel, I've written a 15,000 word story for Mencken. Tomorrow I go to Paris to see Mel Cane before he sails, but I'll return here. I'm going to talk to him about (say nothin' of this to *nobody*) the possibilities of a Paris divorce. It's quite clear now that there never will be a reconciliation—tho' I hope & believe that Grace & I will remain friendly. Quite possibly we'll actually be friendlier than if we were tied together.

I hope the new book (the title of it begins to look more like *Exile* than *Sunset* or any of the other previous choices) won't be over 110,000 words long, & that it will be finished in the spring—possibly, thus, ready for publication a year from now. Then, I think, when I get back to America, I'll tackle *Neighbor* again. That book has remained with me, like *Main Street*, despite several failures to get it going. I'm terribly glad you've taken Guthrie's novel,[1] & I hope you like it as well as I do. Write me what you & the others think of it.

Mit as we Germans say

Herzlichen Grüss,
Red

Brace wrote to Lewis that he and Mrs. Brace were sailing for London on October 5th and expected to get to Paris about November 5th.

Berlin, Wednesday

Dear Don:

Your letter announcing your sailing came just this morning. I'm most eager to see you, but as after so long a loaf I'm up to my ears in the new book, I feel disinclined to come to London. Also, I want you to see Berlin. Can't you come up? It's only about twelve hours from London, via Hook of Holland.

[1] *Parachute*, 1928.

I'd vaguely planned to go to Russia, but I don't think I shall now; I think I'll stay here and work. The only time I plan to be out of town is this coming weekend, when I'm going to the country with a newspaperman who has a shooting box (as, I believe, such objects are called) in Thuringia. Why not skip up here for a few days, or, later, go to Paris via Berlin and Munich—stopping perhaps in Holland for a day or two on your way here?

Love to Ida. I'm feeling immense—better than I have for two or three years.

Ever,
Red

October 13

Dear Red:

I am more than glad to have your good letter of September 30th, and I am chagrined at how the weeks have slipped by without my writing to you. I had a real three weeks holiday. I think both Don and Hal have sent you some bulletins on how things were going. Sales (of *Gantry*) have really been first-rate—since the first of July 19,400, making a grand total since publication of 229,000, which is, after all, a pretty good total—easily twice that of any other novel published this year. We are trying some striking billboard stuff now as a reminder about the book, feeling that the public has seen so much of it in the newspapers and magazines that they are apt to take advertisements in such places for granted and that the law of diminishing returns is apt to get in its usual deadly work. We are going to keep right after it through the fall, and I think a total of 250,000 is pretty sure. I think, too, that as a document on the subject the book is going to have the life of a non-fiction book in addition to the life it deserves as a novel.

Melville landed yesterday, and I have just talked with him over the telephone. His report of you is fine, and you must know how happy it makes me. It's all borne out, too, by the tone of your letter and the news therein.

The dramatization is not yet in rehearsal. Veiller has had a great success with *The Trial of Mary Dugan*, which went on early in August and which will make his name bulk all the larger as your dramatist. The contract calls for production this year. I was to hear more about it this week and I'll write to you after I do.

Your news about the reason for your trip to Paris is not real news because Grace has been interested to consult me in an entirely friendly manner about her feelings and problems in regard to it. I am *sure* it's a good thing all round. I am doubly convinced that one of the most important steps in her life and yours must be taken carefully for the benefit of everybody concerned. I think this would be true of ordinary people, but with people of your prominence it's essential that there should be no possibility of a comeback. Bernie [1] and Melville know all about it, and you can safely be guided by them. I think Grace is to go to Nevada just after the first of the year, and I hope it will work out on that basis. I think it will be better for her health, for you, and for everybody if it's done that way.

We had a cable from Don this morning that he arrived in London and is at the Mayfair.

I am glad to know about the 15,000 word story for Mencken. Won't you send me a carbon copy or ask Mencken to send me early proofs? And *Exile* strikes me as just the right title for the new novel. I am glad *Neighbor* lingers with you. I have taken the contract for it out of the safe several times and given it a little pat.

Everything is serene with us. We are having a whale of a year's business. Ellen and I have bought a house on the shore of the Sound just above Greenwich where there'll be room and a welcome for you whenever you're ready. We hope to move in the end of the month. Hastings is in Meiklejohn's [2] Experimental College out at Wisconsin trying to find out what it's all about. Write again when it comes handy.

Ever yours,
Alf

October 14

Dear Red:

Continuing my letter of yesterday: The dramatization of *Gantry* is practically complete, and it goes into rehearsal early in November with production in view in December—perhaps just before Christmas. I hear that the first two acts are scrumptious; they're mainly characterization. The trouble Veiller is having now is the transition between the second and third acts.

As rumors increase about the next novel, inquiries about serial rights will also increase and folks will start pestering you. I think we have both learned it is better not to serialize, but if you should decide to, I am con-

[1] Bernard M. L. Ernst, lawyer and partner of Melville Cane.
[2] Alexander Meiklejohn, professor of philosophy and chairman, Experimental College, University of Wisconsin.

vinced you can get more for it when it's done than you can for the idea and be saved an awful lot of bother in the meantime.

Ever yours,
Alf

On October 22nd Lewis cabled that he was sailing for New York immediately, but he cabled again a few days later that he was remaining in Berlin after all.

October 25

Dear Alf:

When I telegraphed you last week that I was sailing immediately for New York, it was because it looked as though Grace would keep changing her mind, keep putting off things for months and months; and Cane had just cabled me that a German divorce, like a Paris divorce, might easily be invalidated, or at least seriously questioned, later, in the American courts. So I decided to go to Nevada myself, and get the thing really done. I had my ticket, and had my trunks completely packed, ready to be off for Hamburg tomorrow morning, when last evening came cables from both Cane and Grace, suggesting that I stay, and that it would make Grace miserable (it was such a fine, sincere wire from her) if she felt that she had made me interrupt the work on *Exile*. She is now, apparently, really ready to go West about mid-January.

It would, of course, be much better to remain here till I get *Exile* done—remain an exile myself till then! So, rather weary after getting everything done for sailing, I decided to get everything undone again and here I am, back at work (and hoping to get my trunks back from Hamburg by tomorrow!). I'll hope to be home before next summer, with the book all done; or, if I don't come myself, to have the ms in your hands early in May, or earlier, all ready for fall publication.

I'm grateful to you for all your news about *Elmer*, advertising, the play, and so on, and please go on giving me details—and please be sure to thank Hal for his letter, and his proof from the billboard people. This seems to me an excellent stunt. But I think you might also do the newspaper stunt which I suggested of a conglomeration of the principal sensational clippings about *Elmer*, because really we *are* justified in saying that since *Uncle Tom* no book has been so discussed.

I want so much to see your new house. Christen a room for me.

I've come—as I think I've written you—to have the most immense personal liking as well as business respect for Ernst Rowohlt—so much so that I hope some day for a Harcourt-Cape-Rowohlt alliance. And asking various littery gents here, I find that they have the same sort of respect for him that people who knew had for Don and you while the firm was still small. . . . Here's the sort of thing he does: Having had *Gantry* translated by quite a good man, he's having Count Montgelas, who spent several years in America, go over the proofs again, at a fair expense.

I'm hoping to see Don before he sails. I wrote him in London asking him if he couldn't come here between London and Paris, then when I expected to sail I got him on the long-distance phone and explained—now I'll explain again all over! I hope to get him here before he sails.

About the story for Mencken: It's just possible that we may want to make a small (60,000) word book out of this and three others. It's the account by a Babbitt, entirely in his own words without any comment by the author, as to how he called on Coolidge in the White House—and not till the last page do we find that he never really saw Coolidge. Of course I love this sort of drool—and it'll be my swan-song to Babbittism. I want to wait till I hear from Menck as to how it strikes him, and then, if he finds it good, I'll send you, as you suggest, a carbon of the story, and see what you think about a book of this stuff.

Alf, I haven't for years felt so serene, well, secure. You'd better get ready to publish several nice lil books by Sinclair Lewis, now that he's gone through his apprenticeship and begun to live. You delicately hint as though you had heard of Dorothy; that's why, though I'm still devoted to German beer and wine, I haven't had and, what is more curious, haven't wanted, a drop of whisky, gin, rum, brandy or any of their delightful but rather destructive little brothers for a long time now. Write me here—I'll be here till about January 1st, at least.

Ever,
SL

995 Fifth Avenue,
New York City
October 25th.

Dear Alfred:

As Hal is as much addicted to telegrams and cables as Jesse Lasky, you probably heard from him this morning. I heard the following: "All right remain Europe writing."

A few more of these colon-upsetting cables and you will receive concerning me an engraved invitation to Campbell's Luxurious Funeral Parlors. The possibility of Hal's return, just as I had calmly settled myself in the obscurity of upper Fifth Avenue until after Wells' Christmas holidays, destroyed the work of two weeks. Hal will kill me if he doesn't stay put. Cane and Ernst are corkers and so are you, but the general wear and tear is frightful.

Have you seen Charlie Shaw's almost scurrilous vignette of Hal in the last Vanity Fair? As he only knew Hal during that insane period last winter, his deductions are undoubtedly fair, but I do hate the idea of them being incorporated in a book.

I am back as you see at the old address but in a higher and sunnier flat, where I hope to remain, Hal willing, until after Wells' Christmas holidays. I want so much to shield Wells from all unpleasantness, and Christmas holidays mean so much to little boys. The day after he goes back to school, I shall take a train for Reno. Meanwhile I shall do my spineless best to eject this arthritic poison from my tired old body—and I have a birthday tomorrow!!!

With trust and affection,

Grace

Berlin, October 27

Dear Hal:

I was delighted to hear from you and to have tidings about the progress of *Elmer*, but I wish you'd given more details about yourself and whom you're seeing and the village scandals, if any.

I'm really feeling immense after all my wandering, especially after a lot of walking in Alsace, the Rhineland, the Schwartzwald, Cornwall, and Shropshire, and I'm settled down to the quietest kind of life, seeing very few people while I work on the new novel. I wish to God I could get you to run away and come over here for a time. I'd be awfully glad to break away and wander with you. Why don't you? It's been so long since you've been in Europe.

Let me hear again, you profuse young correspondent!

Ever,
Red

Without warning Bayard Veiller sent an announcement to the newspapers that he had given up the dramatization of Elmer Gantry.

November 7

Dear Red:

Your good letter of October 25th makes me warmly happy. I am glad to have your testimony about Ernst Rowohlt. Everything that I have heard confirms what you say about his intelligence and interest.

I'd like to see the carbon of the story for Mencken, no matter what he says about it. Of course I'm just tickled to death that *Exile* is going so

[1927]

well and that we may have it for next fall. After all we have done with *Gantry* this year, the lack of a novel from you would be sorely felt in our sales next year. Thanks to *Gantry* and the rest of our list, our sales will pretty nearly reach a million and a half this year—which is a whale of a publishing business.

I just have your cable: "Oughtn't we to sue Veiller. Is Milton getting new dramatist and who." This situation is still a little too tangled for me to take definite action. I have been in close touch with Cane about it. We are in a perfect position legally, as our contract refers only to a dramatization by Veiller, and if the play is not produced by December first all rights revert to us and we keep the $2000 paid on account without any obligations to anybody. Veiller's announcements attracted so much attention that I think we'll have no difficulty in reselling the dramatic rights to one of several producers once we are free to do so. But I want to be careful not to open negotiations with anyone else until after this contract has cleared itself up. There are all sorts of tales about it. Veiller has a great hit on, *The Trial of Mary Dugan*, which is making him a couple of thousand dollars a week. I hear vaguely that the District Attorney has been making threats to close up *Mary Dugan*, and I hear still more vaguely that some of the church people have used this as a club to scare him off *Elmer Gantry*.

Ever yours,
Alf

Berlin, Nov. 12

Dear Alf:

I'm still waiting for word from you *re* Veiller's chucking ms—I've seen only newspaper clips. Something must be done. Could we get Stallings, O'Neill, or Sidney Howard to dramatize it?

I think in January ads you ought to have some more notices of *Gantry*, however small. True, as you say, that many ads this fall would seem simply repetition. But after that period, if we don't advertise, people will think the book is dead—indeed it will *become* dead—& this one I think we could keep alive. I wish you'd give particular attention to it. Nothing moves slower than the religious mind, especially as I know it in the West. If you'll go on advertising, with claims of "still best seller after one year— still most sensationally discussed book of century" I think you may hit a whole new stratum of readers. And drive the idea home: "You, Mr. Church-goer, if you haven't *read Gantry*, instead of taking your pastor's word for it, you don't know what your own church & your own faith really mean today."

And *how about a $1.50 edition,* instead of letting Grosset & D. have all the skimmed milk? One with a preface of the most violent attacks & boosts? Call it Pulpit Edition? Publicity in that.

Exile is going apace. You'll have it by next May, for publication in Autumn 1928, & I hope it won't run over 120,000—perhaps less. And you may have it by late March, for publication in late August.

Both Mencken & Nathan seem most unusually enthusiastic about "The Man Who Saw Coolidge." I've asked Menck to send you proofs. I might, for 1929, either do a volume of 4 such drools by Mr. Lowell Schmaltz, or use this story with the few very best of my published short stories—e.g. "Hobohemia" & "Willow Walk." I wish you'd read this one & perhaps talk it over with Menck & see what you think. . . . I already have plans for three possible other drools by Mr. Schmaltz. So sorry I'll miss Don.

Ever,
SL

Berlin, November 29

Dear Alf:

I've neglected to answer your query about Rowohlt's financial responsibility. So far as I can find out, it's perfect. One thing: he's Emil Ludwig's publisher, and Mr. Ludwig is one of the very best at collecting every cent that's coming to him.

I've finished 50,000 words of the first draft of the new novel and today I'm running away to Russia, but only for a couple of weeks, then back to work. Yes, *she's* up in Russia, drat her!

Ever,
SL

November 29

Dear Red:

I have been out Chicago-way for a week and on my return find a budget of mail from you, including your cable about advertising. I am sorry if some expression I used about advertising has worried you. I suppose it's a sign of middle age and a temperamental inclination to promise less than I expect to perform that crept into my letter to you. We have gone right ahead with advertising. The ad you suggested—a conglomeration of newspaper headlines with "Have you read Elmer Gantry?" in a blank space in the middle—appears next Sunday in the Times here and next week in Chicago.

Unless Milton comes through in the next two days with a proposal of a satisfactory dramatist for *Gantry*, he will receive a formal note from Melville on the first of December informing him that he has not fulfilled his contract and that that contract is null and void. Then we'll be free to move in other directions.

What you say about Rowohlt and *Gantry* is fine. I think there is a chance for a big German sale on it.

One of the nicest books we have published lately is Carl Sandburg's *The American Songbag*. All the old stuff is in it and a lot of Carl, too. I am sending it along to you, hoping it will arrive before Christmas and make you homesick.

Your recent letters sound as if you are hard at work on the new novel. Your tone changes when you get absorbed. Good luck to you and to it!

Ever yours,
Alf

December 9

Dear Brother:

I know your faith and I know your works and you should be informed that through some friends of mine I have had the privilege—and I hope you appreciate what a privilege it is—to read in advance of the mass of the American public an account of a trip to Washington by a good American citizen and a classmate of Coolidge, which, not only because of what it tells of the President and the sound doctrines of American manhood and manners which it inculcates, but also as a revelation of our democracy and the opportunity which this great land affords, is bound to do good, not only now, but for years to come.

The piece is perfectly splendid. I haven't had more fun over anything for a long time. I think it would make a little book. I have asked Don to read it and see what he thinks. I don't believe I would combine it with anything else unless it were exactly in the same key. Will you cable if it is all right for us to publish it next spring as a little book at $1.00, à la Irvin Cobb's *Speaking of Operations*—? One reason for doing it is that it is really genial and a pleasant farewell to Babbittry for you.

I hope you had a good time in Russia. Ellen and I are hoping that you and "she" will come over here in the spring and settle down with us for as long as you please. Our new house is lovely. A piece of the Sound is just across the road from us. It's quiet; there aren't many neighbors, but lots of people are in reach if and when we want them. There's even a little farmer's cottage, which I bought so that no one else could get it, which might do nicely for a honeymoon or for finishing a novel, with meals and service from our house if that arrangement might be more fun.

Ever yours,
Alf

P.S. Our spring list goes to the printer Monday. We shall put *The Man Who Knew Coolidge* into the list, and shall expect you to cable immediately on receipt of this if you do *not* agree to our publishing it this spring. Don enjoyed it as much as I, and points out that it should be done this spring, as the splendid title will lose much of its force if the piece is published after the Presidential campaign starts with Calvin out of the running and on the shelf.

Cable from Berlin Dec 11

Harbrace
New York

Just returned Russia. If you publish Coolidge skit alone twill be merely timely pamphlet also being serialized Mercury have smaller sale. Can and wish unite it with three similar pieces be called something like Soul of Lowell Schmaltz as complete novel to have enduring sale. Probably never be desirable for me do more than one such stunt and shame waste it with this quarter finished effort. Now that Mencken and you approve could do rest even better yet not make whole long enough be boring. Can write this stuff incredible speed and have whole mailed in four weeks to be published coming spring as fortyfive to sixty thousand word book two dollars or one seventy five. Never had stronger hunch and advise you agree turn little item into big book. Had conferences State Publishing House Russia. Believe can arrange convention we get royalties my and other books they publish including my back royalties if you pay equal royalties on such of theirs you publish. You can also arrange same behalf other American publishers. Shall write terms etc if you cable that I free start proceedings which you OK later.

Lewis

December 12

Cable to
Sinclair Lewis
Herkuleshaus
Berlin

While could get more dollars this spring from Schmaltz volume you describe we feel most readers may know all they want to of him from this piece. Urge Man Who Knew Coolidge as title anyway. You know rest of material and must decide but keep present title. We will reciprocate Russian royalties. If you write terms will lay before Publishers Association. Think most publishers will pay on modern books but not on pre-revolution noncopyrights like Tolstoi.

Harcourt

Cable from Berlin Dec 13

Harbrace
New York City

Alright keep title Man Who Knew Coolidge but expect book fifty thousand words. Shall make it exactly that length. Am sure Russians expect royalties only new books. Dont lay formally before Publishers Association till I send details. Must still correspond Russia.

Lewis

December 14

Dear Red:

There will probably be a lull now in the exchange of cables about *The Man Who Knew Coolidge*. We also have the description of the new material, and it sounds fine. Of course we'll make a $2.00 book. This volume seems to me to be of the order of *Mantrap* rather than of the order of *Gantry*, and we shouldn't spend as much money in advertising this as *Gantry* or *Exile*. The sales may be large; if so, it is apt to be because people will find reading it great fun and recommend it to each other. If after we have the book out and the problem of more advertising comes up, we can make a special arrangement about that as we have on various occasions.

This stuff is so amusing that I think we're all doing the right thing to pick up what odd change we can out of it this spring. If *Exile* should get done for the autumn, well and good. If you need more time to work it over lovingly, that will be all right anyway.

Don't force the new material to 50,000 words if it doesn't come naturally. The various scenes and occasions of the Schmaltz monologues enable you to cover a wide range, but it's much better to have too little than too much of such highly humorous, satirical material.

Ever yours,
Alf

December 22

Dear Red:

About the dramatic version of *Gantry:* As I wrote you before, we were not free to move in the matter until Milton's failure to produce Veiller's version by the first of December actually outlawed his contract. Finally, after a week or two of negotiation, I signed a contract last week with Patrick Kearney, who dramatized *An American Tragedy*, to make a play from *Elmer*.[1] He is het up about the book, has good ideas for the play, and he's the best we could find.

The January Mercury with "The Man Who Knew Coolidge" went on the stands yesterday. We are setting March as a tentative publication date but may switch that around, according to when we can get the complete material in pages to show to the Book-of-the-Month Club. We ought to give them a chance at it, and one month may be better than another for them. Experience seems to show that both the Book-of-the-Month Club and the Literary Guild are exceedingly useful as advertising besides the actual cash which a sale to them brings in.

We are winding up the best year we have ever had, with sales running a little over a million and a half. And you're winding up the best year you've ever had. So everything is lovely, and the goose hangs high.

Ever yours,
Alf

Berlin, Dec. 23

Dear Alf:

Within four days I expect to start off to you all the rest of *The Man Who Knew Coolidge*. I mailed to you a few days ago the revised first part with the front matter. I expect the whole thing to come out 48 or 50,000 words.

Sometime next week I hope to be able to send you practically the whole manuscript of the articles which Dorothy Thompson is doing for the New York Evening Post and the Philadelphia Public Ledger—likely to be sold by them to the Boston Transcript and other papers also—on Russia. To me it seems the best stuff I have ever read on Russia, but probably I am prejudiced. It really gives a clear idea of such matters as the Red Army, the evolution of a new High Society in Russia, how one really lives there, and a lot of other things. I think it would really make a peach of a timely book, particularly interesting to all business men who are

---

[1] After a try-out in Cleveland, Patrick Kearney's dramatization of *Elmer Gantry*, under direction of William A. Brady, was presented by Joseph E. Shea at The Playhouse Theatre, New York City, August 9th, 1928.

wondering whether they can do business with Russia; and as to the complete authenticity of her material, I can vouch myself.

As soon as I finish *The Man Who Knew Coolidge* I am—after a week's vacation in the mountains—going to get right back to *Exile* and I hope to have it ready for publication at latest January first 1929. It would probably be as well not to publish it next fall, because the book after that is very likely to be *Neighbor* and I should think that would entail a couple of years' work.

Dorothy and I myself seem to find the new part of *The Man Who Knew Coolidge* at least as good as the first, and getting rather more away from immediate timeliness, so that I think there is a ghost of a possibility with this of another 200,000 sale—anyway, be prepared for such a possibility.

Feeling fine despite going so hard and I want to send all of you my warmest Christmas greetings.

Ever,
Red

[1928]
January 6

Dear Red:

We are looking for the complete manuscript of *The Man Who Knew Coolidge* by the next steamer, and we shall attend to careful proof-reading here. We now have a first-rate person for that sort of thing in the office. She may do it, or we may have Feipel do it and then superimpose her judgment on his. I wonder what the Britishers and Germans will make of this book—if it will match their sense of humor.

We are in our usual position as regards the contract. I have sent you one on the basis of *Mantrap*. I couldn't help snickering at finding that we are again trying to get you to take a little more and you're arguing for a little less. I think you had better let us have our way this time and sign the contracts that are sent to you on the understanding that if we need more room for advertising we'll lower the royalty on a certain number of copies to 10% and spend the difference in special exploitation.

The Dorothy Thompson articles [1] will have our prayerful consideration. It sounds good to me.

Love to you both.

Ever yours,
Alf

[1] Later in the year the articles were published by Henry Holt and Company under the title *New Russia*.

Lewis remained in Berlin longer than he had planned, all the while working on Dodsworth. *And then mid-March there was a letter from him from Italy.*

>c/o American Express Company,
>Naples, March 19

Dear Alf:

Here!—and here instead of Sicily because there are villas to be had, and, I learned, few if any in Sicily. Indeed I'm moving into one today—small but charming, and very quiet, with the most beautiful view of the sea and Vesuvius and the village-lined distant shores, and a big garden to walk in and breakfast in. I have the villa for exactly seven weeks—after which, England and the caravan.

I have finished 105,000 words of the first draft of *Exile*, and hope to have the whole first draft finished before I leave here—on the caravan trip, it will be easier to concentrate on rewriting than on first draft. I feel so content and well. And I'm thinking of *Neighbor*, and of the dim possibility of going to California—say, next September—and seeing if one could obtain without too much cost, a tiny fruit ranch which would make a real home, with American background, yet with something of the climate and the beauty of Italy, and which would almost or quite pay for itself. But that's far ahead, and to be talked of when I reach NY. I wouldn't want an expensive pretentious place like Jack London's, but it would be nice to have one in which there might be some tiny income instead of all outgo. And which one could leave in charge of the farmer-boss and go abroad once in two years. I mention all of this only to indicate a rather contented and happy outlook on the future—now!

Even with the Nevada business, it looks as though it would cost me a fair amount less this year than last. More sanity in spending. For example, the rent of the villa is only $250 for seven weeks—as against $600 a month for that dratted big house in Washington in the fall of 1926—and two servants at about $50 a month for the two, instead of, as in Washington, three servants costing, if I remember, over $200 a month! And a more charming place!

About the book—no, *Home* would not be the right title, doesn't sound right. Nor is *The Yearner*—as the book comes out, though the wife is a yearner she is so much less important in the book than the husband, who is in no tiny degree a yearner, and the title might seem to refer to him. The title I most want, *A Man Alone*, has been used,[1] and recently. Fortunately, there is no hurry. If you *should* have to announce it ahead

---

[1] George Agnew Chamberlain: *Man Alone*, Putnam, 1926.

of time, better stick to *Dodsworth*[1] as title. It fits the book, as you'll see. You say "I'd guess this would be a good time to get away from the name title." Well in the first place, I'll certainly get away from it after this time —whether my next is *Neighbor* or some shorter ad interim novel to do while laboring over the long task of preparation for *Neighbor*. And second, as I've pointed out, with the success of hundreds of such titles as *Nicholas Nickleby, David Copperfield, Martin Chuzzlewit, Oliver Twist, The Newcombes, Ethan Frome, David Harum*, to say nothing of the well-known novels called *Babbitt* and *Elmer Gantry*, there is a question whether any title *can* in the long run—after the first introduction—be more distinctive, satisfactory, and memorable than a name title. (Oh yuh, one might also mention *Pere Goriot* & *Mme. Bovary*.)

Do you know that the great General Conference of the Methodist Church meets in Kansas City this year—I think in May? This is the conference of the whole blooming Methodist Church (North); it meets only once in four years; it elects bishops and decides vast policies; and it must be attended by thousands, preachers and laymen. Now they're going to talk a lot about *Elmer Gantry*, particularly as they meet in Kansas City. Why don't you arrange to have all K.C. booksellers have large stocks of *Elmer*—if necessary on consignment—with special advertising. For a lot of these Methodists, including some who have preached on the book, will not have seen it, and might buy it if it were there at hand, whereas they've never had the chance in their little towns.

I can see special advertising to the effect: Greetings to the General Conference: You have read and talked about *E.G.*—maybe preached about it—but have you read the book itself? You have heard that Gantry is a scoundrel, but do you know that in Frank Shallard and Mr. Pengilly, one a liberal and one a fundamentalist, Mr. Lewis has produced two of the noblest and most inspiring of preachers in fiction? No novel about the church has ever been more talked of—none has ever been more praised or more denounced—*read it* and see why.

As all these Methodists will go back to every quarter of the country and talk, it's not just a question of how many they buy themselves but what they start. I can even imagine a billboard, near the entrance of each of the churches at which they hold meetings, giving some such gospel message as I have outlined above. I think this would be awfully worth doing, whatever the cost. (Heh? Sure I'll come in on cost.) Might give new life to the book. If you use the billboards, put on them "To be bought in *almost* every bookshop in Kansas City"—because the Methodist Book Concern probably does not handle the book. Mightn't it be worth

---

[1] The other titles Lewis considered for the book were *Evening, Exile, Sunset, Blind Giant*.

the expense to send some one, possibly even Hal, to Kansas City for this stunt? . . . And there might be a good news story in it.

How about my suggestion that Ellen and you join me for a week or two this summer? Be room.

Ever,
SL

For about four months, during which Lewis lived in the villa in Naples and then went to England, he had little occasion to write his publishers. He was actively engaged in completing Dodsworth.

April 11

Dear Red:

It has been a long time since I've written you, although I hear occasional echoes of what you are doing abroad. *The Man Who Knew Coolidge*[1] is launched and on the whole, as you probably know, the reviews are favorable. Canby and Hansen were both enthusiastic and the Times treated you to a front page. Your old friend in Chicago, Fanny Butcher,[2] turned both thumbs down.

The General Conference of the Methodist Church is to be held in Kansas City in Convention Hall during the entire month of May. We are going in for an extensive billboard campaign which will cover the whole city. It would have cost just about as much to have tried to take isolated billboards near the Convention Hall and churches, and we have made up our mind that it would be better to do the job thoroughly. Consequently, there will be 49 billboard displays in Kansas City including 13 illuminated boards in the center of the town. Altogether it will run to $1000, but we feel sure it will be worth it since, as you said, "all these Methodists will go back to every part of the country and talk." We will, of course, have as many copies of *Elmer Gantry* in the bookstores by May 1 as we are able to force on them.

I find life now in New York as entertaining as ever, but this winter has been somewhat exhausting. Claire has been abroad for the last two months and probably won't be back till June. I don't believe you will run across her trail because she's in southern France and then is going to Spain. It's hard to keep the girls at home these days.

Yours,
Hal

On April 16th Mrs. Lewis obtained a Reno divorce.

[1] Published April 5th.
[2] Reviewer and columnist on the *Chicago Tribune*.

Savoy Hotel
London, W.C.
May 6

Dear Hal:

So good to hear from you. You probably know by now that Dorothy Thompson and I will be married, here in London, a week from tomorrow. You'll see her, if you're in New York, probably about mid-August—which means you will see me mit. We'll probably buy a farm somewhere in New England, Maryland, or California. Perhaps you can take a day or two off and run around with us, looking at places. I wish I had a place like Carl Van Doren's.

Yes, sure: bring the royalty on *Gantry* down on the next 5000, to pay for my half of the Kansas City display. Let me know what comes of the stunt, and what the newspapers say that the preachers say.

Cape tells me there is a fine advance sale on *Man Who Knew Coolidge* here—he publishes on May 11.

I feel fine. I'm looking forward so keenly to caravanning all summer here, but also I'm beginning to be keen to see America again, and I'll be excited to sail and to see you-all.

Ever,
Red

Salisbury, England
July 13

Dear Alf:

The journey continues to be a great success. We had a little rest from camping by spending a week here in Salisbury catching up on work and letters—including finishing the first draft of *Dodsworth* and doing some revising on it; then had a week of touring in Dorset, Devon, and Cornwall—glorious country. After a couple of days here again catching up, we start for Wales.

We're becoming awfully keen to get home, and we spend large wide hours talking about the possibilities of a farm in America. See you soon!

Ever,
SL

Cable from Paris Aug 17

Harbrace
New York City
May take four months finishing Dodsworth. Better not plan publish before April.

Lewis

Lewis and his wife, Dorothy Thompson Lewis, returned to the United States August 28th. They stayed at the Harcourt house in Riverside, Connecticut, for a time, and after looking for a country place, they purchased a 300-acre farm near Barnard, Vermont, where they stayed until early November, while he continued his work on Dodsworth. Then they came to New York and stayed at their apartment at 37 West Tenth Street. There he finished the manuscript and delivered it to his publishers before Christmas. About the middle of February 1929 the Lewises went to Florida. All this while contact between Lewis and the office was in person or by telephone.

TEN
The Nobel Prize

[1929]
February 18

Dear Red:

Here's another letter from Rowohlt persisting in true Continental merchant fashion in his plea for a lower royalty on *Dodsworth*. I think 10% is not too much to ask. We made a concession on *Mantrap* because that was somewhat out of line with your other novels. I would be inclined to stand pat on our proposal. I wrote him ten days ago that we'd have to stick to 20% for serial & 10% for book. What he is offering now is 10% on the paper bound books and the same number of pfennigs per copy on the cloth bound books. We have noticed in recent royalty reports from Germany that the sale of cloth bound books seems to be increasing there, and of course it's better to have the royalty on the higher priced book. If we hadn't made the concession on *Mantrap*, we wouldn't have had this difficulty.

We just have your telegram that you are at Homosassa. I hope you like Florida and that you both catch big fish.

Ever yours,
Alf

The Lodge,
Homosassa, Fla.
Feb. 21

Dear Alf:

Stick by the 10% for book and 20% for serial. If Rowohlt won't take it, some one else will—though I'd like to continue with him.

The fishing is fine, the weather glorious, and I'm having a real rest, though I am spending part of each day writing. We may stay away till mid-March, looking in at Palm Beach and possibly even Havana. We'll be here for about another week.

If you still have copies of the special edition of *Dodsworth*, I wish you'd send me one P.D.Q. Put down Cabell, Edith Wharton, and Louis Bromfield on the list of people who ought to have copies for boosting. *Dodsworth* ought to go to my Swede publishers as early as possible.

Try *Middletown*[1] and *Love in Chicago*[2] on the German publishers.

Luck!
SL

March 14

Dear Red:

I am glad to have an address for you, and I have just telegraphed you: "Advance fifty thousand. Times Hansen Phelps highly favorable Mencken disappointed Tribune stupid. Have ordered our best and heaviest advertising so far. Outlook really fine." The advance of 50,000 is first-rate. It means that we have been able to get the impression around generally that *Dodsworth*[3] is a sure-fire big book. It's extraordinary how fast the notion got around to the public that they didn't want *The Man Who Knew Coolidge*. When you consider that we had sold 240,000 *Gantry* and that we planted only 20,000 *Man Who Knew Coolidge* in advance of publication, it is astonishing how few the public bought. It would almost seem as if an unfavorable impression about that book spread from one end of the country to the other inside of 24 hours. I mention this so you will understand that a really favorable impression of *Dodsworth* has spread throughout the book trade or we couldn't have an advance of 50,000.

Baker and Taylor ordered 10,000 and the News Company 10,000. We can't expect re-orders until next week. They will begin to show up by the time you get home, and we'll have some real indications then. Meantime, all I can say is that everything looks fine, that the office enthusiasm for the book is at fever heat, and because so many other people here now have a hand in it, it is only fair for me to say that you're certainly getting an enthusiastic publishing job.

I have to go West on a variety of errands about the first of April. Let me know definitely when you'll be home so that we can have a real visit before I leave.

Love to you both.

Yours,
Alf

[1] By Robert S. and Helen Merrell Lynd, HB&Co., 1929.
[2] By Charles Walt, HB&Co., 1929.
[3] Harcourt's letter was written on publication day, March 14th.

[1929]

Hotel Ponce de Leon
St. Augustine, Florida
March 15

Dear Alf:

Many thanks for your wire, received yesterday. Dorothy had to go to Pittsburgh to lecture—she left yesterday—but I'm going to remain here a week or ten days to finish a short story for Ray Long, then join her in NY.

We've had a grand vacation—though on it each of us did a short story and an article. We stayed at Homosassa for nearly two weeks, writing part of the day but going out fishing for five or six hours daily, with lunch cooked by our guide in some wild spot in the jungle; then we bought a flivver—which I'm going to ship up to Vermont from here, as an extra car for next summer—and believe me the new Ford is a marvelous car, too—and we motored from Homosassa to St. Petersburg, Tampa, Winter Haven, Mountain Lake (where one of Edward Bok's millionaire neighbors is a celebrated manufacturer of pink pills), Avon Park, Okechobee, and Palm Beach, where we stayed about a week, with a jaunt down to Miami. Then up here, where I shall play the sedulous hermit for a week and return looking like Danl Boone.

If anything interesting happens, you can get me here by wire for another week. See you soon.

Ever,
SL

Hugh Walpole and Francis Brett Young would probably be interested in *Dodsworth*. Jonathan ought to send 'em copies.

March 20

Dear Red:

I talked with Dorothy on the telephone yesterday. It is too early for real re-orders on *Dodsworth* yet. I enclose proofs of a few of our latest advertisements, from which you will see that F.P.A. likes it, and so does Fanny Butcher. In fact, her review comes nearest to understanding what it is all about than that of anyone else so far! We have spent or ordered spent about $6000 in advertising at the moment and have as much more scheduled through the next three or four weeks. The book is well displayed everywhere around here, and in walking to the station last evening I saw three people carrying copies—which is a darn good sign. I have asked Jonathan to send copies to Walpole and Brett Young.

Yours,
Alf

In the next two months there was little correspondence between Lewis and the office. Mrs. Lewis arrived in New York on or before March 19th, and Lewis joined her at their Tenth Street apartment probably the end of the month. Only one brief note was written to him there by the office in mid-April. There is no indication as to the exact date they left for Twin Farms.

Twin Farms
Barnard, Vermont
May 26

Dear Alf:

Will you please have another check for $1000 deposited to my account at the Guaranty, and confirm the deposit to me, as soon as convenient. . . . Carpenters' bills, masons' bills, all that, but Lord! what a lovely place we're coming to have, and this second farmhouse of ours, which we are modernizing to use as a guest house, is going to be even lovelier than the present main house in which we live—we may move over to the other one when it's done. The whole place is even more beautiful than I had remembered, with spring here. When are Ellen and you coming? . . . You head for Woodstock, and ask at the post office how to get to Barnard; at Barnard, the general store, ask how to get here.

It seems to me that the three ringed portions in the enclosed correspondence from Hugh Walpole would make about as perfect an ad as could be.

I've been thinking more about the possibility of having *Babbitt* in the Modern Library. That library—and it seems to be improving steadily—reaches just the sort of people who would keep *Babbitt* alive; and I don't think G & D (Grosset and Dunlap) do. Would it be possible to have it BOTH G & D and the Modern Library?

I feel about one million per cent better up here than in New York. Curiously, I don't get in the least lonely. Evenings we read and sneak off to bed at 11, instead of one or two. And now I'm going out and chop some wood—well, not *much* wood!

Ever,
SL

Will you please send me here a *Gantry* and four copies of *Dodsworth*. I find that our otherwise admirably furnished residence lacks these necessities.

ALSO, did I tell you that Peggy Bacon wants to do an illustrated edition of *Babbitt?* This might be a stunning success—I see it on good paper, selling probably at five dollars. If we did this, we wouldn't, of course, consider the Modern Library stunt, at least for a long time. I wish you'd talk this over with Peggy, if you see her. Jonathan writes me that he is thinking of getting out a five shilling collected edition of my books. It seems to me that we ought, with the Bacon-illustrated *Babbitt* as a beginning, to think of something of the same sort. I believe we could get more out of (at least) *Main St.*, *Babbitt* & *Arrowsmith*, than we are now, just leaving them to be buried among the Zane Grey books in the G & D collections. Let's talk it over.

SL

May 29

Dear Red:

I am pleased to be able to report that our advertising girl beat us both to it on the Hugh Walpole comment on *Dodsworth*. When I went to her about it, she showed me the enclosed proof.

It is fine to know that you're both well and happy in Vermont. It must be lovely there, and I am looking forward to the time when I can get away to see you and the place. I certainly can't leave till after Don gets home about the middle of June. He reports much interesting business in London. He has made a telephone appointment with me for this afternoon, the idea of which I find rather exciting.

If you look at the Peggy Bacon pictures in *New Songs for New Voices*[1] and particularly when you see those she's done for Carl's Rootabaga stories,[2] you will find, I think, that they lean too much on the side of caricature to suit *Babbitt*. I like her pictures enormously; in fact, I bought from her a dozen of the originals for *New Voices* to give to Ellen, who is really responsible for that volume. Don't you think somebody like Webster would do a better *Babbitt* than Peggy Bacon?

I am digging out just what Grosset and Dunlap have been doing with the old books. I have some ideas of my own about a scheme for handling all our cheap editions, which I think will ripen in the course of the year, and which, if it does ripen, will interest you almost as much as it does us. I'll save that to talk about when we meet.

I enclose some more proofs of recent advertisements of *Dodsworth*, from which you will see that we have started the steamer gift campaign. The book business generally is flat. *Dodsworth*, the new Viña Delmar

[1] Edited by Louis Untermeyer and David Mannes, HB&Co., 1928.
[2] Carl Sandburg: *Rootabaga Country*, HB&Co., 1929.

short stories,[1] and Strachey's *Elizabeth and Essex* seem to be about the only books that are selling in the bookstores.

Yours,
Alf

During the next month, while Lewis was in Vermont, communication between him and the office was by telephone.

June 25

Dear Red:

Did you get a letter from Jonathan dated May 13th on the subject of a five shilling uniform edition of your books? Jonathan talked to me about it in London, but I didn't commit myself, thinking we should all talk it over when I got back. But meanwhile he wrote to you and sent me a copy of the letter. I think the idea is a good one, and I have talked about it with Alf, who thinks so too. It seems a good way to keep all the old books going.

I had a pleasant and busy four and a half weeks in London. Georgian House seemed a little dingier, but no less comfortable. It was three years since I had been there.

I expect you're enjoying the farm. Love to you and to Dorothy.

Ever yours,
Don

July 3

Dear Don:

Welcome back! And welcome to Vermont if you ever get time to come here. Yes, I had Jonathan's letter and agreed with him that it would be a good thing to do the five shilling edition of my books. And what about H.B.and Co. doing the same thing? As I have written Alf, I am not at all satisfied with the way Grosset & Dunlap are handling my books. It seems to me that they just let them ride along with a lot of Zane Grey and detective stories. Yet there should be, in *Main St* and *Babbitt*, with their incredible advertising value, a steady yearly sale of—I don't know how many tens of thousands.

Alf says G & D are boosting them in their special dollar series. Well, I hear very little of this series in comparison with the Modern Library and the Doubleday-Doran dollar series. And I note in the enclosed ads of that series that not even one of my books is mentioned. We must make

---

[1] *Loose Ladies*, 1929. All three books mentioned were published by Harcourt, Brace.

[1929]

plans to see if we can't utilize the rep of these books better, maybe, eh? This letter, of course, is equally for Alf and you.

Ever,
Red

July 10

Dear Red:

Your letter about cheap editions has been on my desk for a few days because of the Fourth of July weekend and because I wanted to get some figures from Grosset. Grosset does not publish your books in his Dollar Library, a list of which you sent, but in his 75¢ reprints. Your books belong in the Dollar Library as regards distinction, but the Dollar Library is carried only by regular bookstores, a few department stores, and a few of the more important newsstands. Grosset has 30 salesmen on the road, two-thirds of whom are visiting drugstores, newsstands, and places which do not carry his Dollar Library or the Modern Library or the Doubleday Doran "Star Dollar Books." It's his judgment, and I agree with him, that your books are popular enough to profit by the wider distribution. He is to take on *Elmer Gantry* in September and is going to try that in both his Dollar Library and his 75¢ Library. He is coupling with the 75¢ edition of *Gantry* a new campaign on *Babbitt* and *Main Street* with a series of posters saying, in effect: "You all know Babbitt. You've all said, 'She comes from Main Street.' Read the books that gave these words their meaning."

There is one aspect of all this which seems important to me. The chief reason Grosset has extended his retail distribution and display machinery so widely is that it is a settled part of his policy not to advertise his cheap editions direct to the public. He thinks this would cut off his supplies from publishers and authors, as it tends to foul the market for the books at the higher prices. It might be said that you and we are lucky to have sold so much of your market at $2.00 and $2.50 that there hasn't been a great market left at 75¢. I am dubious particularly about the advertising of books like *Trader Horn*, with its hint that the public was a fool to buy such a book at $3.50 when if they had waited a while they could get it for $1.00. I don't like the tendency. It may lead to American publishing getting into the condition of British publishing, for their first publication is often merely for reviewers, the circulating libraries, and a small public, to earmark the book as important, with the real sale and real publishing effort put on the three-and-six, the two-and-six, the two shilling, the one shilling and the ninepence editions. I'd hate to have things get to that condition here.

The reprint situation seems to me to be changing. I have some new ideas about it up my sleeve, but they can't develop for a year or two. Meantime, I don't like to get our machine sidetracked into selling cheap books with a small return both for us and for the author.

Dodsworth keeps on. We sold 10,000 in June, and it's going at a little better rate this month. Sales are just beyond 85,000 in this country. We have been busy, and things are humming here. Some first-rate novels have shown up and a top-notch lot of non-fiction is on the carpet. The latter includes Clemenceau's Memoirs, the third volume of Parrington, Geoffrey Scott's Boswell, Pringle's Roosevelt, and Lloyd Lewis's Sherman [1]—which would be hard to beat for next year.

We'll talk more about reprints when we meet. I am looking for the chance to get up to see you.

Ever yours,
Alf

Barnard, Vermont
July 16

Dear Alf:

Your letter about the Grosset situation is very complete and satisfactory, and obviously it will be well to go on, certainly for the present. There's only one sale the Grosset system fails to get for me—that prestige sale which is more valuable, even in eventual sales, than the current figures indicate.

Can't we, presently, handle this by getting out a collected edition of my books to be handled by the regular bookstores? I see something at about $1.75 a volume; I see us starting with *Main Street, Babbitt, Arrowsmith, Gantry,* and *Dodsworth,* then adding the minor items only if the first plunge is a success. Keep this in mind, talk it over with Don and Gus, and we'll discuss it when I see you.

All goes well though most placidly. The new house, which will have cost me about $10,000 beyond the first purchase price, will be done in about three weeks—and, thank God, the huge expense will then cease.

---

[1] Georges Clemenceau: *Grandeur and Misery of Victory,* 1930.

Vernon Louis Parrington: *The Beginnings of Critical Realism in America,* Volume III of *Main Currents in American Thought,* was published October 1930, more than a year after the author's death.

Geoffrey Scott was editing the Colonel Ralph Isham collection of *Private Papers of James Boswell from Malahide Castle* and planned to write his own biography of Boswell. When he died shortly after this, both tasks were unfinished.

Henry F. Pringle: *Theodore Roosevelt,* 1931.

Lloyd Lewis: *Sherman: Fighting Prophet,* 1932.

It will be a wonderful guest house and could, if we ever wanted to, be sold as a separate unit, leaving us this place and a couple of hundred acres. It has the most splendid view—but then I hope you'll be up here to see it yourself.

I'm returning the G & D posters etc. today. I think they make a mistake in advertising *Main St* etc. just as they do Zane Grey—in trying to sell my books on a lowbrow basis when, actually, they have always sold on just the opposite basis. I think they get that wrong slant from dealing so much with the lowbrow books they publish and forget that even the corner store on Main St does have a lot of school teacher and women's club real or would-be highbrow buyers.

We'll be here all summer except from August 5th to about August 10th, when I'll be at Middlebury College. When you get sick of the NY smell, do come shooting up whenever you feel like it.

Ever,
SL

July 30

Dear Red:

I just had a nice visit with Ramon Guthrie. He seems to be wabbling a little about his work, but I think he is back here in pretty good shape and that some one of the books he has on the stocks is apt to fall into order rather promptly. He says he is coming up to see you, and I think it would be a grand thing for him. He is also talking of getting a teaching job, which he can do without its taking much out of him, to take the bread-and-butter worry off his neck while he gets a book or two into shape. I think this is a good idea, and we are keeping our eyes open for some connection. You might keep it on your mind while you are at Middlebury. If you mention his name now and then, there is apt to be someone there who knows of an opening.

Harcourt, Brace and Company celebrated the tenth anniversary of its incorporation yesterday. It was too hot for anything but a very mild celebration. Don and Gus and Joel came out to Riverside and had dinner with Ellen and me, and we sat around and talked about our mistakes.

Ever yours,
Alf

Lewis made a hurried visit to New York after his session at Middlebury College in Vermont and arranged to have Harcourt, Brace publish the work of his young protégé, Fred Rothermell.

August 12

Dear Red:

We have been trying to close the office Saturdays while it is so hot so I am just able today to send you the contracts for Rothermell's novels. Of course we are glad to follow your judgment in a case of this sort.

More power to your elbow, which I hope had enough pleasant exercise to justify your visit to our metropolis during this hot term. The more I think of the boy's story the more I like it.

Ever yours,
Alf

Barnard, Vermont
August 13

Dear Alf:

I enjoyed my brief bat in New York—my only one in three months—but I enjoyed still more getting back to this lovely coolness and quiet.

I'm enclosing the Rothermell contract, one copy, signed. He will be sending you both mss, and then you can see which one you would like to publish first and, if it prove to be *Superman* instead of *Fifth Avenue,* you can just change name on the contract. He's revising both mss and I'm going over both of them again before he sends them.

I rather think that it will be *Superman* that you will want to publish first, but we'll see. Meantime, as soon as he gets these two revised, he will go back to a third novel, which he has half finished. Lord I envy him that industry of 30!

Come on!

Ever,
SL

There were no letters for a period of three weeks, and at the end of the summer Harcourt and his wife took a trip to New England and dropped in to see Lewis at his farm.

Barnard, Vt.
September 7

Dear Alf:

Jimmie Sheean writes me from Palestine asking me to O.K. his contract with you.[1] I shall be glad to do this, if you will send it on.

[1] Vincent Sheean: *Gog and Magog,* HB&Co., 1930.

[1929]

We want to see you and Ellen up here soon again, when we are not swamped with other guests. We hardly had a moment for a real chin.

Cordially,
SL

Barnard, Vermont
September 16

Dear Alf:

André Siegfried [1] will be in New York soon—indeed he may already have arrived. He was here for a few days and told me of something that might make a great book for you. His father, later a Senator of France, came to America in about 1860. He became acquainted with Lincoln; was an intimate of the White House; went there almost daily; talked with cabinet members about the most crucial affairs. All this is related in a diary which, I understand, Siegfried has and which has never been published. Wouldn't it, with a proper (and not too short) preface by his distinguished son, make a bully publishing item? Talk to Siegfried about it.

And another idea. Is there today any really up-to-date Hoyle? I once tried to find one and couldn't. There are plenty of books on bridge, but is there any book giving, and properly, the new rules for all forms of bridge, poker, roulette, chemin de fer, baccarat, all forms of rummy, etc. etc.?

I wish you would send me, roughly, the sale of *Dodsworth* to date, and the approximate amount of money now due me from HB and Co. I must begin to think about financing the writing of the new novel, which is going to be *Neighbor* with the new slants created by the fact there ain't no labor today—in itself a dramatic thing: and I don't want, if I can help it, to have to write at all for Ray Long [2] or any magazine while I'm doing it. Of course this year, with the rebuilding of the new house, I've needed a lot of current money. That's all paid for now—or will be with the next check, due me from Ray on October 1st—and next year there isn't a single thing we *need* to do on the place—though always, as you so well know, there's endless things one agreeably *can* do.

If Ann (Watkins) would only sell the *Dodsworth* movie, even if she only got $20,000 for it, that would amply take care of financing next year. But as I don't want, under any considerations, to touch any of my sav-

[1] Harcourt, Brace had published Siegfried's *America Comes of Age* in 1927.
[2] By this time the name of *Hearst's International Magazine* had been changed to *Cosmopolitan Magazine*, and Ray Long was still editor.

ings, if she doesn't sell it, I'm afraid I may have to do a little magazine work to get through.

It's gorgeous here now—the autumn has just set in with days so fine that I have to use Xian Science on myself to stay indoors before the typewriter. The trees have turned only a little, and from now on, unless we hit a soggy rainy spell, it will be finer and finer, till about October 15.

Ever,
SL

September 19

Dear Red:

Thanks for your note of the 16th. I have heard from André Siegfried and expect to see him tomorrow.

I'll get after Ann about the possibility of some motion picture income. About your financial situation, your balance on the first of July has been whittled down, by your withdrawals and by the $1000 a month to Grace, to $10,619.00. Since the first of July, *Dodsworth* has earned $4000. This does not account for royalties from England or translations. I should guess there would be at least $5000 from those sources. I'll really stir around about some motion picture money. I agree with you that it is too bad to work for Ray Long when you're ready to get at a big job. I'll let you know when anything develops.

Ever yours,
Alf

Barnard, Vermont
September 20th

Dear Alf:

Will you please send me another copy of *Middletown?* I gave mine to André Siegfried, who had never heard of the book and who was most excited by it.

Are we going to see you up here again before we leave on the 9th of October? I am going to Toronto to the A. F. of L. Conference. Reason: *Neighbor.* Dorothy and I were sorry to have seen you for such a very short time and had hoped you would get up here again before we left. The weather is lovely.

Ever—
S.L.

[1929]

September 23

Dear Red:

I had a nice visit with Siegfried Friday. He is coming out to Riverside for the weekend after next.

We are exceedingly busy here, and I shan't be able to get up before the 9th of October. I am glad I did get the glimpse of you last month. The autumn must be gorgeous in your little valley.

Ever yours,
Alf

October 3

Dear Mr. Lewis:

Sidney Williams of the Philadelphia Inquirer has asked us for articles by some of our authors. He plans to run a series this winter on the subject of "Why People Should Own and Read Books." It would be limited to about 200 words and run in a box with a cut of the author's portrait. If you aren't too busy would you be willing to write such an article for him?

How about writing me a line or two about what you are doing, your plans, etc. I am flooded with questions as to what you will do next and what you are writing now. I hear you are going to Toronto soon. Is that right?

Please give my best to Mrs. Lewis.

Sincerely,
John D. Chase [1]

Barnard, Vermont
October 15

Dear Denny:

No, I won't write 200 words for Sidney Williams. What in the deuce could anyone say on such a silly question? Norman Hapgood has taken a whole book to answer a far more limited question: Why Janet (or anyone) should read Shakspere.[2] A good book, but it won't influence the Janets, I am afraid. Tell Mr. Williams to run the Borzoi ads, and tell the public that one should read books because the Russian aristocracy do—or carry 'em anyhow.

I am beginning a novel with American labor as the scene, but inasmuch as the thing looks enormous and the task so vast as to be discouraging, I may never finish it, so let's not say anything about it. I am going

---
[1] Chase was then publicity director of Harcourt, Brace.
[2] *Why Janet Should Read Shakespere*, Century, 1929.

to Toronto and I went to the Marion cotton mills, but two trips don't make this novel.

If the world yearns for news, tell it I am staying in these Vermont hills until the snow drives me out by threatening to barricade me in. I am writing short stories—or have been—just to keep my hand in until I get up energy to begin this new novel. I am reading innumerable books on the labor movement in the United States, in between visiting the local rotary clubs—because I want to know Vermont, the first place I have ever had a real home in. I am also overseeing my wife overseeing the gardener plant delphiniums.

Sincerely,
SL

Get acquainted with Fred Rothermell, whose *5th Ave.* you are to publish & who goes to N.Y. to see the firm tomorrow.

October 25

Dear Mr. Lewis:

Thanks for your note. We're always glad to have any news about you that we can use. Every now and then I get a request for an article from you. Do you want me to refuse these for you or send them along to you? Here is another—

In getting up a free lance feature article on the question as to whether the successful business man can retire before old age or ill health forces it, and work out a satisfactory existence, I would like a comment from Sinclair Lewis. As the author of *Dodsworth* he certainly is, of course, one of the profound observers of the retired business man here and in Europe.

In Mr. Lewis' opinion, would Dodsworth, having felt restless before retirement, be apt to have developed and found himself in his old routine and tracks? What would have been the effect of keeping in harness, after it seemed irksome and empty? Would not his friendship and tastes, the pattern of his life have remained more fixed and satisfactory? What effect on his marriage? Likely to remain intact although empty?

This article is to be written for the New York World or the Sunday Magazine Section of the Herald Tribune. If these things are merely a nuisance send me a blanket refusal and we'll be hardboiled.

Sincerely,
John D. Chase

[1929]

Barnard, Vermont
October 26

Dear Denny:

If anybody wants an article from me and wants to pay 75 cents a word, I may, and may not, be interested. But, being a professional writer who has to earn his living thus, one of the things I most ain't interested in is writing other people's articles for them. If the gentleman wants to know Mr. Lewis's opinion about what Mr. Dodsworth would do, he might read the book. Yes, please be hardboiled with all these requests.

It's gorgeous here now, even though most of the leaves are gone. There's a spaciousness about the hills that's somehow exciting. I'm going to stay on for another week or ten days.

Ever,
SL

Barnard, Vermont
October 26

Dear Alf:

I think the royalty statement sent out October 25th is in error about *Dodsworth*. I haven't the *Dodsworth* contract here—it is in New York—but as I remember it, on this contract we did not have the former arrangement of 10% to 50,000. If so, there should be another $6250 on my balance.

Your seeing Fred Rothermell and his getting acquainted with Raymond and Helen Everitt [1] have been fine for him. It starts him going at an accelerated pace. I think you'll have something superb there, with another two or three years of training.

Have you been able to start anything about the *Dodsworth* movie? I hope not to have to do a bit of hackwriting next year. After seeing the Marion strike, and spending a few days at the American Federation of Labor convention, I'm keener about this novel than anything since *Arrowsmith*. And at the A F of L convention I met exactly the right man for the De Kruif-Birkhead of my novel—Carl Haessler of the Federated Press; college man, Rhodes scholar at Oxford, imprisoned as conscientious obj during the war, ever since up to his ears in the labor movement; sense of humor; delightful to work with; eager to do the job. He is to join me here, and we'll go snooping about the country together.

Dorothy had to start out lecturing three days ago, but the snow has not come yet, and I'm going to stay here (with the Rothermells, who are

[1] C. R. Everitt was an editor at Harcourt, Brace.

to have the house for the winter, and with Carl and a temporary cook) until the roads get bad, making plans for the novel so that we won't waste motion when we start out. I hope to have the novel (which will be longer than the new edition of the Encyc Britannica) finished a year from now, ready for publication (naturally, as The Big Book of the Season) in early spring 1931—just when labor is busting loose again and raising hell.

Shouldn't Cape be making a report on *Dodsworth* sales in England? There doesn't seem to be any on the royalty statement.

I wish you could slip up here for a few days—it's even more restful than in summer. But probably about the time you hit the Vermont border, you'd be riding into a blizzard!

Ever,
SL

October 29

Dear Red:

I have yours of the 26th. The royalty statement on *Dodsworth* is right. I am afraid you have it confused with *Neighbor*. I enclose a summary of advertising through September. Of course, you can have the details for each month if you want them. We just have Cape's royalty report for sales last spring, too late, of course, to get into this account. The earnings on your books are £954.

I'm delighted that you're settling down to the new novel and that you're staying in Vermont doing the ground work. It sounds fine about Carl Haessler.

We had a good session with Rothermell. That's going to be all to the good.

I can't get a smell of interest in a *Dodsworth* movie, although I have put out feelers in a number of directions. I am hoping to see Laurence Stallings before the first of the year, and maybe I can work it round that way.

Ever yours,
Alf

Barnard, Vermont
Nov. 5

Dear Don:

Sorry to have to bother you with making the investments for me the other day but otherwise I would never have got in on the bargain stocks—as I hope they will prove to be!

I'll be here about two more days, and arrive in NY about the 15th, with Boston and Rhode Island for about a week in between.

Ever,
SL

The Lewises spent part of the winter in New York, at their apartment at 37 West Tenth Street. In January they headed for California, stopping off at Reno, where Lewis successfully petitioned for a more equitable method of paying the agreed alimony to his former wife.

[1930]
February 6

Dear Red:

I am just back from a grand fishing trip in Florida, and Melville tells me the news of the outcome of the Nevada business. I hope you and Dorothy are both fine and getting along comfortably with your mutual pregnancies.

This note is to say that if you find yourself in or near Hollywood, Viña Delmar is in Beverly Hills. She is quite a person. She'd like to meet you, and I think you'd enjoy each other.

Ever yours,
Alf

Monterey, Calif.
Feb. 15

Dear Alf:

I'm glad you had a good fishing-trip in Florida, but that state is a blinking swamp compared with this one-and-only earthly edition of paradise. I re-realize that, showing California to Dorothy, who had never been farther west than Kansas City.

The ordeal in Reno was considerable; I was on the witness stand through morning, afternoon, and evening. But I had an admirable lawyer, and the Judge was at once just and sympathetic.

We've taken a house here in Monterey for two months, during which I expect to have the labor novel pretty clearly formed in my mind. It's a charming old Spanish house with a walled garden, in which we sit, among spring flowers, while you have the joys of rain and snow and fog. Dorothy feels fine and is taking it easy.

I'll put Viña Delmar's address in my address book, and if we get to Hollywood—which is by no means certain—we'll shout for her. Ida Brace called up yesterday from San Francisco. She may come down here, and if she does, we'll hope to have some good parties.

Ever,
SL

Dear Alf: I've turned patriot and am rooting in the best Californiac manner. Feeling grand.—DT

February 20

Dear Red:

Grand to have your note of the 15th from Monterey! Melville had told me about the Reno modification. It's too bad to have had the worry.

You'll like Monterey. I think the curve of the bay and the ride over the hill to Carmel are quite lovely. Good golf course, too, if you want to start that. I suppose you know Lincoln Steffens? He is just finishing his autobiography [1] for us, and his wife, Ella Winter, is a great girl.

I am glad the plan for the labor novel is rounding out. I can imagine a little how you hate to take the plunge into the deep water of such a job as that, but I guess you can't help it—and that's fine. It needn't be too damned all-inclusive.

Love to you both!

Ever yours,
Alf

Monterey, Calif.
February 24

Dear Alf:

We like Monterey a lot—find it better to live in than Carmel, because the latter is so arty, and when we want the sea, it's only a few minutes over by motor. (I bought a second-hand car in San Francisco, and when we get ready to leave, we'll sell it, possibly driving as far as Los Angeles first.) We have a small but comfortable old house, with a beautiful garden, into which I wander a dozen times a day. It's like June here, now, and has been ever since we got here—with snow and below zero in NY.

We've seen Steffens and Ella Winter a number of times—had them here for dinner a few nights ago. But the people we see most of are Gouverneur and Mrs. Morris. He's a corker. I'm trying to get him to think of doing—as only he and Edith Wharton could—a sort of Forsyte Saga of American High Society, from the simple Bar Harbor days of

---

[1] *The Autobiography of Lincoln Steffens*, 1931.

cutunder buggies and the polka, to these days of gin and racing cars with the names dominating American society in 1890 almost entirely replaced by new ones. He could do it, too, though most of his life he has written only rather light stories. But he knows, and he can write. If I persuade him, I may get us a first look at it, without binding either side.

Ask Paul if he has been looking into this Coffey-Humber cancer cure stuff. It sounds important to me. Might repay him to make a trip out here to look into it. And he would see the Jacques Loeb Marine Laboratory here. I wish he'd come.

Anything stirring on *Fifth Avenue* (Fred Rothermell's book, not that horrible thoroughfare) and any news of his new novel? He could probably use another $250 advance most handsomely by about now—I know he had just enough to scrape through till spring.

Ever,
SL

Ever have a chance to talk to Stallings about a *Dodsworth* movie—or play and movie?

March 1

Dear Red:

I get a good deal of pleasure out of the comfort and fun you both seem to be having in Monterey. What you say about Gouverneur Morris is really interesting. He certainly can write and if he would do a Forsyte Saga of American High Society, it might be a grand book. It might even be non-fiction if you and he could think of some theme to hold the material. The idea interests me a good deal. Do try to get it earmarked for us.

Paul and Rhea are fine, but he is headed for Europe this summer, leaving about the first of May for five or six months, to look into several matters there which will be grist for his articles as well as for the next book.

Fifth Avenue hasn't shown any real signs of life. I have never seen the fiction market so congested or the trade book business so poor, aside from a few titles. Alec Grosset told me last night that their January business was only a little more than half of what it was a year ago. The stores were left with a great lot of undigested stock the first of the year, and the whole trade seems to be selling plugs and overstock. It will take all spring for things to straighten out. You're lucky not to have a new book ready just now. I haven't seen Stallings in almost a year. Helen [1] is in New

---
[1] Stallings's wife.

York just now and is going to have lunch with me next week. Laurence is still in Hollywood and will be, I think, until about the first of April.

Ever yours,
Alf

Monterey, Calif.
March 12

Dear Alf:

I doubt if Gouverneur Morris will ever really settle down and do the Ameriforsyte book. He thinks of it, but he says he would need a complete free year—and as I imagine he spends 50,000 a year, there would be no question of an advance being of any significance in this case.

You didn't say whether you had been moved to send Fred Rothermell a voluntary $250 advance. I imagine it would mean more to them now than a thousand at any time later. I'd be glad to send it to them, but they won't take it—too proud—a fine and too rare quality in a young author. I hear from him that he has completed the astronomer novel. Has he sent it in?

I've seen McNamara, Mooney, and Schmitt in San Quentin—Dorothy and I went to San Francisco for a week—and had a good talk with them. If one % of people out of prison were as fine and interesting as they, life would be more worth while.

Ever,
SL

The Lewises returned to New York during April, and after a brief stay at their Tenth Street apartment, went up to Twin Farms. Mrs. Lewis, who was expecting a child, returned to New York early in May to be near her doctor. Lewis stayed on in Vermont until the end of May.

May 19

Dear Red:

I have a note from Will White about a novel I sent him, in which he says: "Remember me affectionately to Red Lewis, who is the best all-around, single-handed, catch-as-catch-can, no-holds-barred, Greeco-Roman writing man that the American Continent has produced, willing to meet all comers. *Elmer Gantry* fouled him but he knocked out all the rest, God bless him."

Ever yours,
Alf

[1930]

37 West 10th Street,
New York, June 14

Dear J.E.S.:

Thank you for the memorandum. I enclose my answer to the Grande Revue.

SL

[*Enclosure*]

New York, June 13

M. Georges Roth
Paris 17me

Dear Sir:

In answering the questionnaire submitted by you on behalf of La Grande Revue, I am afraid that I cannot commit myself to any cult of letters or school of literary aesthetics, whether it call itself "populism," "humanism" (a movement which has achieved a certain popularity, recently, in America, and which appears to be in some ways the antithesis of the tendency which you represent), or anti-humanism—because the opponents of humanism threaten, also, to become a cult. It is my conviction that art fulfills itself in many ways "lest one good custom should corrupt the world."

The fact that in my own work I have perhaps, up until now, met with the populist demand to concentrate on depicting the popular classes of the nation, in terms, largely, of behavior, does not encourage me to elevate my own interests, or way of looking at life, into a rule for all novelists. I could not, for instance, write like Mr. Aldous Huxley, nor of Mr. Huxley's characters, but I find that *Point Counterpoint* is an admirable novel. And although I am inclined to think, with you, that contemporary novelists have become excessive in psychological analysis, sometimes to the sacrifice of all form, I bow my head to Mr. Joyce in his greater moments, and am deeply grateful for the work of Virginia Woolf.

Nor do I think that the peculiar preoccupations of many of our younger writers are due to any conscious literary movement, but are rather symptomatic of the times in which we live, and will change with the times. I do not believe that literary movements are made by organized will, by literary cliques, but are made by life itself, and by men of genius.

Certainly the world is flooded at present with bad novels, but I am inclined to blame for this, not the choice of material with which the authors deal, nor their departure from accepted artistic forms, but rather democracy which has made the masses articulate and the plethora of publishers who encourage everyone, including the ungifted and unillumined, to express himself.

Sincerely yours,
Sinclair Lewis

Following the birth of their son Michael in New York the end of June, the Lewises returned to Twin Farms. The correspondence that ensued dealt mainly with translation rights of Lewis's work.

August 1

Dear Red:

You never sent me your suggestions for editors for a five shilling edition of your novels. If you want us to go ahead with this, I wish you would let me have your suggestions because we might as well try first to get just the people you would prefer.

What do you think of the current gyrations in publishing—George Doran going to Hearst and Liveright going to Hollywood? I suppose more significant than either of these is Baker and Taylor's statement to Gus yesterday afternoon that this July's business was the worst in their experience. I am happy to say that our textbook department took up the slack. Of course things are apt to look worst just before they begin to get better. There may be nothing to the general impression that business will improve in the autumn. If it doesn't, I have a notion we may be in for at least two lean years. If so, we should perhaps wait until conditions are definitely better to do the five shilling edition.

I think the whole situation will be clear by a year from now, and if there were a new novel from you for a year from this autumn, it would pretty surely be "the good five cent cigar the country needs."

Ever yours,
Alf

So. Pomfret, Vt.
August 6

Dear Alf:

First, about the possible introductions to the library set of my books. I am enclosing an elaborate list of possibilities. If and when we decide to do this, I think Dorothy would be an admirable person to handle the approach to these people—especially the Germans, French and English, and if she handled these, she'd have to handle the Americans too, to avoid crossed wires. I don't suppose the set would be published before autumn 1931, so there is no hurry. If you decide on it, let her know—she's keen to do it—and let her know how much you would be willing to pay these introducers.

Second, after months of thinking, it seems to me more important to make this a really fine edition—say $3.00 or $3.50 a volume, or even more—rather than a five shilling edition like Jonathan's. The cheap edition can, however, come later, if this goes over. In the first place, people who want to pay only $1.25 will get these in the Grosset and Dunlap edition or secondhand. Second, the people who are really interested in sets, in making and preserving a library, are most of them willing to pay enough to get fine books on *paper that will last*. Third, with such an edition, we need be in no hurry selling it—take five years if necessary, perhaps adding a volume or two—and in the end get the money back with a good profit AND have the prestige.

About the Russian business: Herewith carbon of a letter I am sending to the Gosizdat—State Publishing House.

It's been consistently cool up here while you've had such hellish weather, and all of us feel splendid.

Ever,
SL

[*Enclosure*]

South Pomfret, Vermont
August 7

To the State Publishing House
Moscow, U.S.S.R.
Dear Sirs:

Months ago I received the enclosed letter from you, suggesting that with my next novel, I send you advance proofs so that you could publish it simultaneously with America. But as you will see by the letter itself, the signature and part of the letter had been torn off before I received it—whether by accident or by some postoffice censor I do not know. I have been waiting, expecting another letter, but as it has not come, I shall answer as best I can, and hope that this letter will be delivered to the proper official.

The Gosizdat is in error in understanding that I am writing about the class-struggle of California textile workers. In the first place, there are no textile workers in California; in the second place I am not writing about either California or textile workers. As a matter of fact I do not know just exactly what I shall next write about. But when I do finish my next novel, I shall be glad to have my publishers send you proofs well in advance of our publication here, and I understand that I shall then be paid royalties.

But meantime, I wish to inquire about royalties on the many books of mine which you have already published. When I was in Moscow in the autumn of 1927, I received word from the Gosizdat that you would be glad to pay royalties on these books. I also, without success, tried to arrange a non-official convention between the Gosizdat and the American publishers whereby Russian authors would receive royalties for their books published in America. I have heard nothing more of either of these projects. As I said, I should be glad to send you advance copies of not only my next but all future novels, but in the meantime, I should be glad to receive royalties on the already published novels—which are, as I understand it, not classed in Russia as bourgeois novels but as more or less revolutionary in their final effect.

Yours sincerely,
Sinclair Lewis

8/7—Later

Dear Alf:

How roughly does my royalty account stand now? Have I anything coming? What *happened* to Liveright & Doran?

Ever,
SL

August 11

Dear Red:

Thanks for your letter of August 6th. Credit in your royalty account to June 30th is $866.00.

There are lots of rumors about George Doran. I think the truth of the matter is that he and Nelson Doubleday couldn't get along together, so Nelson broke the arrangement. I guess Liveright's business is in a precarious condition. It was on the verge of being sold to Coward-McCann, but that fell through. There are all sorts of negotiations and rumors going on about it. Liveright is going, or has just gone, to Hollywood to work for Paramount-Publix.

Don't quote me as authority for this diagnosis. I think it is pretty nearly the truth. I know it is true that four or five other publishing houses would welcome being merged or bought. Our trade business is very slack, but the textbook business is going along beautifully.

Yours,
Alf

[1930]

Barnard, Vermont
8/13

Dear Alf:

I don't think very much of most of my short stories. Hence, while it might be all right to have them published in France *after* they've had not one but several of my novels, I think that now, as introduction, they'd be bad. The same applies to our publishing here a volume of short stories. The critics laying for me would have too good a chance. *But* I do think that when we do the set, we might have one volume of short stories in it to give variety & interest.

I also have your letter of Aug. 11, about $866 on hand. I *may* grab this off you to help meet Sept. ¼ of income tax, but I'm not sure.

Ever,
SL

August 19

Dear Red:

Don is just back from a holiday and I have waited for his return to discuss yours of the sixth about a collected edition and possible editors. Before we get into that, I note what you say about publishing your short stories. I haven't read any of them in a long time. There are two or three I remember vividly, but maybe there are not enough top-notchers to make a book.

We can't see a library set of your books now—that is, at $3.00 or $3.50 a volume. I was talking with Alfred Knopf a few days ago, and he said he'd come to the conclusion that modern life has in a way spoiled the best part of the publishers' or authors' market; that the really bookish people who used to buy collected editions of standard works have their houses full of them; that as he went round and saw such people, not only were the bookcases full, but the tables and the book racks in the guest rooms and the whole place. We were talking, as a matter of fact, about starting a campaign to get people to weed out inconsequential books and send them to libraries and such. If you take that situation in a time when people feel poor, it would be almost impossible either to get the booksellers to stock or the public to buy a handsome edition. We couldn't ask $3.00 or $3.50 for a book printed from the original plates, even with an introduction.

About what we call for the sake of definition the $1.25 set to be printed on good thinner paper and bound nicely, looking a good deal like the Cape edition but with introductions, we are ready to do that whenever you are ready. I suppose it would be a bad time to try it just now, but business certainly ought to be better by the time we could get the books ready.

If Dorothy will handle getting the introductions, that will be fine. She would be good at it from every point of view. We'd be glad to pay her $50 a volume for getting the introductions, and the fee for the introduction itself ought to run from $100 to £50.

Will you consider all this and let me know what you think?

Yours,
Alf

Barnard, Vermont
Aug. 21

Dear Don:

Alf writes me that I have a balance mit you of about $866. Will you please deposit this to my account at the Guaranty Trust & let me know? God will bless you.

Dorothy & Mike (*and* the father) are corking. Is there any chance that Ida & you will be motoring this way before October 1st? Then we go off to Yurrop.

Ever,
Red

Barnard, Vermont
8/21

Dear Alf:

Dorothy or I will write you about the set in a day or two—all rite, $1.25 edition, not $3—publish, I shd think, fall of 1931, with maybe novel spring 1932. *Re* short stories, see 2 of the best I've ever written—"Noble Experiment" in August & "Bongo" in September Cosmopolitan. I really think we mite do a volume of these in the set.

Come on up here! It's lovely now.

Ever,
SL

September 6

Dear Red:

We have received a report and check from Ernst Rowohlt. Their remittance of 14,375.65 Marks comes to $3417.09. Your share of this remittance is $3103.12. We are depositing this amount to your account at the Guaranty today.

Ever yours,
Don

Barnard Vt Sep 9

Telegram to
Donald Brace
New York
Has Rowohlt check for three thousand been deposited yet. Please wire as I wish to draw against it.

Sinclair Lewis

September 22

Dear Red:

The following is a translation of a cablegram we have just received from Rowohlt:

We request you to withdraw by cable the posted check. Charge any expense to our account. We are cabling you September 25th 5000, September 29th 5000 and balance on October first. Settlement in this form unfortunately required on account of non-receipt of substantial amounts because of economic and political condition.

Don and I have decided that we have no choice but to do as he requests, as there is no advantage in having his check thrown back on our bank and he promises to cable the money. Since Dorothy is going abroad, perhaps she can straighten this thing out. We could both give her power of attorney to act for us in regard to your German rights.

Ever yours,
Alf

September 26

Dear Alf:

I'm disturbed about Rowohlt's capers—though probably there is a little something on his side in that general financial conditions seem to be very bad in Germany just now. I think your idea of having Dorothy look into the whole matter, with power of attorney from both of us, is excellent. It may be that she will find out that Rowohlt is doing as well as the rest. Has the cable of the 25th, with 5000 M. come in yet? Needless to say, if you get stuck on this I'll pay back to you all you paid me as my share, but give me a few weeks on this, as otherwise I'll have to sell some stocks.

Us Vermont farmers certainly have our troubles, don't we. Why don't we go into authorship which is, I am informed, a trade singularly free of all financial and other complications—authors think not about taxes but only about cloudlets, adultery, rose-buds, the laughing hands of Little Ones. Do you know of a good school for learning authorship?

Ever,
SL

Barnard, Vermont
October 10

Dear Alf:

Dorothy and I sneaked off for three days to Montreal and had a bottle of champagne and a black duck. Dorothy won't be going to Germany till about January 1st. She'll go down to Westport (I think I've written you that we take F.P.A.'s house for the winter) next Tuesday—October 14th; but I'll stay here a week or ten days longer to get the house closed up.

Ever,
SL

On November fifth the news broke that Lewis was awarded the Nobel Prize. He was at Westport when he received the announcement and he came down immediately to the office where reporters and newsreel people were present at a public interview.

Lewis's statement to the press:

I feel the highest honor and gratification at being the first American to be awarded the Nobel Prize in Literature, and I am accepting it with pleasure. Until this morning, when the press associations telephoned to me, I had no notion even that I was being considered. In the few hours since then, I have several times been asked two questions by telephone. The first is what I intend to do with the prize. My answer is that I shall use it to support a well-known young American author and his family, and to enable him to continue writing. The second question regards my refusal of the Pulitzer Prize in 1926 and acceptance of the Nobel Prize in 1930.

The reason is the enormous difference between the two prizes. The

[1930]

Nobel Prize is an international prize with no strings tied. It is awarded on the basis of excellence of work. In the terms of the will of Mr. Nobel, the prize was to be awarded for "the most distinguished work of an idealistic tendency," which has come to be interpreted by the Swedish Academy, which has the award of the prize, as merely meaning that such work shall not be simply a commercial and machine-like production reaching vast popularity. The Pulitzer Prize, on the other hand, is cramped by the provision of Mr. Pulitzer's will that the prize shall be given "for the American novel published during the year which shall best present the wholesome atmosphere of American life, and the highest standard of American manners and manhood." This suggests not actual literary merit, but an obedience to whatever code of good form may chance to be popular at the moment. As a result of this, the Pulitzer Prize has been given to some merely mediocre novels along with other admirable novels. It is sufficient criticism of the prize to say that in the last few years it has not been awarded to Cabell's *Jurgen*, Dreiser's *An American Tragedy*, Hemingway's *A Farewell to Arms*, Wolfe's *Look Homeward, Angel*, or Cather's *A Lost Lady*.

Another trouble with the Pulitzer Prize is that whereas the winner of the Nobel Prize is chosen on the basis of his entire work up to the time of the award, the Pulitzer Prize is supposed to be given for the best novel appearing during a single year. Consequently in one year the committee may have to choose between four or five first-rate novels, and the next year between four or five third-rate novels. I am bringing in this matter of the Pulitzer Prize only because I am being asked regarding it. Were it possible, I should say nothing whatever except that I am extremely proud to have been awarded the Nobel Prize.

November 5

His Excellency Wollmann F. Bostrom
Swedish Embassy
Washington D C

I have great honor and pleasure in accepting the Nobel Prize in Literature and I shall be happy to go to Stockholm to receive the prize on December tenth. Will you please express to the Swedish Academy my profound gratification.

Sinclair Lewis

There was division of feeling when the Nobel award was announced, especially as it was the first time the Literature prize had been given to an American writer. Lewis was feted on the one hand and criticized on the other. He and Mrs. Lewis sailed for Stockholm on the Drottningholm *late in November.*

Harbrace
New York

Radio from SS Drottningholm Dec 5

Please mail advertisements Grand Hotel Stockholm

Lewis

Harbrace
New York

Cable from Stockholm Dec 10

Have you arranged for publication full text my address Nobel Committee next Friday. If so where when. Otherwise please try get Sunday sections Times or Herald Tribune. Speech as it will be reported press certain cause repercussions and very important exact text appears somewhere America. About four thousand words. Wire me Grand Hotel where send.

Sinclair Lewis

Cable to
Sinclair Lewis
Grand Hotel
Stockholm

December 10

Times wants full text. Is cabling you direct. Mail me copy. We are proudly thinking of you.

Alfred

Cable to
Sinclair Lewis
Grand Hotel
Stockholm

December 13

Warmest congratulations splendid speech. One column first page Times full text page twelve.

Alfdon

Lewis, always a controversial figure, continued the tradition in his acceptance speech, the New York Times *headlining it, "Sinclair Lewis hits old* school writers, champions new." He denounced academicism and lauded the work of Theodore Dreiser, Sherwood Anderson, Eugene O'Neill, and Willa Cather, any one of whom he felt could have been chosen. The artist was isolated and creative work belittled in the United States, he said, while universities still lived in the dead past.

[1931]
c/o Guaranty Trust Co.,
London
January 21

Dear Alfred:

I am actually writing this in Berlin, but as I shall go to London in a week, to remain there for two months, possibly, I give the address above.

Thank you (at this rather late date, which is the first on which I have had time to write letters) for your prompt attention to the Stockholm speech, and for your cable.

Stockholm went off very well. It was, of course, an ordeal, but the members of the Academy and Mr. Laurin did everything to make our stay pleasant and to protect us from whatever public events were not absolutely necessary. Naturally our trip was somewhat depressed by Dorothy's illness.

Her condition was evidently one which has been developing for some time, and her terrific seasickness on the voyage over, the attack of high fever in Stockholm, which kept her in bed during more than half of our stay there, these were really preliminary to the sudden attack of appendicitis which resulted in the operation—entirely successful—in Berlin. The result has been that I have spent about half my time since I left America by her bedside; and we have just returned here from ten days of living remote from the world of telephones and interviewers, in the wooded Thuringian mountains.

This enforced quiet has given me a chance to think, coolly and objectively, about matters which have been bothering me for a long time. I would have spoken to you about them before we left America, but the opportunities for undisturbed discussion were so few and so brief and, perhaps more important, my own mind wasn't then fully made up.

It comes down to this. I have the impression, and the impression is backed up by too many facts to be merely fanciful, that the firm of Harcourt, Brace and Co., and you personally, feel that they have just about done their duty by Sinclair Lewis. And I feel that I have just about done my duty by Harcourt, Brace and Co. I am sure that you have for some time known how I feel. My outburst to you at lunch at my flat last spring was a sign of it. If I hadn't felt so tied to the firm, by the fact that we all began our careers together, I would have been more definite then, though also, probably, more polite.

My feeling of that time has greatly increased in the last months, and especially since the award of the Nobel Prize. To put it brutally, I feel that the firm let me down, let my books down, in regard to the prize award. It seems to me that you failed to revive the sale of my books as you might have and that, aside from this commercial aspect, you let me down as an author by not getting over to the people of the United States the way in which the rest of the world greeted the award. It would have meant the expenditure of considerable money on your part to have done this, but never in history has an American publisher had such a chance.

I think, to take only one example, that it is unfortunate that you should have permitted the readers of Heywood Broun's column to suppose that his supercilious words on the subject were representative. You have had in your hands, or you could have procured, material from the whole world: Arnold Zweig's brilliant essay, for instance, spoken on the radio in Berlin and then published in the German Literatur; the comment of L'Europe Nouvelle in France; essays in Das Tagebuch in Germany; Dr. Karlfeldt's analysis of my work before the huge and distinguished crowd at the formal prize giving, with all the royalty there; and many others in a dozen countries. You might, by advertising, have counteracted such editorials as the one in the New York Times. A few cables abroad would have placed all this material at your disposal.

Just before I sailed, in the few minutes conversation at our house, I turned over to you the interesting and important Swedish and German clippings which I already had, and you agreed (or so I understood it) to place some full-page advertisements simultaneously with the actual giving of the prize in Stockholm. As far as I have been able to discover, you have done absolutely nothing with this. And when in the January number of the American Mercury you do mention me and the prize by a curt notice down in a corner, it is as though the prize were a useful comment by a third-rate critic.

In Europe, *Dodsworth* and several of the other novels have had an enormous stimulation by reason of the prize. Even in the tiny village of Oberhof, in the Thuringian forest, from which we have just returned, in the one little bookstore there were posters—yes, plural—about me and a lot of copies of *Dodsworth* and *Babbitt*. All over Europe the award was used as a basis for Christmas advertising: "The book to give for Christmas this year is the latest novel by this year's Nobel Prize winner."

It comes down to this: If you haven't used this opportunity to push

[1931]

my books energetically and to support my prestige intelligently, you never will do so, because I can never give you again such a moment.

There are all sorts of other things that have distressed me. At lunch, just after the award, you said that you would immediately reprint and advertise another edition of all my books, uniform but without introductions.[1] If you have done so, I have seen no signs of it. The Grosset and Dunlap editions, burying my books among those of Zane Grey and Gene Stratton Porter and paying me only five cents a copy, have reaped whatever reward there was in the prize.

But there's no good going over all these matters. I'm sure you will agree with me that the most important thing in any business relationship is mutual confidence. I think that element no longer exists with us—on either side. And for me this lack of confidence is most important, because it is keeping me from starting work on a new novel. I haven't made this decision under the influence of any other publisher whatever. I have had offers, but I have refused even to consider them.

Our parting is complicated by many things, one of the most important of which is that you have a contract for my next book—unnamed. But I recall having heard you say many times that you would never try to hold an author who did not wish to be held. Also, this contract I volunteered to make, at the time when Harrison Smith left you,[2] and I did it to protect you and the firm from the many rumors that I was leaving you and going with him. I am asking you to be as generous as I was then, and to send me back the contract, cancelled.

Please believe me that it has cost me weeks of thinking and worry to plan and write this letter. If we had not gone through so much together, I would have written it long ago. Actually, I suspect that my decision may be a relief to you, and that in parting we may become better friends.

I would be grateful to you if you would reply immediately.

Sincerely yours,
Sinclair Lewis

February 3

Dear Red:

I have your letter of January 21st. Of course we don't want to hold your next novel by the semi-compulsion of a contract. Here is the agreement for the "next book" and also the one for *Neighbor*, which I include

---

[1] The Nobel Prize edition of all of Lewis's books was published one week after Lewis wrote this letter.
[2] Smith left Harcourt, Brace the end of 1928 to found his own firm, Harrison Smith and Jonathan Cape Ltd.

so that your title will be completely clear. I've endorsed them "cancelled by mutual consent." If you will acknowledge their receipt and confirm their cancellation, this will clear the record until you find it convenient to return your copies with a similar endorsement.

I know you have some idea of how sorry I am that events have taken this turn. You and we have been so closely associated in our youth and growth that I wish we might have gone the rest of the way together. If I've lost an author, you haven't lost either a friend or a devoted reader.

Yours,
Alf

Index

Adams, Franklin P., 35
Adams, Henry, 109
Addams, Jane, 57
Adler, Alfred, 168
Aley, Maxwell, 72
Allen, Frank Waller, 58
American Play Company, The, 60, 90-91
Anderson, Sherwood, 32, 48, 214, 299
Angell, Norman, 75
Archer, William, 94
Arliss, George, 187
Arrhenius, S. A., 168
Ashford, Daisy, 46 fn.
Astor, Lady, 131
Astor, Lord, 131
Atherton, Gertrude, 194-195
Aumonier, Stacy, 135
Austin, Mary, 56, 84, 193
Avery, Sid, 67
Ayres, Ruby, 74

Babbitt, B. T., 105
Babbitt, George F., 105, 106-107, 138
Bacon, Peggy, 272, 273
Baldorolden, Dr., 102
Barrie, J. M., 46 fn.
Barrows, Ellen, 176
Beard, Mary, 98
Beaverbrook, Lord, 131, 135
Bechhofer, C. E., 140
Belloc, Hilaire, 154 fn.
Belloc, Hilary, 154
Benchley, Robert, 37, 42, 162
Benet, William Rose, 35, 92, 138
Bennett, Arnold, 43, 148, 151, 182, 238
Berlin, Irving, 5 fn.
Bierce, Ambrose, 194, 195
Birkhead, Rev. L. M., 206, 211, 217, 238
Bjorkman, Edwin, 59

Blackman, Rev. Earl, 217, 232, 233, 234, 236, 238
Blackwood, Algernon, 88
Block, Ralph, 153, 155, 161
Bok, Edward, 271
Booth, Franklin, 30
Bordet, Jules, 168
Bostrom, Wollmann F., 297
Boswell, James, 276
Boyd, Ernest, 182
Brady, William A., 262 fn.
Brailsford, H. N., 74
Brandes, Georg, 168
Brandt, Carl, 7, 8
Bristol, E. N., 4, 6
Brody, Mrs., 188
Bromfield, Louis, 270
Brooks, Van Wyck, 35
Broun, Heywood, 25, 28, 35, 36, 37, 39, 182, 184, 219, 300
Brown, Arthur William, 8
Brown, C. B., 202
Brown, Curtis, 132, 148
Brown, Sir George McClaren, 151
Bryant, Louise, 8, 170
Buchan, John, 130
Bullard, Arthur, 38, 41
Bullitt, William C., 237
Butcher, Fanny, 266, 271
Butler, Nicholas Murray, 210
Byron, Lord, 174

Cabell, James Branch, 13-14, 23, 25, 37, 270, 297
Cabot, Hugh, 195
Cabot, Richard, 195
Cadman, Rev. S. Parkes, 225
Call, Arthur D., 38, 41

Canby, Henry Seidel, 113, 172, 177, 178, 188, 266
Cane, Melville, 89, 250, 251, 254, 256, 257
Canfield, Dorothy, 12, 24, 127, 185
Cape, Jonathan, 71, 96, 102, 104, 105, 110, 111, 112, 127, 129, 130, 131, 132, 134, 152, 168, 172, 174, 175, 179, 184, 234, 267, 271, 273, 274, 284, 291, 293
Cather, Willa, 214, 297, 299
Chamberlain, George Agnew, 264 fn.
Chambers, Robert, 38
Clemenceau, Georges, 74, 276
Cleveland, R. M., 202
Cobb, Irvin, 259
Cohen, Octavus Roy, 64
Conrad, Joseph, 43, 88
Cornwell, Dean, 8
Cournos, John, 94
Cowles, Mrs. W. S., 110
Croce, Benedetto, 168
Curtiss, Philip, 40, 45
Curwood, James Oliver, 83 fn.

Davis, James J., 230
Dawson, Mrs. N. P., 35, 97
de Kruif, Paul, 121, 122, 123, 125, 126, 127, 128, 129, 132, 135, 136, 139, 140, 141, 144, 145, 146, 147, 148, 149, 150, 157, 160, 164, 165, 166, 167, 168, 170, 172, 174-175, 178, 184, 201, 202, 204, 210, 211, 212, 287
Dean, Charlotte, 114, 115
Debs, Eugene, 91, 98, 138 fn.
Dell, Floyd, 35, 39, 44
Delmar, Viña, 273, 285
D'Herelle, Dr. Felix H., 168
Disraeli, Benjamin, 109, 174, 179
Domher, L., 170
Doran, George H., ix, x, 46, 94, 95, 156, 290, 292
Doubleday, Nelson, 292
Dreiser, Theodore, 214, 297, 299
Drinkwater, John, 94
Duncan Sisters, 74

Ernst, Bernard M. L., 253
Ervine, St. John, 113

Famous Players, 7, 8, 153, 155
Farrar, John, 178
Fay, Bernard, 243
Feipel, Louis N., 113, 114, 186-187, 263
Ferber, Edna, 47
Feuchtwanger, Lion, 250
Fishbein, Morris, 178, 195
Fitch, Clyde, 57
Fitzgerald, F. Scott, 63

Flandrau, Charles, 40
Fletcher, Sir Walter, 131
Flexner, Abraham, 168
Foley, District Attorney, 239, 240
Follett, Wilson, 35, 168
Ford, Harriet, 60, 61, 62, 78, 81
Forman, Henry, 41
Forster, E. M., xii, 166
Frederic, Harold, 63 fn.
Freud, Sigmund, 168

Galantiere, Lewis, 48
Gale, Zona, 42, 114
Galsworthy, John, 43, 47, 48, 49, 50, 56, 60, 63, 65, 94, 105, 110, 182
Gardner, Gilson, 28
Gardner, Mrs. Gilson, 28
Garland, Hamlin, 203 fn.
Gaston, Herbert E., 3, 6
George, W. L., 41, 43, 71, 74
Gibbs, Sir Philip, 129, 131
Gilman, Lawrence, 35
Glasgow, Ellen, 214
Goethe, 174
Goodman, Philip, 172, 173, 175, 176, 178, 180, 185, 222
Gosse, Edmund, 43
Graham, Tom, 168 fn.
Grahame-White, Claude, 74
Grant, Ulysses S., 177
Grasset, Bernard, 174
Greenslet, Ferris, 130
Grey, Zane, 15, 273, 274, 277, 301
Grosset, Alexander, 242, 275, 276, 287
Gruening, Ernest, 186 fn.
Gruger, F. R., 8, 12
Guthrie, Ramon, 236, 238, 239, 243, 244, 251, 277

Hackett, Francis, 19, 35, 52
Haessler, Carl, 283, 284
Haggard, Sewell, 143, 145, 146, 147, 148, 149, 153, 154, 155
Hahner, Marcella Burns, 133, 171, 227
Haldeman-Julius, E., 205
Hammond, Percy, 62
Hamsun, Knut, 61
Hansen, Harry, 266
Hanson, Dr. W. C., 216
Hapgood, Norman, 57, 130, 281
Hardy, Thomas, 43
Harkness, Sam, 217
Harraden, Beatrice, 94
Harriman, Karl, 144, 145, 146
Harrison, Oliver, 176 fn., 177
Hartman, C. Bertram, 136

INDEX

Hays, Arthur Garfield, 240
Hays, Will, 241
Hemingway, Ernest, 297
Herbert, Victor, 5 fn.
Hergesheimer, Joseph, 10, 13, 37 fn., 38, 54
Hildebrand, Arthur, 166, 167, 183
Hirst, F. W., 74
Hodder-Williams, Sir Ernest, 71, 74, 75, 76, 80, 127
Holt, Guy, 25, 48
Holt, Roland, 6
Hood, Fred R., 66, 185
Hopkins, Arthur, 241
Hoppé, E. O., 79, 92
Howard, G. Wren, 132
Howard, Sidney, 257
Howe, Frederic C., 25, 28, 155, 167, 204, 244, 245
Howells, William Dean, ix
Hoyns, Henry, 9, 16, 27, 28
Hughes, Hatcher, 210
Hunt, Frazier (Spike), 130, 145, 147, 148, 153, 175, 178, 179, 211
Hurst, Fannie, 52
Hutchinson, A. S. M., 101
Huxley, Aldous, 289

International Feature Service, 136
Isham, Colonel Ralph, 276 fn.

Jefferson, Thomas, 167
Jenkins, Burris, 217
Jenkins, Herbert, 27, 28
Johnson, Dawson, 92, 174
Johnson, Owen, 109
Joyce, James, 168, 289
Jung, Carl, 168

Karlfeldt, Erik, 300
Karstner, David, 98
Kaufman, George, 130
Kearney, Patrick, 262
Kelley, Edith Summers, 75, 87, 128, 130, 131, 132, 138, 140, 141
Kelly, George, 210
Kendall, A. I., 141
Kennedy, Margaret, 178
Kerr, Philip, 131
Key, Ellen, 45
Keynes, John Maynard, xii, 24, 25, 28, 32, 84, 99
Kidd, John, 16, 65
Klaw, Marc, 74
Knopf, Alfred, 206
Kochnitzky, Leon, 170

Korner, Harry, 16
Kroch, A., 227
Kyne, Peter B., 158

LaFollette, Fola, 162
Laski, Harold, 25, 65, 71, 74, 77
Leeuwenhoek, Anton van, 141
Levy, Ethel, 74
Lewis, Grace Hegger, x, 9, 10, 26, 31, 32, 33, 36, 56, 71, 78, 79, 80, 82, 83, 84, 91, 93, 100, 101, 105, 106, 108, 109, 113, 114, 116, 117, 122, 123, 124, 128, 129, 131, 132, 133, 134, 135, 137, 139, 140, 141, 142, 144, 154, 160, 168, 171, 173, 176, 178, 179, 180, 183, 185, 189, 197, 198, 199, 200, 201, 202, 204, 207, 209, 216, 222, 223, 231, 237, 243, 249, 251, 252-253, 254, 255-256
Lewis, Lloyd, 276
Lewis, Wells, 72, 78, 93, 134, 144, 255, 256
Lewisohn, Ludwig, 41, 236
Lincoln, Joseph, 55, 83 fn.
Lindbergh, Charles A., 242
Lindsay, Vachel, 57, 58
Lippmann, Walter, 35
Liveright, Horace, 91, 94, 98, 186, 206, 240, 290, 292
London, Jack, 194, 264
Long, Ray, 95, 96, 130, 144, 145, 271, 279, 280
Lorimer, George Horace, ix, x, 13, 14, 37, 52, 107-108
Lovett, Robert Morss, 77, 203, 205
Loving, Pierre, 230
Lowndes, Mrs. Belloc, 74
Ludwig, Emil, 258
Lynd, Helen Merrell, 270 fn.
Lynd, Robert S., 270 fn.

McComas, Mrs. Francis, 38, 41
McIntyre, O. O., 35
McNamara, J. B., 288
Macaulay, Rose, 57 fn., 75
Macauley, Ward, 131
Macdonald, Ramsay, 130, 150
Mackenzie, Compton, 43, 105
Mannes, David, 273 fn.
Mannin, Ethel, 201
Mansfield, Katherine, 81
Marbury, Elisabeth, 60, 62
Margolies, Sam, 63
Massingham, H. J., 74
Masters, Edgar Lee, 86
Matthews, Brander, 210
Maugham, Somerset, 105
Maupin, J. C., 217
Maurice, Arthur Bartlett, 109, 167

Maurois, André, 174, 179
Mayer, Rabbi H. H., 217
Mayo, William J., 195
Meiklejohn, Alexander, 253
Melcher, Frederic G., 66
Mellish, Howard, 220
Mencken, Henry L., 19, 35, 39, 40, 43, 62, 95, 157, 163, 170, 172, 175, 176, 214, 216 fn., 233, 234, 236, 251, 253, 255, 256, 258, 260, 270
Merrick, Leonard, 43
Middleton, George, 162
Millay, Edna St. Vincent, 88, 89, 91
Miller, Joaquin, 194, 195
Millin, Sarah C., 178
Milton, Robert, 241, 257, 262
Montgelas, Count, 255
Mooney, Thomas, 288
Moore, George, 43, 94
Moore, Guernsey, 30
More, Paul Elmer, 100
Morehouse, Edward, 105
Morley, Christopher, 35, 169
Morris, Gouverneur, 195, 196, 197, 286-287, 288
Munro, Wallace, 111, 112

Nathan, George Jean, 216 fn., 258
Negri, Pola, 195, 196-197, 198, 199
Nevinson, H. W., 74, 84
Nicholson, Meredith, 92
Nicoll, William Robertson, 74, 75
Nobel, Alfred, 297
Nobel Prize, ix, xi, 61, 296-301
Nohowel, Mrs. Frank P., 61
Nonpartisan League, 3, 6, 26
Norris, Charles G., 47, 142

O'Brien, E. J., 186
O'Brien, Frederick, 146
O'Higgins, Harvey, 60, 61, 62, 78, 81 fn., 89
O'Neill, Eugene, 257, 299
Onions, Oliver, 74
Oppenheim, E. Phillips, 74
Osbourne, Lloyd, 129
Overton, Grant, 182, 238

Palmer, Loren, 180-181, 183
Palmieri, Teodoro, 238
Papini, Giovanni, 133, 136
Parmelee, Maurice, 131
Parrington, Vernon Louis, 276
Pasteur, Louis, 141
Patti, Adelina, 141
Pawling, Sydney S., 71

Phelps, Hansen, 270
Phelps, William Lyon, 35, 42, 46
Piccoli, Rafaello, 89, 90
Pinker, James B., 71
Porter, Gene Stratton, 83 fn., 301
Preston, Keith, 114, 178
Pringle, Henry F., 276
Proust, Marcel, 139, 142
Pulitzer, Joseph, 209, 214, 297
Pulitzer Prize, xi, 46, 49, 203-216, 296-297
Pusey, Edward Bouverie, 195

Quinn, Michael F., 128, 132, 133

Rascoe, Burton, 19, 48, 182
Ray, Man, 169
Reed, John, 8
Reidenbach, Clarence, 217
Reynolds, Paul, 197, 198
Roberts, Rev., 217
Robinson, Boardman, 130
Roosevelt, Theodore, 110, 276
Rosenwald, Julius, 64
Roth, Georges, 289
Rothermell, Fred, 277, 278, 282, 283, 284, 287, 288
Roux, Pierre Paul Emile, 168
Rowohlt, Ernst, 250, 254, 256, 258, 259, 269, 294, 295
Ruck, Berta, 74
Russell, Bertrand, 129
Rutherford, Rev., 217

Sandburg, Carl, 134, 183, 201, 214, 259, 273
Sarg, Tony, 162
Savage, Harry, 243
Saxton, Gene, 185
Schmidt, Matthew, 288
Scott, Evelyn, 84
Scott, Geoffrey, 276
Sedgwick, Ellery, 12
Seldes, Gilbert, 168
Selfridge, Harry Gordon, 63
Shaw, Charles, 256
Shaw, George Bernard, 43, 49, 82, 84, 165, 166
Shea, Joseph E., 262 fn.
Sheean, Vincent, 278
Sherman, Stuart, 35, 42, 67, 100, 108, 116, 127, 151, 170, 177, 178, 180, 184, 203 fn., 206
Sherwood, Robert, 225, 226, 227
Shiveley, Rev., 217
Shorter, Clement, 74
Shubert, Lee, 81

INDEX

Shubert Brothers, 60, 62, 81 fn.
Siddall, John M., 56, 57
Siegfried, André, 279, 280, 281
Simpson, Percy, 72
Sinclair, May, 94, 105, 108, 110, 111, 168
Sinclair, Upton, 75, 109, 140
Slaughter, Mrs. William, 102
Smith, Harry Bache, 5, 21
Smith, Winchell, 110, 111
Smyth, Clifford, 108, 110
Soule, George, 38, 92
Stallings, Helen, 287
Stallings, Laurence, 178, 182, 214, 241, 257, 284, 287-288
Stearns, Harold E., 82, 98
Steele, Wilbur Daniel, 85
Steffens, Lincoln, 286
Steichen, Edwin, 169
Sterling, George, 194-195
Stewart, Donald Ogden, 92, 135
Stidger, William L., 193, 194, 207, 216, 233, 234, 238
Stieglitz, Alfred, 169
Stoddard, Richard Henry, 195
Stokes, Brett, 105
Stokes, Frederick A., 156
Strachey, Lytton, xii, 75, 76, 99, 100, 274
Straton, John Roach, 235
Sturgis, Major General, 125
Suckow, Ruth, 95, 96
Sunday, Billy, 250
Swinnerton, Frank, 74, 75, 92

Tarkington, Booth, 39, 59, 212
Thompson, Dorothy, 250, 255, 262, 263, 267, 268, 271, 274, 280, 283, 285, 286, 288, 290, 294, 295, 296, 299
Thompson, Grace, 133, 134
Thomson, General C. B., 150, 152, 153, 155
Tinker, Chauncey B., 136, 138
Tobenkin, Elias, 24
Tolstoi, Leo, 261
Toohey, John Peter, 38, 39, 40, 45
Turpin, Alice, 174
Twain, Mark, ix

Untermeyer, Louis, 134, 169, 273 fn.
Updegraff, Allan, 75, 92, 140, 236

Valentino, Rudolph, 196, 199
Van Doren, Carl, 47, 85-86, 170, 178, 267
Van Doren, Irita, 237, 241
Van Loon, Hendrik Willem, 156, 214
Van Vechten, Carl, 142
Veiller, Bayard, 241, 252, 253, 256, 257
Voltaire, 167

Walker, Stuart, 81
Walpole, Hugh, 43, 65, 74, 75, 92, 94, 104, 105, 112, 113, 126, 271, 272, 273
Walt, Charles, 270 fn.
Warner Brothers, 110, 115, 117, 153, 155, 161
Warwick, Countess of, 130
Washburn, Claude, 34, 35, 81, 85, 87, 129, 140, 183
Wassermann, Jacob, 41
Watkins, Ann, 241, 279, 280
Webster, Harold Tucker, 273
Wells, H. G., 43, 49, 56, 75, 105, 110, 111, 130, 134, 135, 168, 182
Wells, Leonard S., 218
Wells, Thomas B., 55, 167-168
West, Rebecca, 75, 94, 168, 235
Wharton, Edith, 43, 82, 139, 142, 168, 180, 203 fn., 214, 270, 286
Whitall, James, 75
Whitcomb, Richard, 125
White, William Allen, 48-49, 288
Williams, Blanche Colton, 186
Williams, Geoffrey, 71
Williams, Sidney, 281
Wilson, Woodrow, 174
Winter, Ella, 286
Wolfe, Thomas Clayton, 297
Wolff, Kurt, 176, 184, 188, 222
Woods, Al, 58, 60
Woodward, William, 142, 172, 235
Woolf, Virginia, xii, 289
Wright, Harold Bell, 19, 83 fn.
Wycherley, Margaret, 74
Wylie, Elinor, 138, 151, 227
Wylie, Horace, 227

Yeats, William Butler, 38
Young, Francis Brett, 271

Zweig, Arnold, 300

B LEWIS, S.
Lewis, Sinclair,
1885-1951.
From Main Street to
Stockholm; letters of
Sinclair Lewis, 1919-1930.